100 THINGS
COLORADO FANS
SHOULD KNOW & DO
BEFORE THEY DIE

T0164279

100 THINGS
COLORADO FANS
SHOULD KNOW & DO
BEFORE THEY DIE

Brian Howell

30 YEARS
TRIUMPH
BOOKS

Library of Congress Cataloging-in-Publication Data available upon request

This book is available in quantity at special discounts for your group or organization. For further information, contact:
Triumph Books LLC
814 North Franklin Street
Chicago, Illinois 60610
(312) 337-0747
www.triumphbooks.com

Printed in U.S.A.
ISBN: 978-1-62937-691-2
Design by Patricia Frey

For Melissa, Connor, Isabel, Lucas, and Mason

Contents

Introduction

I had never met Rashaan Salaam before we had lunch together at Boulder's Fate Brewing Company in December 2014. The former Colorado football star was a bit guarded, since we'd never met, but we connected over age and George Rogers. We had both turned 40 in October—he was exactly three weeks older—and had both idolized Rogers, a running back for the New Orleans Saints and Washington Redskins, in our youth.

By the time the food arrived, Salaam had relaxed a bit and we spent the next hour talking about his youth, his pro career, his post-football struggles and successes, and, of course, his Heisman Trophy–winning season of 1994. After all, I was doing the interview for a story on the 20th anniversary of Salaam becoming the only Heisman winner in CU history.

The 20th anniversary was a big deal, but Salaam was looking forward to going to New York for the 25th anniversary.

"They do something special for your 25th," he said before smiling and adding, "I've got five more years to get in shape."

This book is being published in 2019—the 25th anniversary of Salaam's Heisman-winning season, and it's sad for me that he won't be there for the festivities in New York City. Along with CU fans everywhere, I was devastated when I woke up the morning of December 6, 2016—nearly two years to the day after our lunch—and learned that Salaam had died from a self-inflicted gunshot wound to the head. He was only 42 years old.

Meeting Salaam that day in 2014 was a highlight of my journalism career and covering his funeral in 2016 was one of the hardest days of that career. I'll never forget standing in Mountain View Memorial Park near Salaam's parents, other family members, and former CU teammates, and watching his body placed into the grave and buried.

I knew from our interview that Salaam had some struggles. He told me he used to get down on himself over some of his choices and failures, but added, "I don't beat myself up any more. Those days are way over." Although I didn't know him well, I never saw his life ending in suicide. Nobody ever really sees it coming, I guess.

I've learned more about Salaam after his death and have come to admire him even more than I did as a college student watching him rush for over 2,000 yards and climb the top of the mountain in college football. More than anything, I cherish that day I got to have lunch with one of the greatest players in CU history, because I learned he was much more than a great running back. He was a good man, with a good heart and a heck of a smile.

Growing up in Littleton, Colorado, I watched Eric Bieniemy, Darian Hagan, J.J. Flannigan, Alfred Williams, Chad Brown, Salaam, and others contend for national titles under legendary head football coach Bill McCartney. I watched Chauncey Billups star on the basketball court at Denver's George Washington High School before his remarkable two years at CU and his stellar NBA career. And, I followed Ceal Barry's exceptional teams in women's basketball.

In 2010, I began covering the Buffaloes, and have had the pleasure of meeting and getting to know so many of the great Buffs I watched in my youth, including Barry, Bieniemy, Hagan, and McCartney. I've been able to meet other legends, too, including Mark Haynes, Hale Irwin, Steve Jones, and Herb Orvis.

Along the way, it's been a thrill covering the newest wave of stars who will one day be labeled as legends, including Emma Coburn, Spencer Dinwiddie, Phillip Lindsay, and Sefo Liufau.

Writing this book has allowed me to revisit many of those interviews and relationships, but it also afforded me the opportunity to learn more about the flagship university in my home state. It's allowed me to learn about great men and women of the past, including Byron "Whizzer" White, Claude Walton, Shelley Sheetz, and Fred Folsom.

This book highlights many of the great moments, players, coaches, and contributors in CU history, while also touching on turbulent times in the athletic department's history, such as the financial crisis of 1980 and the football recruiting scandal in the early 2000s. It tells the story of an athletic department that has experienced some highs and lows, but has thrived for more than 130 years because of not only great athletes, but great people who have given their heart and soul to the Buffaloes and brought pride to the university, the city of Boulder, and the state of Colorado.

On that December day in 2014, I learned a lot more about one of those people. I'm not sure Salaam ever truly appreciated the impact he had on others, but he was grateful for the influence that the coaches, teammates, and the Boulder community had on him.

"I love the University of Colorado," he said.

1 National Champs

Four Buffaloes got their hands on The Rocket, but the most electric player in college football escaped and raced down the sidelines. Notre Dame's Raghib "The Rocket" Ismail fielded a Colorado punt at his own 9-yard line and during his 91-yard journey to the end zone, he ripped the hearts out of the Buffaloes.

"When I saw the ball going right to him, that's scary," Darian Hagan, CU's quarterback, said years later. "You've got the best returner in the game—one of the best players in college football—you give him the ball in open space, things can happen, and not good things."

Only 65 seconds remained in the Orange Bowl in Miami on January 1, 1991, when Colorado's Tom Rouen punted the ball to Ismail. Leading 10–9, all CU needed to do was hold on to win the game and the national championship. When The Rocket crossed the goal line, it appeared CU's dream had turned into a nightmare.

"It's a huge downer," said Hagan, who had left the game just before halftime with a knee injury. "You're just like, 'Wow I can't believe this. I can't believe we gave this guy a chance to do the things he's been doing his whole career—make big plays.'

"I just sat there on my crutches and wanted to start crying. Then I looked over at coach [Bill] McCartney and he was pointing to the flag."

More than 70 yards away from Notre Dame's celebration in the end zone, a yellow penalty flag rested on the field. A clipping penalty on the Irish negated the Ismail touchdown and preserved the Colorado lead. Six plays later, the Buffs' Deon Figures intercepted a Notre Dame pass and ran around until the clock expired.

McCartney and the Buffaloes, who finished with an 11–1–1 record, exploded onto the field in celebration, as the 10–9 victory in the Orange Bowl secured the Associated Press national championship and put Colorado at the top of the mountain in college football.

"Our focus [during the season] was to get better and it ended up just perfect," center Jay Leeuwenburg said.

Unfortunately for the Buffs, they had to share the throne. Long before the Bowl Championship Series (BCS) and College Football Playoff (CFP) began crowning the Division I champion on the field, it was two major polls deciding the winner. College football writers voted in the Associated Press (AP) poll, while head coaches voted in the United Press International (UPI) poll. CU was No. 1 in both polls going into the bowl games. Following all the bowls, CU narrowly won the AP vote over Georgia Tech (11–0–1), while the Yellow Jackets narrowly won the UPI vote. CU's main rival, Nebraska, was the only team in the country to play both teams, losing to CU 27–12 and then to Georgia Tech, 45–21, in the Citrus Bowl. Cornhuskers head coach Tom Osborne put Georgia Tech at the top of his ballot for the UPI poll.

"I feel we were slighted, and we were slighted by the guys up north," Hagan said. "I don't know if they thought they were better than us and they deserved to be in that [Orange Bowl] game, but they didn't beat us. We beat them handily in their stadium. To not get a vote from them, that kind of hurt us a little bit. But we're not bitter. We still went out there and strapped it on and played with our emotions and our heart and we won games and were there right where we should have been."

For the Buffs, the 1990 season was, in many ways, an extension of 1989, when they went 11–0 during the regular season and lost to Notre Dame, 21–6, in the Orange Bowl. The 1989 squad was fueled not only by its talent, but by the memory of their fallen teammate, Sal Aunese. The starting quarterback in 1988, Aunese would have been a senior in 1989, but was stricken with inoperable stomach cancer and passed away on September 23, 1989—three games into the Buffs' season. In honor of Aunese, the 1989 team set a goal of winning the national championship. That team was arguably better than the 1990 Buffs, but the loss to Notre Dame in the Orange Bowl left the Buffs with unfinished business. Although several key players from 1989 had graduated, the Buffs were still loaded with talent in 1990.

"I think we still had a lot of confidence in our ability to get back to the national championship game and this time to get it," Hagan said of the 1990 team.

With the exception of the loss to Notre Dame, the Buffs were dominant in 1989. Eight wins in 1989 came by 21 points or more and 10 of them by at least 17 points. Hagan said the Buffs got a little too confident with their 1989 dominance and, coming into 1990, "I guess I thought we felt we were invincible." The 1990 season was anything but easy for the Buffaloes, who faced adversity from the start.

Ranked No. 5 by the AP to start the season, the Buffs tied No. 8 Tennessee, 31–31, in the opener. After a four-point win against an average Stanford team, the Buffs lost at No. 21 Illinois, 23–22. Three games in, the Buffs had slipped to No. 20 in the rankings with a 1–1–1 record. Losing to Illinois was a wake-up call for the Buffs.

"I think it really turned our season around," tight end Sean Embree said. "We knew after that we weren't going to be beat and we couldn't be beat."

CU didn't lose again, but had to battle nearly every week. After the loss to Illinois, the Buffs won the next three by a combined 15 points—including a narrow escape at Missouri. The famous "5th Down Game" allowed CU to pull off a 33–31 victory.

"We pretty much got everyone's best effort that year," linebacker Chad Brown said.

5ᵗʰ Down

Colorado's title dream nearly came to an end on the slippery turf of Faurot Field in Columbia, Missouri, on October 6, 1990. Despite being heavy favorites against Missouri—a team that finished 4–7 that season—CU trailed 31–27 in the closing minutes.

With 38 seconds to play, CU's Charles Johnson completed a pass to tight end Jon Boman, who was wide open, but slipped at the 3-yard line. "I'm thinking, 'Man, I'm going to score a touchdown here,'" Boman said. "And the next thing I know, it was like someone shot my legs out from underneath me from the stands. You had no chance on that turf; it was just terrible. It would have probably been a touchdown."

The awful condition of the field neutralized the game for Missouri and made life difficult on the Buffs. "I think we switched our cleats two or three times to try to find the right shoe that could give us traction and we never found that," Boman said.

Boman's slip set up the final, wild sequence. From the 3-yard line, Johnson got the Buffs lined up on first-and-goal and spiked the ball to stop the clock with 28 seconds to play. On second down, Eric Bieniemy ran up the middle and was stopped at the 1-yard line. CU called timeout with 18 seconds to play and head coach Bill McCartney told the team the plan to run a play, spike the ball to stop the clock if needed, and then run a final play. Center Jay Leeuwenburg said, "Coach, we can't do that, because that will be fifth down." McCartney told Leeuwenburg to "shut up and play center." Leeuwenburg, as it turned out, was one of the few in the stadium who knew what was going on.

After the timeout, Bieniemy was stuffed at the 1-yard line on what should have been third down, but the down marker still showed "2." Johnson then spiked the ball to stop the clock with 2 seconds left. The game should have been over, but officials all thought the spike came on third down. The 1990 season was the first in which college teams could stop the clock by spiking the ball, and confusion took over in that moment.

The Buffs got a fifth down, and Johnson took the snap and dove toward the end zone, barely getting the ball across the goal line. Missouri fans celebrated the win, but officials signaled touchdown.

Colorado got the controversial 33–31 victory and continued the title quest. CU has always maintained that if the field was in good shape, the game never would have come down to that controversial finish. It did, however, and it produced one of the most remarkable finishes in college football history.

"I was just glad [Johnson] made it in," Boman said.

For the players, the 1990 season was an eye-opening experience, as they realized the difficulty of winning each week.

"It was a season of trials and tribulations," backup quarterback Charles Johnson said. "But, it was a season of incredible growth and maturity of a program. We won in '89 because we had great coaches and great talent. In '90, we won a national championship because we had matured as a team that wasn't the hunter; we were the huntee at that point. We didn't realize it at first, but we quickly discovered it."

Each step along the way, the Buffs found a way to get a win. Running back Eric Bieniemy scored a touchdown in the final minutes to win at Texas. Figures had two interceptions, including one in the end zone at the end of the game, to secure a six-point win against Washington. Johnson, playing for the injured Hagan, scored on the final play at Missouri. After escaping at Missouri, the Buffs seemed to hit their stride, rolling past Iowa State and Kansas. Rising to No. 10 in the rankings, the Buffs then knocked off No. 22 Oklahoma at Folsom Field. Hagan's 85-yard touchdown pass to Rico Smith in the fourth quarter solidified that victory.

The pivotal day in the season came the following week, on November 3, when the Buffs visited third-ranked Nebraska. Ranked No. 9, and with only three weeks to play in the season, the Buffs needed help to get back into the national title picture. On that day, No. 1 Virginia was upset by Georgia Tech (a key victory in the Yellow Jackets' title run), and the Cavaliers lost three more times to fall out of the title picture. In addition, No. 4 Auburn lost by 41 at Florida and No. 5 Illinois lost by 26 to Iowa.

CU did its part by upsetting the Cornhuskers on a rainy and miserable day in Lincoln, Nebraska. Down 12–0 going into the fourth quarter, the Buffs got four Bieniemy touchdowns in the final 15 minutes to win 27–12. Bieniemy, who finished third in Heisman Trophy voting that season, had fumbled five times in the first three quarters. CU, as a team, had seven fumbles (losing three) and an interception.

"We go in at halftime and, as a man on the offensive line, coaches start talking about changes," Leeuwenburg said, "and we all just said, 'No. We are kicking their ass; we're not changing a damn thing. All we're changing…' and we all just kind of looked at EB and said, 'Hold onto the damn ball and we'll win.' That was pretty much halftime. Then we went out and we did the same damn thing and he scored four touchdowns in the fourth quarter and we win."

With four of the top five teams in the country losing on November 3, CU vaulted to No. 4 in the AP poll. The next week, the Buffs rolled past Oklahoma State, while No. 2 Washington and No. 3 Houston both lost. After No. 1 Notre Dame lost the following week, the Buffs vaulted to No. 1 heading into the Orange Bowl. For the second year in a row, it was the Fighting Irish standing in CU's way of a national title.

"It was definitely some revenge," Hagan said. "It was a chance for us to make it up to Sal and get the victory. It was an opportunity for us to know that we could play with anybody in the country now. We thought we were a better team than the previous year. We were rolling, everybody was healthy. We were really, really excited for the game."

Early on the morning of the game, Hagan was jolted from a deep sleep and had to wake up his roommate, Johnson. "I had a dream I'm going to get hurt and you've got to finish the game,"

Hagan told Johnson. "We're going to win, but you've got to finish the game." Johnson brushed it off and went back to sleep.

When Hagan went down with his knee injury at the end of the first half, he and Johnson couldn't believe the dream was coming true. "All my teammates and coaches were saying, 'CJ you ready for it?'" Johnson said. "I'm thinking, 'Nope, Hagan is going to come out and lead us to victory.' The realization that that wasn't going to be the case and I had to step in was a big moment for me—it was a big moment for our team and of course the history of our program."

Notre Dame led 9–3 when Johnson took over, and his first pass badly missed the mark. He was perfect from there, finishing the game 5-for-6 for 80 yards. Johnson also led the Buffs on their lone touchdown drive, as Bieniemy scored on a one-yard run with four minutes and 26 seconds to play in the third quarter to give CU a 10–9 lead that would hold up as the winning margin. To win, CU took advantage of five Notre Dame turnovers, but also had several unexpected heroes, such as Johnson.

With 7:32 to play in the second quarter, Notre Dame scored its only touchdown, but CU's Ronnie Bradford blocked the extra point. That proved to be the difference in the final score.

"I came off the edge and I didn't get touched and when I took that third step and flattened out, I saw the holder still had the ball in his hand and he hadn't quite put it down," Bradford said. "I laid out and I'm thinking, 'Okay, I've got a good chance to block this thing.' I went to a spot and that's the thing we always practiced. It was just a great get-off, good timing, and I came off the edge and ended up blocking it.

"It's always a good feeling to know that you contributed to the success of that game and made a difference."

The fact that so many players contributed throughout that season made it special then, and perhaps more so as time has passed. More than a quarter century after claiming the only football national championship in CU history, those Buffs are still connected by what they did that season.

"Guys who were on that team, they were groomsmen in my wedding, they were there when my kids were born," Brown said. "It's not just something that we talk about. It's something that's actually real and profound and lifelong."

That team was a star-studded lineup that included Hagan, Bieniemy, Mike Pritchard, and several NFL linemen on offense. The greatest collections of linebackers in CU history—Alfred Williams, Kanavis McGhee, Greg Biekert, and Brown—teamed with Figures, Leonard Renfro, Joel Steed, and others on defense. Nine players from that team were selected in the 1991 NFL Draft, including Pritchard (13th overall) and Williams (18th) as first rounders. Four more were drafted in 1992 and five more in 1993. That list doesn't include Rouen, who had a 13-year NFL career. Of course, the team was also led by McCartney, the legendary head coach who took CU to a place it had never been before—and hasn't been since.

On talent, alone, that was one of the greatest teams to ever suit up at Colorado. But it was the ability to fight through adversity, take everyone's best shot and find a way to stay standing that made that group a special team that is still revered by Buff Nation.

"It was very magical," Hagan said. "We just played all together and we played for each other. We played with one heartbeat. That was our slogan. We didn't really talk about Sal a lot, but in the back of our minds, that's what we were playing for. We were playing for Sal. We wanted to get back to that grand stage and get that victory, because of the letdown the year before. You don't get second chances in life and when we got that second chance, we took advantage. I just thank God we were able to do what we did."

Coach Mac

Hagan, Bieniemy, Williams, and a host of other stars led Colorado to the 1990 national championship and it was a spectacular year. The real star of that team, however, may have been the head coach. "We had a special leader in Bill McCartney," quarterback Charles Johnson said. "He was uncompromising. He was just a special leader. And two, he recruited special guys. We came from all kinds of backgrounds, but special guys who bought into something an incredible, superior leader sort of put out as a vision. The nerve of Bill McCartney to put out, as a goal, or his vision, to win a championship. What right did he have to do that at the University of Colorado? But he recruited guys who bought in, who wanted the exact same thing, and the result of it was a national championship."

The 1990 national title was the pinnacle of McCartney's head coaching career—and of CU football history—but it was part of an exceptional 13-year run, from 1982 to 1994. McCartney is CU's all-time leader in games coached (153) and wins (93). He led the Buffaloes to three Big Eight Conference titles, nine bowl game appearances, and six top-20 finishes in the national rankings.

At the time he was hired, though, McCartney's vision for CU seemed more like an unattainable dream. The Buffaloes had just been through the dismal, three-year tenure of Chuck Fairbanks, who went 7–26 and then abruptly resigned on June 1, 1982, to take over the New Jersey Generals of the newly formed United States Football League.

To replace Fairbanks, CU targeted Drake University head coach Chuck Shelton, whose team had stunned the Buffs twice in Boulder, in 1979 and 1980. Brigham Young University head coach LaVell Edwards, who had won seven Western Athletic Conference titles in 10 years with the Cougars at that point, interviewed for the job, as well, but withdrew his name from consideration. CU athletic director Eddie Crowder was impressed by Shelton, who led Drake to a 10–1 record in 1981 and had five seasons of head coaching experience. Shelton was the front-runner, but CU brought McCartney in for an interview. He had spent the previous eight years, from 1974 to 1981, as an assistant coach at Michigan,

Coach McCartney beams as he's escorted off the field after defeating Notre Dame in the 57th annual Orange Bowl Classic in Miami on January 1, 1991.
(AP Photo / Ray Fairall)

including five seasons as defensive coordinator. McCartney helped the Wolverines and head coach Bo Schembechler to five 10-win seasons and seven bowl games in eight years. He didn't have college head coaching experience, but he was coming from a big-time program and that gave him the edge.

"When it came down to a final decision, it was a question of Shelton having the benefit of being a head coach, and McCartney having the benefit of being at the competitive level of Michigan," Crowder said. "That one little point turned it in favor of McCartney."

Crowder wasn't so sure about the choice, though.

"This was a collective decision by our administration, and I'm not sure it's the right one," he said. "I can tell you one thing, I would have been delighted had we hired Chuck Shelton."

According to Shelton, Crowder was ready to hire him, but administration backed McCartney. "Some other people got involved who do not know the definiteness of how things should take place," Shelton said. "Some controls were put on Eddie and I became a victim of those controls, as did he. There are some problems at Colorado. The relationships between the faculty and football program and the students and the football program have been bad. Some of the regents also are unhappy with the football program and they wanted to be thorough."

While Shelton had impressed Crowder, McCartney went into his interview with "about 15 people representing all kinds of factions on campus and the alumni," he said, and told them what they wanted to hear. He signed a four-year contract to lead the Buffaloes into the future.

"I promise you a program based on integrity and honesty, with the top priority on graduating students," he said. "That's how we're going to measure success. I see Colorado as being a lot like Michigan in being able to attract the superior student-athlete. Our standards are better here than most, but that has to be looked at as an advantage."

McCartney had always been a winner. He played in two Orange Bowls, in 1959 and 1960, as a center and linebacker at Missouri. He then coached boys basketball and football at Divine Child High School in Dearborn, Michigan, leading the Falcons to state championships in both sports in 1973. He had a 30–5 record in four seasons as the Divine Child football coach before his successful run at Michigan.

In becoming the head coach at CU, it didn't matter whether he was the first choice or not, but three years into his tenure in Boulder, he appeared to be the wrong choice. On the field, the Buffs continued losing, going 7–25–1 during his first three seasons—a record nearly identical to Fairbanks' tenure. That included a dreadful 1–10 record in 1984. McCartney's strong religious views were becoming an issue, as well.

"Factions of our team started feeling like coach McCartney was playing favorites towards kids that were more religious and we did a prayer at the end of practice," Gary Barnett, a McCartney assistant and future CU head coach, said during ESPN's 30 for 30 documentary, *The Gospel According to Mac*. "I don't know that it was mandatory, but I think the players felt like it was mandatory. The ACLU got involved, he got a lot of criticism, and it was a mess."

In September of 1985, pressure from the American Civil Liberties Union (ACLU) led CU to issue a five-point policy separating religion from the athletic programs. McCartney's faith was always prominent in his life, however. In 1990, he founded the Promise Keepers men's ministry.

During his tenure, McCartney also dealt with numerous legal issues involving his players. To win, McCartney believed he had to recruit "the great black athlete," and he did. But, in doing so, he brought young, African American men into a predominantly white campus and city. Those players were often the target of racial discrimination.

"You knew people were going to say certain things: 'The only reason why you were here was to play football. You didn't deserve to be here. Why are you here?'" said Hagan, who came to Boulder in 1988 after growing up in South Central Los Angeles.

Frustrated and angry, some of the players fought back, leading to many of them getting arrested and CU being labeled as a team of thugs. Several players told McCartney they wanted to leave. McCartney stood up for his players, though, urging the community to accept young men who were not only in Boulder to play football, but to get an education.

"In order for us to be successful at the University of Colorado, we first had to be successful in Boulder," Hagan said. "We had to be able to walk around our community and be involved in our community without being targeted."

Knowing McCartney was an advocate for them, the players bonded. Eventually, the coach got past his rocky start and began winning. McCartney could motivate like nobody else, and it led to him recruiting dynamic athletes such as Sal Aunese, Hagan, Bieniemy, J.J. Flannigan, and more. With higher caliber athletes on the roster, McCartney used his fire to motivate the troops each week.

"Mac was just a great team motivator," former equipment manager Jeff Kosley said. "When he would prepare the team in pregame, he'd get everybody together before going out, and the hair would just stand up on the back of your neck. It was just magic, the way he would get people focused and get the team ready to play that game."

McCartney came to CU determined to win, and he didn't care who was in his way. He singled out Big Eight Conference power Nebraska as CU's rival, and then beat the Cornhuskers in 1986, 1989, and 1990. After winning just seven games in his first three years combined, McCartney led the Buffs to a 7–5 record and a trip to the Freedom Bowl in 1985. Nine of his final 10 seasons as head coach at CU concluded with a bowl game appearance.

McCartney stunned the entire CU community when, on November 19, 1994, he announced he would resign at the end of the season. The 1994 team went 11–1 and was one of the best in CU history, and the Buffs were set up for several more years of national prominence. "This is the time," he said, with his wife, Lyndi, at his side. "It's the right thing for us to do as a family." Several weeks later, McCartney would cap his career with a 41–24 win against Notre Dame in the Fiesta Bowl that left his Buffaloes as the third-ranked team in the country.

McCartney came to CU at one of its lowest points, and he left the program near the top of the college football world. He won a national championship, earned a spot in the College Football Hall of Fame in 2013, and has been inducted into the CU athletics and Colorado sports halls of fame.

"He's our iconic coach," longtime sports information director David Plati said.

Nearly a quarter century after his retirement, it was not the victories and the championships that left the greatest impression on his players, though. McCartney came to Boulder to win football games, but also to mold boys into great men. Several of McCartney's players went on to the NFL. Some, including Bieniemy, Hagan, and Jon Embree (CU's head coach in 2011 and '12) embarked on successful coaching careers. Some players, including Chad Brown, Johnson, Mike Pritchard, and Alfred Williams, went into broadcasting. Many others went on to success in other occupations and as husbands and fathers.

"Coach Mac gave me an opportunity to go to school, earn a degree, and he gave me an opportunity to pursue my dreams of playing football," said Bieniemy, who, as of 2019, was still the all-time leading rusher in CU history and a successful coach in the National Football League. "Coach Mac is a special man, and he always will be. He did a great job not only recruiting, but also he did a great job of helping young kids mature into men in every phase of their lives. That's all you can ask for in a head coach at that level. That's the love and respect that I know I will always have for him. He gave me an opportunity. That opportunity paved the way to help me achieve the goals that I've accomplished today in life. I'm sure every player that has played for coach Mac has a similar, successful story."

3 Whizzer

As a star football player, president of the student body, and a Rhodes scholar, Clayton "Sam" White set quite the standard during his days at the University of Colorado. His younger brother somehow met and surpassed that standard.

Byron "Whizzer" White was arguably the greatest athlete to ever suit up for the Colorado Buffaloes, while also making headlines nationally for his academics, matching his brother as a Rhodes scholar, serving in World War II, and then spending 31 years as a justice of the Supreme Court of the United States.

Upon White's death on April 15, 2002, at the age of 84, U.S. President George W. Bush described White as "a distinguished jurist who served his country with honor and dedication."

It was an amazing life and journey for White, who grew up in Wellington, Colorado, a small town north of Fort Collins known for its sugar beet farming. During his youth, White and his brother, who was five years older, learned the value of hard work. When it was time for beet topping in October, the youth in the

Wellington area would take off from school to work in the fields. White's father, Albert, and mother, Maude, instilled a strong work ethic in the boys. Albert, who served three terms as Wellington mayor, had a lumber business during the boys' youth. During the summers, when the boys weren't working on the beet farms, they were working at the lumber yard. As they got older and stronger, they worked for the Colorado and Southern Railroad.

"There was very little money around Wellington," White said in 1962, when he was appointed to the Supreme Court. "I suppose you could say that by the standards of today we were all quite poor, although we didn't necessarily feel poor because everyone was more or less the same. Everybody worked for a living. Everybody."

While Albert and Maude knew the value of work, they also saw value in the boys being well-rounded. Byron and Sam were always encouraged in activities they wanted to pursue, whether it was football, basketball, baseball, music, or drama. Both boys were in school bands and both performed as actors in plays. Nothing was more important than education, however, as Albert told his sons, "I would rather see you win one medal or scholarship than 40 football games."

When Byron left home for college at CU, Albert gave him this advice: "Young college men have to learn to make a living. They will run this country when the time comes and, if they don't do a better job than we are doing, they aren't going to get by. If people think athletics are more important than real preparation for life, they haven't lived right."

Byron certainly took those words to heart. He earned straight As all through his years at Wellington High School. At the time, CU offered scholarships to students who were valedictorians at their high schools. Sam and Byron both earned that scholarship.

At CU, Byron earned As in 180 of his 186 course hours; the rest were Bs. In December of 1937, at age 20, Byron earned the prestigious Rhodes scholarship—a postgraduate award to study for two years at the University of Oxford in England. "I'm happy, I'm gratified," he said. "It took my breath away." The White brothers are two of only five CU football players to become Rhodes scholars.

While achieving stellar academic success, Byron waited tables to earn money for his board, served as student body president and starred for CU's football, basketball, and baseball teams. He was a .400 hitter for the baseball team and helped the basketball team finish as runner-up in the 1938 National Invitation Tournament, but it was football that made Byron a star.

Prior to Byron's arrival at CU, Earl "Dutch" Clark was regarded as the best player to ever come through the region. A native of Fowler, Colorado, Clark was a star at Pueblo Central High School before gaining fame at Colorado College. In 1928, he became the first player from Colorado to earn first-team All-American honors. Byron viewed Clark as a hero, and had the good fortune of learning from Clark. During Byron's freshman year at CU, Clark took a job as the Buffaloes' basketball coach. He then helped the football team during spring practices. It was during that spring, in 1935, that Byron first gained some confidence that he could succeed at the college level.

"The first time the coach called, 'Fresh meat for the varsity,' I was scared stiff," Byron said. "About the third scrimmage, I conquered this fear by saying over and over to myself, 'Other players have taken this; I can.'"

He sure did. In the fall of 1935, it was clear to anyone watching him that Byron was a stellar player. A group of sportswriters decided he needed a nickname. Leonard Cahn of the *Denver Post* called him "Whizzer." Byron never liked the nickname, but it stuck. A knee injury limited Whizzer during his sophomore year in 1935 and it nearly ended his football career. Doctors recommended that he stop playing contact sports. Instead, White believed he simply needed to strengthen his knee. He joined the CU basketball team to do just that.

White started to really shine in 1936, and in 1937 he was a bona fide star, leading the country in rushing (1,121 yards) and scoring (122 points), while also throwing for 475 yards. White also returned punts and kickoffs, punted, and played defense. He had eight interceptions in his final two seasons. Long before social media and 24-hour sports TV networks made it fairly easy to gain recognition, it took something spectacular to grab the attention of the sporting world. In 1937, Whizzer was spectacular.

That year, sportswriter Irving Dix wrote, "There are those who stoutly contend that White is the nation's greatest triple threat in collegiate ranks. As a ballcarrier he is amazing. Terrific speed and a pair of hips that seem to swing on hinges have piled up yard after yard for him. His punting is phenomenal and his passing deadly. In addition to all those talents he's known as a quarterback who seldom makes a mistake."

White was a consensus first-team All-American, the first in CU's history and the only Buff to earn All-American honors before 1952. He was also runner-up to Yale's Clint Frank for the Heisman Trophy—awarded to the top player in college football.

In those days, Clark and White were the first true football stars in the western region of the country.

"Those were the two names you heard in the '20s and '30s that made a splash that other people noticed outside of this area," CU sports information director David Plati said.

CU had gained some national attention with a 9–0 record in 1923—followed by an 8–1–1 mark in 1924. The 1937 season was different, however, and it was because of White. The 1936 season was the first year of the Associated Press polls and in 1937, the Buffs were ranked nationally for the first time, finishing at No. 17. They also played in a bowl game—losing to Rice in the Cotton Bowl—for the first time.

"You could almost make the case that Byron White did put CU football on the map nationally for the first time," Plati said.

In the weeks leading up to White's final college football game, in the Cotton Bowl, he earned the Rhodes scholarship and was selected by the Pittsburgh Pirates (later renamed the Steelers) in the NFL draft with the No. 4 overall pick. He was paid what was then a record $15,000 salary to play for the Pirates as a rookie in 1938. White led the NFL in rushing in 1938, with 567 yards, and then went to Oxford in January of 1939 to resume his studies. With the start of World War II in 1939, he returned to the United States later that year and studied at Yale Law School. He played two more seasons in the NFL, 1940–41 with the Detroit Lions, and led the NFL in rushing in 1940.

In 1942, White joined the Navy and would be awarded two Bronze Stars for his service. While working in naval intelligence, he became friends with John F. Kennedy and future Supreme Court justice John Paul Stevens. White finished his law degree at Yale in 1946 and then worked for several years as a lawyer. After Kennedy was elected U.S. President in 1960, he named White as deputy attorney general. Then, in 1962, President Kennedy nominated White for the Supreme Court. He was just 44 years old when he took that position on April 12, 1962.

"That was a really big deal for the state of Colorado, especially with Byron coming from here," Plati said. "That not only meant a lot to the university; that meant a lot to the state."

White would serve on the Supreme Court until June 28, 1993, when he retired at age 75.

Sam, by the way, was rather accomplished in his own right as a medical researcher. According to the *New York Times*, "Dr. White developed the field of blast biology, the study of how explosions affect people immediately and over time. His studies, many highly classified, helped determine how to aim atomic bombs, treat blast victims, and improve bomb shelters." Byron often looked up to Sam, who proved to set a great example for his younger brother.

Byron wound up forging a remarkable path of his own, however, and is arguably the greatest Buff in history. White was named to the College Football Hall of Fame in 1954 and was the lone inductee for the inaugural year of the CU Athletics Hall of Fame in 1998.

"He represented the epitome of the reason we have athletic programs at a major university, that is to allow a talented young person to learn how to achieve the highest levels of success, whether in athletics or serving our country and society in a capacity such as the Supreme Court," former CU athletic director Dick Tharp said after White passed away. "We will miss his presence but, at the University of Colorado, we will always have a sense of his presence in our programs."

4 Rashaan Salaam

Recognizing the star in their midst, United Airlines flight attendants upgraded Rashaan Salaam to first class for his trip from New York to Denver in December of 1994. The Heisman Trophy won by Salaam that weekend got its own first class seat next to him.

It was a monumental weekend for Salaam and CU, as he became the first player in program history to be honored with the Heisman, presented annually to the top player in college football. Nothing excited Salaam more than the surprise he got upon returning home, however. Salaam had asked David Plati, who made the trip to New York, if any teammates would be at the airport. Because of final exams on campus, Plati said there likely wouldn't be anyone there.

"When we exited the plane, boom, there's all of his offensive linemen," Plati said. "It was really, really a cool thing to be a part of. From there, we went to a sports bar and had chicken wings. He had that infectious smile, but I've never seen him smile as much as he did when we came back from New York with the Heisman. I wouldn't say he was shy or introverted, but he never liked the spotlight on himself. He always thought all his accomplishments were because of everybody around him, specifically the offensive line. He loved the fact that he could share any glory that he had with his teammates, particularly the offensive line."

Byron White may have been the greatest athlete to ever play for CU, but Salaam would be in the conversation, and his 1994 season ranks with White's 1937 campaign for the best single-season performances in program history. In 1994, Salaam rushed for a program-record 2,055 yards—becoming just the fourth player in college football history to top 2,000 yards in a single season—and 24 touchdowns. He added another 83 yards and three touchdowns in a Fiesta Bowl win against Notre Dame and was the fifth unanimous All-American in CU history, helping the Buffs to an 11–1 record. In addition to the Heisman, Salaam won the Doak Walker Award (presented to the nation's top running back) and was named to the Big Eight Conference offensive player of the year.

"It was a great year," Salaam said in 2014, just ahead of the 20th anniversary of his Heisman win. "I played with some great players, played for a legendary coach, a Hall of Fame coach. It was a special time in Colorado. Football was king in the town, we had some exciting games. It was a very exciting college football experience that I had."

After playing eight-man football at La Jolla Country Day School in San Diego, Salaam didn't take long to prove that he might be okay in the 11-man game, too. During Salaam's third practice at CU, even before the team put on the pads, Plati was standing next to his mentor, Fred Casotti, a longtime CU sports information director and associate athletic director who was, at that time, working as the official historian. "Fred turns me to and he said, 'This kid is going to win the Heisman,'" Plati said. "He never said that about anybody else the entire time he was alive when I was there. He called it. Rashaan had incredible athletic talent."

Still, Salaam had to bide his time. He played sparingly as a true freshman in 1992 and then, in 1993, gained 844 yards and eight touchdowns as a backup to Lamont Warren, who rushed for 900 yards.

"It became apparent that he was the guy," Plati said. "That's why Lamont Warren left early to turn pro because he saw the handwriting on the wall with Rashaan."

Warren, who led the Buffs in rushing three years in a row, was a talented player who was drafted by the Indianapolis Colts the next spring and spent nine years in the NFL. Salaam was on a much different level, however, and had good genes. His father, Teddy Washington (who later changed his name to Sultan Abdus-Salaam) played running back at CU in 1963 before transferring to San Diego State.

Growing up in San Diego, Salaam figured he would go to Lincoln High School, which had produced Hall of Fame running backs Marcus Allen and Terrell Davis. Instead, his mother, Khalada, sent him to La Jolla. "She was hoping they didn't have a football team," Salaam said. "To go out there and find they had eight-man football, I had to take advantage of it."

In basically two-and-a-half seasons, he rushed for 4,965 yards and 112 touchdowns. He was recruited by several colleges and was planning to go to California until coach Bruce Snyder left for Arizona State. Salaam wound up at CU, but struggled in his first season.

"My first year at the University of Colorado, I was horrible," he said. "I didn't even letter. Coach Mac was in my corner, but it was a rough adjustment. I never doubted myself; I just knew I had to get some reps. I couldn't wait for spring ball to go out there and show the coaches that year I'm ready."

During his final two seasons at CU, Salaam made himself a household name in college football. Yet, as his star grew brighter, he tried to avoid the spotlight. That wasn't easy, as Heisman trophy talk heated up midway through the 1994 season.

"I'm scared, man. I really don't want to win it because I know how much pressure is put upon me," he said as the Buffs, at 7–0, prepared to face Nebraska. "I just want to play football. I just wish the Heisman was given to the best offensive team…. That would be more appropriate. It doesn't make sense for a person who might put up 1,700 or 1,800 yards to get the trophy to himself because it's not a one-man sport; it's a team effort."

On a star-studded team that featured many of the best players in CU history, including quarterback Kordell Stewart and receiver Michael Westbrook, Salaam stole the show. In 1994, he topped the 100-yard mark in 10 of 12 games (in the two he didn't, he scored four and three touchdowns, respectively) and the 200-yard mark four times.

"Rashaan is the kind of guy you like to block for as an offensive lineman," Tony Berti, CU's left tackle in 1994, said. "He was clearly talented, but he was such a great team player. It was never about Rashaan; it was about what he could do for the team and how he could make the team better."

Salaam's team-first attitude endeared him to his teammates, who were all pulling for him to reach the 2,000-yard mark. Salaam hit the milestone on a 67-yard touchdown run against Iowa State at Folsom Field on November 19, 1994. "It was special, man," he said. "It was gratifying. My family was there, my cousins were there. It felt good."

Even in that moment, however, as teammates mobbed him in the end zone, Salaam was shy about being the center of attention. "He didn't want the notoriety for rushing for 2,000 yards and I thought that was hilarious," Westbrook said. "He was trying to run out of the pile and I grabbed him and snatched him back to the ground. Then we put him on our shoulders and he didn't want to be up there. How shy he was about stuff like that, it makes me laugh because that's just how he was. He never wanted credit for stuff."

As he went to New York for the Heisman ceremony, Salaam wished his teammates could be there with him, but he did enjoy the atmosphere of being surrounded by college football royalty. "I was very excited to get a chance to meet a lot of these great football players you watched all year," he said. "You get a chance to meet them up close. You get a chance to meet some of your childhood heroes that you grew up watching, like Tony Dorsett."

While Salaam was not one to get too caught up in personal glory, winning the Heisman did have special meaning to him. "To get a chance to go out there and play well and win the Heisman was very empowering, because growing up I had no support at all," he said.

Growing up, Salaam never felt that his mother backed his athletic endeavors, and his father wasn't always around. "I had a Disneyland dad," he said. "When he showed up, we'd go to Disneyland. I love him for it; he tried."

As Salaam continued to enjoy the game and excel, his mother supported him and he knew she was proud of him when he won the Heisman. "Of course, definitely," he said. "A lot of people change. Especially my mother. She really started to change as far as how she looked at football."

As the 20th anniversary of his Heisman win approached, Salaam was still a celebrity in Boulder and was one of those players people came to meet. "It put me on a level that's so big," he said. "Winning the Heisman is one of those things, it's a dream come true. I'm very blessed. I'm thankful for the people around me."

Inside, however, Salaam battled demons for years.

Following the 1994 season, he skipped his senior year at CU to enter the NFL Draft and he was selected in the first round (21st overall) by the Chicago Bears. He set a Bears rookie record with 1,074 rushing yards in 1995 and he won the Brian Piccolo Award, given to the Bear who best exemplified the traits—courage, loyalty, teamwork, and dedication—of the late running back. Salaam's career took a sharp decline from there, however. He became addicted to marijuana, suffered a leg injury in 1998, and never worked as hard as he needed to in the NFL.

"I tried to get away with natural ability too much," he said. "I didn't build on it. I was lazy. My body started breaking down, I started getting hurt. I put the wrong people around me in my corner. It was just very immature things."

Following his rookie year, Salaam rushed for just 610 more yards. He played two games with the Cleveland Browns and was cut by three other teams. After briefly playing in the XFL and, in 2004, with the CFL's Toronto Argonauts, his career came to a close.

"I had a chance to reflect on the mess I made with the opportunity I had, the people who I could have associated with and decided not to," Salaam said in 2014. "I just had a lot of mistakes, a lot of errors."

In 2014, Salaam appeared to be coming to peace with his mistakes and how he could turn them into positives. "What I realized is that my whole career I've been too hard on myself," he said. "I did some great things. I made history. I would love to go back and change some things, but I can't. I'm hoping to use my story to go and influence kids."

The demons in his mind caught up to him, however. On December 5, 2016, he died from a self-inflicted gunshot wound to the head. He was only 42 years old.

"It makes me so extremely sad, because he was a really, really good person," Westbrook said upon learning of Salaam's death.

Salaam was a great person and player who left a lasting impression on those who knew him and played with him.

"I came to pay respects to my brother," Chris Naeole, a starting guard in 1994, said at Salaam's funeral. "At the end of the day, I have a lot of great memories, a lot of great thoughts about my friend. I'm just glad to be here today and see him off. That's all I can do is remember the best and celebrate his legacy."

While Salaam's story has a tragic conclusion, his legacy lives on at CU. As of 2018, he was still CU's only Heisman winner. He's been inducted into the CU Athletics and Colorado sports halls of fame. In 2017, CU posthumously retired his No. 19 jersey.

"Everywhere he went, he represented CU and he did it great," Plati said. "He was good with kids and signed autographs until the last person wanted one. He was just an all-around nice guy that cared about the people around him."

5 Darian Hagan

When Darian Hagan was a senior at Locke High School in Los Angeles in 1987, recruiting analysts were divided on what position he might play in college. Some thought he'd be a quarterback. Others thought he'd be better suited for running back or receiver. It was clear, however, that he had the talent to be a star. After a bumpy start in his freshman season, Hagan became one of the brightest stars in CU football history, as the Buffaloes' quarterback during the height of the program's success.

The 5-foot-10, 185-pound Hagan played at CU from 1988 to 1991, the last three years as the starter. He led the Buffs to a national championship in 1990 and a 2–0–1 record against rival

Nebraska. "Hagan has been the catalyst for our success," head coach Bill McCartney said before Hagan's final game in the 1991 Blockbuster Bowl. "He's made so many big plays and risen to the occasion so many times that you can't put into words what they meant."

Hagan threw for 3,801 yards, rushed for 2,007, accounted for 54 touchdowns, and posted a 28–5–2 record as a starter, including a remarkable 19–0–1 mark in Big Eight Conference games. He earned All-American honors in 1989, a year in which he finished fifth in Heisman Trophy voting. That season, he ran for 1,004 yards and threw for 1,002, becoming just the sixth player in college football history to top 1,000 yards in both categories in the same season. Considered the nation's top option quarterback coming out of high school, he didn't disappoint at CU, as he was often brilliant running the offense.

"I had the pleasure, and the challenge at the same time, of playing behind, I think, the greatest option quarterback to ever play college football," said Charles Johnson, Hagan's backup in 1989 and 1990. "Having played the option, we knew there were times when I was going to have to play, because it took such a physical toll on you."

That physical toll did lead to Johnson filling in at times, but Hagan still played in 34 of 37 games during his final three seasons, and he was a magician at times when running the option, taking advantage of his ambidexterity to execute plays that were mind-boggling.

Three of Hagan's most memorable pitches:

- October 28, 1989, at Oklahoma: CU had the ball at the 1-yard line. Hagan took the snap and went to his left, but was tripped up in the backfield. As he fell, he tossed the ball over the head of an Oklahoma defender and into the arms of J.J. Flannigan for the touchdown. CU won 20–3.

- November 4, 1989, vs. Nebraska: Arguably Hagan's most famous play, considering it came in a huge game against the No. 3 Cornhuskers. The Buffs were at their own 30 and Hagan kept the ball as he ran the option to the left. He sprinted downfield, while Flannigan ran a bit behind him and to the left, near the sideline. Hagan was 25 yards down field and probably could have cut to his right to get around a block and take it to the end zone, but instead he cut to his left, saw Flannigan and, on a full sprint, pitched the ball. Flannigan went the rest of the way for the 70-yard touchdown.

- August 26, 1990, vs. Tennessee: CU led 24–17 midway through the fourth quarter when Hagan took the snap from his own 22-yard line. As he ran to the right, he was hit behind the line of scrimmage. While falling, Hagan, who was cradling the ball in his right arm, switched it to his left hand and flipped it several yards to his right and into the hands of Mike Pritchard, who sprinted 78 yards for a touchdown. Hagan has said this was his favorite play during his CU days.

After that play against Nebraska, CBS Sports color commentator Pat Haden said, "We said what made Hagan so dangerous is that he pitches the ball at unusual times. Most quarterbacks will not pitch the ball 40 yards downfield. That's what makes Hagan so difficult to defend."

College coaches all over the country knew Hagan would be difficult to defend, and that's why he was so highly recruited. In addition to CU, he took official visits to Arizona, Nebraska, Oklahoma, and Washington. Hagan had Nebraska—arguably the premier option team in the country—at the top of his list, but McCartney wasn't about to get beat by the hated Cornhuskers. During ESPN's 30 for 30 documentary, *The Gospel According to Mac*, Hagan told a story of how McCartney convinced Hagan and his mom, Wanda Webb, to pick CU. Hagan grew up in South

Central Los Angeles, where gang activity was prevalent, including the bitter rivalry between the Crips—known for wearing blue—and the Bloods—known for wearing red.

According to Hagan, McCartney asked Webb, "What neighborhood is this?"

Webb said, "That's the Crips neighborhood over here."

McCartney then said, "You can't go to Nebraska, son. They wear red. This is a Crip neighborhood. They're going to kill you, son."

Hagan recalled that moment decades later and said, "I didn't even think about that, but I'm like, 'He's right, I can't wear this red. I can't go to Nebraska. But I put on that black and gold and I can go anywhere.' I committed right on the spot."

Darian Hagan runs down the field against Notre Dame in the '91 Orange Bowl. (Getty Images / Rick Stewart / Stringer)

Hagan's first year at CU, in 1988, was a struggle, however. Sal Aunese won the starting job and Hagan rarely played as a backup. With Aunese starting, Hagan didn't work hard to learn the game plan or study film.

"He saw his job as going in, finishing the game, and having some fun. Typical freshman," CU quarterbacks coach (and future head coach) Gary Barnett said of Hagan in 1989.

That lack of preparation cost Hagan and the Buffs in the 1988 Freedom Bowl, when he came off the bench during a 17–17 game and threw an interception that led to a game-winning field goal for Brigham Young University. After that game, Hagan told his coaches he was done playing quarterback and that he wanted to move to running back. The request was denied, and when Aunese

Valuable backup

Quarterback Charles Johnson threw a grand total of 46 passes and ran for 247 yards during his career at Colorado. Yet, more than a quarter century after he played, he's still revered by CU fans as the stellar backup who played a key role in CU's 1990 national title. Johnson led the Buffs to the famous "fifth down" win at Missouri in 1990, scoring the game-winning touchdown on the final play. He also relieved starter Darian Hagan during the Orange Bowl that season, leading the Buffs to their lone touchdown in the 10–9 victory over Notre Dame that secured the national title. While he didn't play much, Johnson was highly regarded by his teammates, and it was fitting that he played a key role in the greatest season in CU history.

"C.J. really was the father figure for Darian and Darian was the talent," said Vance Joseph, the third-string QB in 1990 who would later, in 2017–18, become the head coach of the NFL's Denver Broncos. "Behind the scenes, [Johnson] was a great leader of the team. Guys went to him for advice, because he was always a very mature, very smart guy. He was way beyond his years as far as maturity. He was a team leader but wasn't playing a lot. It was fitting that he was a big part of that team."

was diagnosed with inoperable stomach cancer in the spring of 1989, the starting quarterback job suddenly belonged to Hagan.

Surrounded by great leaders on the 1989 team, Hagan didn't need to fill a leadership role; he just had to go play and run the offense, and he did just that. "When I became the starting quarterback, I was trying to learn the ropes of the offense and not do anything to derail any of our seniors and their dreams," he said.

Instead, he helped them achieve their dreams and he became a legend. In 2002, Hagan was inducted into the CU Athletics Hall of Fame. In 2013, he was inducted into the Colorado Sports Hall of Fame.

"When you play with great guys and you do some things that people get excited about, things happen for you," he said in 2013. "I would dedicate [my Hall of Fame induction] all to my former teammates. Pretty much all I had to do was hand the ball off or pitch it."

Following his career at CU, Hagan was selected in the ninth round of the 1992 NFL Draft by the San Francisco 49ers, as a receiver. He didn't make the team, though, and spent five seasons playing for three different teams in the Canadian Football League.

In 2004, Hagan returned to CU, hired by Barnett—then the head coach—as an intern and he's been at CU ever since. In 2005, he was promoted to a full-time assistant coaching job. Since 2004, Hagan has worked with five different head coaches: Barnett, Dan Hawkins, Jon Embree, Mike MacIntyre, and Mel Tucker. Under Hawkins and MacIntyre, Hagan coached the Buffs' running backs, and he remained in that position after Tucker was hired in December of 2018.

After playing with CU's all-time leading rusher, Eric Bieniemy, Hagan coached the running backs who, as of 2019, ranked second and third on the list: Phillip Lindsay and Rodney Stewart.

"I was honored to be able to get coached by Coach Hagan," Lindsay said. "Coach Hagan brings a lot to the table for us."

For Hagan, coaching has been a labor of love. "It's not even a job to me," he said. "It's a big playground. I get to go out and have fun with it."

Part of the fun was making Boulder and CU his long-lasting home. Hagan had plenty of options of where to play when coming out of Locke High School, but since choosing CU in the fall of 1988, he's been a legendary and loyal Buffalo.

"The University of Colorado is a special place for me; always has, always will be," he said. "If I was 18 years old again and had to do it all over, I would do it all over again."

6 Eric Bieniemy

On a warm night in Austin, Texas, on September 22, 1990, everything that made Eric Bieniemy great was put on display. Bieniemy's strength, power, elusiveness, and determination all contributed to him rushing for 99 yards and three touchdowns against the host Texas Longhorns. His greatest contribution to this game, however, came without the ball in his hands.

Texas held a 19–14 lead as the third quarter came to a close, and the Longhorns had the ball. During the quarter break, the 5-foot-7 Bieniemy (who may have been closer to 5-foot-6) gathered the CU offense and approached the defense, challenging them to stop Texas. The CU defense responded by holding Texas to a field goal, and then Bieniemy scored two fourth-quarter touchdowns to deliver a 29–22 win that proved to be a monumental victory during CU's run to the national championship.

"The significance of this is that one guy can make a difference," McCartney said. "One guy like that can change things, and our entire season turned around because of this one kid being ignited and sparking and inspiring others."

The talented and passionate Bieniemy made a difference often during his CU career, from 1987 to 1990. Nearly three decades after he completed his career at CU, he was still the program's all-time leader in rushing yards (3,940) and total touchdowns (42). His 1990 season was one of the greatest in CU history, as he rushed for 1,628 yards and 17 touchdowns, finished third in the voting for the Heisman Trophy, and earned unanimous All-American honors. That game against Texas, when he had 99 yards, was the only time in 1990 that he failed to rush for 100-plus yards.

Bieniemy's career coincided with the greatest run of success in CU history, but he wasn't simply along for the ride. The Buffs were stacked with talent in those years, but Bieniemy was at or near the top of the list.

"During the time that I coached there, Bieniemy had the single greatest impact of any guy that I coached," McCartney said years later. "He had a fire in his heart that you couldn't put out. From the very first time he came on campus, he had an intensity about him, a commitment to him, a resolve that was extraordinary.

"He was fearless. Guys like Bieniemy, they light a fire in the guys around them. I always thought of him as having the most impact."

Bieniemy's road through Colorado wasn't smooth, however.

Like many of the African American players on the team in that era, Bieniemy dealt with racial incidents in predominantly white Boulder. Born in New Orleans and raised in West Covina, California, Boulder provided a new experience for Bieniemy and many of his African American teammates. A couple of times early in his career at CU, he considered transferring and during his freshman year, Bieniemy responded to a racial slur by getting into a fight at a bar. He was arrested, pleaded no contest to disorderly conduct, and had to do community service.

"I should have walked away from it but I didn't," he said in 1989. "It was a racial slur. I have my pride, but I had more to lose than he did. It has happened a few times since and I have walked away. I learned from the experience. You feel like you're alone, all by yourself with these problems, then you realize there is always going to be prejudice. Where I came from, you had every ethnic background. Boulder was culture shock for me. It was a white world and they made me feel like I was trespassing. I didn't do anything to them. I was black."

Eric Bieniemy runs for a big gain against the Missouri Tigers in a 1989 game the Buffaloes won 49–3. (Getty Images / Tim DeFrisco / Stringer)

Bieniemy also had several traffic violations that led to a suspended driver's license, a broken leg that limited him to eight games as a junior in 1989, and an off-the-field incident during the summer of 1990 that led to McCartney suspending him for the season opener. In 2018, when he was the offensive coordinator of the NFL's Kansas City Chiefs, he reflected on his troubles at CU and said, "I wouldn't change any of my experience there, even with some of the negative stuff that took place. It helped shape me as a person and helped me grow. You learn from your mistakes."

On the field, Bieniemy was sensational. His major flaw was that he suffered from fumble-itis. He fumbled 21 times during his career, including five times during a 1990 game against Nebraska; he made up for it with four fourth-quarter touchdowns in a 27–12 win. He also had a momentum-killing fumble in the 1990 Orange Bowl loss to Notre Dame.

Bieniemy's remarkable passion and competitiveness carried him through all the trials, though, as he became one of the greatest players in CU football history. He was one of the most thrilling players to watch and gained a tremendous amount of respect from his teammates. "He's a snot-nosed kid," All-American guard Joe Garten joked in 1990. "When he puts on those pads, he thinks he's 6'8", 320 pounds, and nothing can stop him. He fears failure."

Bieniemy was selected in the second round of the 1991 NFL Draft by the San Diego Chargers. He played nine years in the NFL, primarily as a backup, for the Chargers, Cincinnati Bengals, and Philadelphia Eagles. Following his playing career, Bieniemy got into coaching, including two stints (2001–02 and 2011–12) at CU and NFL jobs with the Minnesota Vikings and Chiefs. The same passion that made him great as a player helped him enjoy success as a coach.

"I'm a football coach and I'm very blessed and fortunate to be in the situation that I'm in," Bieniemy said in 2016, his fourth season with the Chiefs. "There's nothing like coaching. I'm very blessed and fortunate to be affiliated with football since the age of six. Not too many people can say that. I don't have anything to complain about at all. I am enjoying life."

7 Anderson Brothers

As brothers only 20 months apart in age, Bobby and Dick Anderson fought, but they were friends. They competed, but they were teammates.

"We grew up playing with and against each other," Dick told the *Boulder Daily Camera* in 2006. "But just about all the teams we played on won. I'm sure when we were young, we were a little aggressive toward each other, but we supported each other."

From that competitiveness and support blossomed not only two of the greatest individual players in CU football history, but the best brother duo the Buffaloes have ever seen.

One played offense and the other played defense, but they both made a significant impact and reached high levels of success. Both were All-Americans, NFL draft picks, and members of CU's All-Century team in 1989. Both have been inducted into the CU Athletics Hall of Fame and the Colorado Sports Hall of Fame. Then, in 2006, Bobby joined his brother in the College Football Hall of Fame; Dick was elected in 1993.

"It's fun joining Dick in the Hall," Bobby said in 2006. "He always led the way for me, and this is no different."

The Andersons were born in Midland, Michigan, but moved to Boulder in their youth and became stars at Boulder High School. In 1963, when Dick was a senior fullback and Bobby was a sophomore quarterback, they led the Panthers to the state football championship.

At BHS, the Andersons were coached by Emerson Wilson, a fullback with the Buffs from 1953 to '55. Wilson led CU in rushing in 1953 and still owns the school record for the longest play from scrimmage—a 95-yard touchdown run against Kansas State in 1954. Although the Andersons were blessed with talent, they often credited Wilson for taking them to another level.

"The one thing Emerson established immediately with you was to strive for excellence," Bobby said after Wilson died in 2010. "The first thing he'd talk to you about was winning the conference championship and the state championship. He always said at Boulder High, you should expect nothing less."

Both brothers carried those high expectations with them to CU, where they played for legendary coach Eddie Crowder.

Dick came to CU in 1964 and thought he would play fullback for the Buffs, but Crowder moved him to safety and put Wilmer Cooks—who was pretty darn good in his own right—at fullback.

"If I were doing it again, I would have Dick Anderson's hands on the ball on offense at least 10 times a game," Crowder told *The Denver Post* years later. "We didn't have a full grasp of his potential. But when he ran with the ball, he had magic."

The move to safety turned out okay. From 1965 to '67, Dick racked up 266 tackles and 14 interceptions. He's still tied for the single-season school record for interceptions (seven in 1967) and ranks third in career interceptions. He also punted throughout his career. Dick was a consensus All-American and All-Big Eight Conference selection in 1967, and he was named to the Big Eight Hall of Fame in 1978 (Bobby was inducted two years later).

Dick was a third-round pick of the NFL's Miami Dolphins in 1968 and played 10 seasons with them. He was the NFL Defensive Player of the Year in 1973, a three-time Pro Bowler, and two-time Super Bowl champion. He was a key member of the Dolphins in

1972—the only team in history to go undefeated (14–0) and win the Super Bowl. He was later named to the Dolphins Honor Roll and to the NFL's All-Decade team for the '70s.

"As it turned out, [the move to safety] was the best thing that ever happened to me," Dick told *The Denver Post.* "I might not have played in the NFL as a running back. I don't think I could have played 10 years as a running back."

Bobby was a national recruit out of Boulder High in 1966 and nearly went to the University of Florida, but ultimately joined his brother at CU—which is where his heart was all along anyway. "Being a Colorado Buffalo always was in my blood," he said years later. "I always wanted to be a Buff and I'll always be a Buff."

Freshmen were not permitted to play varsity at that time, but when Bobby was eligible in 1967, he beat out senior Dan Kelly for the starting job at quarterback. "If Anderson progresses normally, he can become a very fine quarterback," Crowder said before the 1967 season. "He's big and has enough speed and his passing looks satisfactory."

Bobby scored three touchdowns in his debut, a 27–7 win against Baylor on September 16, 1967. He capped his first season by scoring two touchdowns and winning MVP honors in a 31–21 win against Miami in the Bluebonnet Bowl, despite not starting. He overslept and missed the team bus to the stadium, caught a ride from a University of Houston coach, and entered the game before halftime. Bobby remained as the starting quarterback until a surprising move by Crowder in 1969. CU got off to a 1–1 start that season, but was plagued by injuries at running back. When the Buffs hit the snowy turf at Folsom Field on October 4 against Indiana, Bobby wasn't playing quarterback. Three days before the game, Crowder told Bobby he was moving him to tailback and didn't tell anyone until game time. Bobby ran for 161 yards and three touchdowns in a 30–7 win.

"Eddie said he needed my experience at tailback," Bobby recalled years later. "In the back of my mind, I wanted to play quarterback. I had been at quarterback for 23 games, but I said I'd do whatever was best for the team. I played my last nine college games at tailback."

Really, it wasn't a stretch to move Bobby to tailback. He was one of the country's best running quarterbacks anyway and led the Buffs in rushing three years in a row, from 1967–69. Bobby completed his CU career with more rushing yards (2,367) than passing yards (2,198) and ran for 34 touchdowns, while passing for only nine. He and Darian Hagan are the only players in CU history with at least 2,000 yards passing and rushing. At the time of his graduation, Bobby was CU's all-time leading rusher and he was a consensus All-American at tailback in 1969. His jersey—No. 11—is one of just four to be retired by CU.

In the 1970 NFL Draft, Bobby was selected 11th overall by the Denver Broncos and he played six seasons with the Broncos, New England Patriots, and Washington Redskins. He battled injuries throughout his NFL career, however, and played just 54 games. After retirement, he worked on CU radio broadcasts for nearly 30 years, from 1977 to 2005.

Because they played different positions and because of Bobby's injuries in the NFL, it's tough to compare the two, and David Plati joked, "You really couldn't compare them until they probably started playing on the Celebrity Golf Tour, so they could go head to head in the same thing."

While their paths were a bit different, Bobby and Dick are comparable in that they were legendary Buffs and hometown heroes.

"It's not just CU; Boulder takes a lot of pride in the Anderson family," Plati said. "They've meant a lot to Boulder."

8 Mr. Big Shot

After Chauncey Billups signed his letter of intent in 1995 to play basketball at Colorado, Buffaloes head coach Joe Harrington had a message to fans: be patient.

"He's playing against guys two, three, four years older than he is," Harrington said. "That makes a difference at this level [with] the teams we play in the Big Eight and the non-conference opponents we have next year."

Be patient? Not a chance.

CU fans had been through 25 years of mediocre-to-bad basketball and patience wasn't on the menu. Just 18 years old, Billups was already a legend. A native of Denver's Park Hill neighborhood, he was a two-time state champion at George Washington High School, a McDonald's All-American, and arguably the greatest high school recruit to ever sign with the Buffaloes, picking CU over some of the top programs in the country.

Billups' first game suggested Harrington might be on to something, though, after the freshman had 14 points on 2-for-13 shooting in a 71–47 loss at UC-Santa Barbara. Then, Billups and the Buffs came home for his first games in the Coors Events Center. In his home debut, the 6-foot-3 guard scored the first nine points and finished with 31 in a win against Northwestern State. Two days later, he came within one assist of a triple-double (19 points, 10 rebounds, nine assists) in a win against Tennessee State.

The Billups era was underway, and while it was short-lived, it was as good as advertised.

Billups left CU for the NBA after his sophomore season, but in his two years in Boulder, he averaged 18.5 points, 5.6 rebounds,

Chauncey Billups in a '97 NCAA Tournament game against North Carolina.
(Getty Images / Doug Pensinger / Staff)

and 5.1 assists per game. He earned All-Conference honors twice and All-American recognition as a sophomore.

Marcus Washington, who was a CU football player at the time, said Billups and his teammates were often in the front row at Folsom Field for football games, and the football team returned the favor. "I don't think the football players, as a whole, missed any basketball games when Chauncey Billups was playing," Washington said. "I know I didn't miss a home game. It was amazing to watch Chauncey, being an in-state kid. It was amazing to watch him do what he did. You knew his freshman year he was NBA caliber."

During Billups' freshman season, the Buffs were a dismal 9–18 and Harrington resigned in the middle of the campaign. Ricardo Patton took over and coached the Buffs for the next decade. Billups got Patton's tenure off to a stellar start. In 1996–97, the Buffs had a school-record 22 wins (22–10) and made their first NCAA Tournament appearance in 28 years. Billups had 24 points in a first-round win against Indiana, and they were knocked out by North Carolina in the second round. With a supporting cast that included Fred Edmonds and Martice Moore, Billups had the Coors Events Center rockin' during his years with the Buffs.

"It was loud in there," said Curtis Snyder, who grew up in Boulder, was a CU student during that time, and has worked for several years in the CU sports information department. "I remember for some of the conference games his sophomore year, those were some of the louder games I've been at."

For Billups, that was the goal—to make the Events Center loud.

"I wanted to bring some joy and bring a great atmosphere and some energy to the University of Colorado in a basketball capacity," he said prior to his induction to the CU Athletics Hall of Fame in 2015. "I went to CU to try to put my city and my state on the map as far as basketball is concerned."

CU Events Center

Chauncey Billups is one of several stars to shine in the CU Events Center, which has been home to the men's and women's basketball teams since it opened in 1979. It has also been home to the women's volleyball team since 1988. The arena was originally called the CU Events/Conference Center, but was renamed the Coors Events Center in 1990 after a $5 million donation from the Adolph Coors Foundation. In 2018, the name was changed to CU Events Center. In addition to athletics, the CEC has hosted concerts featuring Bob Dylan, U2, and others, as well as events with president Barack Obama and the 14th Dalai Lama.

Billups certainly did that, and by the end of his sophomore year, it was clear he was destined for a grander stage. He skipped his final two years, declared for the 1997 NBA Draft, and was selected third overall by the Boston Celtics.

"I think CU is lucky to have had him for the two years they did have him," Snyder said. "The overall impact he's had on this state, in terms of basketball, I don't know that anyone else has rivaled that."

Tad Boyle, hired as CU's head coach in 2010, never coached Billups, but has long admired what Billups and his family have meant to the program. Billups has remained close to the program and his younger brother, Rodney, was on Boyle's staff for six years.

"It's immeasurable, the fact that he's accessible to our players," Boyle said. "He's willing to help the program in any way he can. He follows the program and cares about the program. You can't put into words what that means to a coach, but certainly the players that we have."

As great as Billups was at CU, his legend grew in the NBA— although it took a while. During his first four seasons, Billups was traded three times and was a part of five organizations: Boston, Toronto, Denver, Orlando, and Minnesota. In the summer of 2002, he signed as a free agent with the Detroit Pistons, and his career took off. With the Pistons, Billups was a leader and clutch performer, earning the nickname "Mr. Big Shot." In six full seasons with the Pistons, he was a three-time All-Star and led them to the 2004 NBA title, while taking Finals MVP honors. He led the Pistons to the Finals in 2005, as well, but they lost to San Antonio in Game 7.

Early in the 2008–09 season, Billups was traded to Denver and made a triumphant return home. He earned two more All-Star Game appearances and helped the Nuggets reach the Western Conference finals in 2009. Billups retired in 2014 after 17 seasons with seven different teams, averaging 15.2 points and 5.4 assists per game. His jersey numbers have been retired by CU (No. 4) and the Pistons (No. 1).

"I think what Chauncey means to Colorado is the fact that he's a homegrown guy who did very well, both while he was here and certainly when he left the University of Colorado," Boyle said. "When you think about basketball in this state, he's probably the first guy that comes to mind because of his success in high school, his success in college, and his success in the NBA."

Through all of his success, Billups has remained loyal to his home state and his Buffs and he is one of the state's most legendary athletes.

"I would just say thank you to all my Colorado fans here that have really propelled me to stardom," he said in 2015. "I was a childhood name, a childhood star around here in this town. It's only because of the fans and how they viewed me and how they pushed me and how they encouraged me to continue and keep getting better. I'm forever indebted to the fans here in Colorado for the success that I've had in my career."

9 Sal Aunese

After the 1984 football season, head coach Bill McCartney made a bold decision that would change the future of the program.

McCartney was three years into his tenure as head coach and had posted a dismal 7–25–1 record, including 1–10 in 1984. Something had to be done to get the Buffs on the winning track, and McCartney made the decision to ditch the pro-style offense and install the run-oriented wishbone, a triple-option attack. There were only a few major college teams in the country running the wishbone, and one of those wasn't far away. Coach Ken Hatfield introduced the wishbone to Air Force in 1980, after his team went 2–9 in 1979. By 1982, the Falcons won eight games, and in 1983 they won 10. McCartney hoped for similar results.

"After doing extensive research, I feel the wishbone is the right thing for us," McCartney said in the spring of 1985. "I'm excited to crank it up."

That year, the Buffs were one of the most improved teams in the country. With converted running back Mark Hatcher at quarterback, the Buffs went 7–5 and received a bid to the Freedom Bowl—CU's first bowl game in nine years. Hatcher played well, but to take the next step as a program, CU needed a true option quarterback. McCartney and his staff went after one of the best in the land—Sal Aunese of Vista High School in California.

In 1986, Aunese was rated the fifth-best quarterback prospect in the country by Max Emfinger's National High School Scouting Service. Arguably the best option quarterback in the country, Aunese was heavily recruited by several schools, including national power Nebraska, CU's chief rival. McCartney and the CU staff put the full-court press on Aunese, who was also considering Hawaii.

"The day before signing day, we knew Tom Osborne, the head coach at Nebraska, was coming in to see Sal and he was going to spend three or four hours with him that day," Gary Barnett, CU's quarterbacks coach, said during the ESPN 30 for 30 documentary, *The Gospel According to Mac.* "I sat outside the door when Sal met with him and I was there when the meeting was over. We wanted Sal to know that we were going to be there all day; that's how important he was to us."

The talented Samoan signed with the Buffs, sparking a celebration by the coaching staff. His debut would have to wait, however. In 1986, a new NCAA rule on eligibility, known as Proposition 48, was added to the bylaws. Prop 48 penalized incoming players who didn't meet certain academic requirements; those players had to sit out a year, with no games or practice, and give up a year of playing eligibility. Aunese was one of three CU freshmen—including running back J.J. Flannigan and defensive lineman Okland Salavea—who were Prop 48 casualties.

With Aunese sitting out in 1986, Hatcher led the Buffs to a 6–6 record and a trip to the Bluebonnet Bowl. A senior in 1987, Hatcher began that season as the starter, with Aunese third on the depth chart. In the third game of the season, at Folsom Field, Hatcher was out with an ankle injury, so Rick Wheeler got the start. The offense sputtered and, late in the first quarter, McCartney put Aunese into the game. He rushed for 185 yards and a touchdown to lead the Buffs to a 26–17 victory against Washington State.

"I can just remember going, 'Wow, I think we found a quarterback,'" Barnett said.

After that win, Aunese started 19 of the next 20 games, missing only the 1987 finale with a shoulder injury. He was 13–6 as a starter from 1987 to '88 and led CU to the 1988 Freedom Bowl. During those two seasons, he racked up 1,009 yards and 14 touchdowns on the ground and 1,526 yards and five touchdowns as a passer. Early in 1988, Aunese directed the Buffs to a 24–21 upset win at No. 19 Iowa, scoring the game-winning touchdown on a one-yard run. Two weeks later, Aunese's touchdown pass to Mike Pritchard with 38 seconds to play lifted the Buffs to a 27–23 win at Colorado State.

On the field, Aunese was delivering as McCartney had hoped, and his teammates were drawn to him. Off the field, Aunese had his trials.

In the spring of 1988, he was arrested and spent two weeks in Boulder County Jail after pleading guilty to misdemeanor menacing from an incident in the dorms at CU. McCartney suspended him for the entirety of spring practices.

Then, four games into the 1988 season, McCartney's daughter, Kristy, told her parents that she was pregnant. Aunese was the father. Aunese didn't have any intentions to marry Kristy, but McCartney and his wife, Lyndi, asked the quarterback to at least be a friend and support their daughter. McCartney also assured Aunese that he would not lose his position on the team, although it created an awkward second half of the season.

Despite the drama surrounding him, Aunese played well and led the Buffs to the Freedom Bowl in Anaheim, California. In that game, played near Aunese's hometown, he struggled mightily in a 20–17 loss to Brigham Young University. He was sluggish and didn't have the usual explosiveness he displayed on the field.

Aunese's health problems continued after he returned to school in January. On March 30—about a month before Kristy's due date—Aunese was diagnosed with inoperable stomach cancer and was told he had only six months to live.

"It's very rare that someone that young gets literally a death notice," said David Plati, CU's sports information director.

On April 24, 1989, Timothy Chase "T.C." McCartney was born. Aunese was a proud father who would visit Kristy and T.C.

often. But, while his son was growing, Aunese was dying. During the summer, quarterback Darian Hagan, who was in line to take over as the starter, visited Aunese in the hospital and couldn't control his emotions.

"He looked like a totally different person," Hagan told ESPN years later. "He had lost 50 pounds and had tubes in his nose, and he was frail. And, you know, Sal wasn't frail. Sal was like a titan, man. He was put together. And seeing him sitting there fragile, I cried."

During fall camp, Aunese made a few visits to the team. They were happy to see him, but reality was setting in.

"The eye-opening experience that really shook all of us—it physically shook me—was when he came to camp," running back Eric Bieniemy said on *The Gospel According to Mac*. "That's when it really hit, like, 'Damn, cancer is kicking his ass and it ain't supposed to happen like this. Not this young man that never has a bad day.'"

With Hagan leading the team, the Buffs started 2–0 in 1989. In the third game, on September 16, the eighth-ranked Buffs hosted No. 10 Illinois. Each of the first three games were held at Folsom Field and Aunese watched them all from a private booth. The Buffs were especially inspired that day against Illinois, crushing the Illini, 38–7. One week later, on the night of September 23, 1989, Aunese passed away at the age of 21.

Aunese was no saint, and he certainly had his share of trials, but his impact on those around him was significant and his legacy has been long-lasting.

Aunese provided Kristy with a son and coach McCartney with a grandson. T.C. was a star at Boulder's Fairview High School before playing at LSU. He then worked as a graduate assistant at CU during the 2012 and 2013 seasons to kick off a coaching career that has including stops at LSU and in the NFL with the Cleveland

Browns and San Francisco 49ers. In 2019, he was hired by the Denver Broncos to coach quarterbacks.

On the field, Aunese provided some exceptional moments for CU and its fans, and he inspired his teammates to a sensational run of success in 1989 and 1990, culminating in the only national championship in CU football history.

"His story, it's tied into a very special time here," said linebacker Chad Brown, who was a freshman in 1989. "Certainly we were talented, certainly we were well-coached. Coach Mac had been building the program up to that point, but I'm not sure the story would be the same without [Sal]."

10 Inspired by Sal

Going into the 1989 season, Colorado's football players knew they had a special team.

An 8–4 record in 1988 was CU's best in 12 years, and several key players were coming back in 1989. Running backs Eric Bieniemy and J.J. Flannigan, a sensational one-two punch in 1988, returned in 1989. Receivers Jeff Campbell and Mike Pritchard were back. Four of the five starting offensive linemen and eight starters on defense were also coming back. The one major difference in the starting lineup was at quarterback. With senior Sal Aunese battling cancer, sophomore Darian Hagan was slated to take over. Hagan was an exceptional talent that might have won the job anyway, though.

"That's something we'll never know," David Plati said. "But, I would imagine Hagan would have either pushed Sal to another level that even Sal didn't know he could have gone to, or Hagan would have won the job. That would have been a severely intense competition."

With a stacked team, the Buffs were set up for a remarkable run in 1989, and they wound up dominating the competition throughout the regular season. Led by Hagan—who finished fifth in Heisman Trophy voting—the Buffs went 11–0 during the regular season, with 10 of the wins coming by at least 17 points.

CU had five players—Hagan, guard Joe Garten, outside linebackers Kanavis McGhee and Alfred Williams, and punter Tom Rouen—earn first-team All-American honors. Three others earned some sort of All-American recognition and the Buffs had 10 players on the All-Big Eight team. Hagan was Big Eight offensive player of the year, while Williams was the defensive player of the year.

Aunese's impact on the team was perhaps greater than all of them, however. The former starting quarterback lost his battle with cancer and passed away on the night of September 23, 1989, during the Buffs' bye week. Prior to his death, Aunese wrote a letter to his teammates:

> *My dearest teammates, coaches, friends, and brothers, whom apart from my family I do hold so close,*
>
> *I come to you all with love and encouragement to continue to do what you, we all, have been doing since our season first started, only to excel and better ourselves mentally, physically, and spiritually. Unity is our strength and love is our guide from here on in. Don't be saddened that you will no longer see me in the flesh, because I assure you I will always be with you in spirit. Hold me dear to your hearts as you know I do all of you. Strive only for victory each time we play, and trust in the Lord for He truly is the way! I love you all, 'go get 'em,' and bring home the Orange Bowl.*
>
> *Love, Sal*

CU was 3–0 at the time of Aunese's death, but played inspired the rest of the way. "You have guys from different parts of the country, different backgrounds," said linebacker Chad Brown, a freshman on the 1989 team. "Sometimes it takes something that is so core to everyone's being—your health, or seeing your teammate lose his health and, in the end, lose his life—to bring all these people with different interests and different backgrounds to kind of galvanize us together."

One week after Aunese's death, the Buffaloes, ranked No. 5 in the country, played at No. 21 Washington at Husky Stadium in Seattle. Prior to the game, every player in a CU uniform knelt near midfield, raised an arm, and pointed toward the sky. Many of them had to wipe away tears before kickoff. They were not to be denied, however, crushing the Huskies, 45–28. At one point, CU led 38–6.

"You have all these young men that are having to deal with mortality and just things that are so much bigger than football," center Jay Leeuwenburg said. "That really brought us together as men."

Paying tribute to Aunese throughout the 1989 season, CU was one of the best teams in the country. The Buffs rolled through the Big Eight Conference with a 7–0 record, including a 27–21 victory against rival Nebraska. It was arguably the best team in CU history, and the Buffs went into the Orange Bowl on January 1, 1990, ranked No. 1.

One win away from the national championship, CU's magical run came to an end against No. 4 Notre Dame. After a scoreless first half, Notre Dame dominated the second half to win, 21–6. "It was a case of opportunities we didn't capitalize on," McCartney said. "Notre Dame's a good team and didn't make many mistakes." Colorado made plenty—including three turnovers—and it led to a heart-breaking conclusion to a remarkable season.

11 Miracle at Michigan

Standing on the sidelines at Michigan Stadium and feeling the energy generated by 106,427 spectators, Michael Westbrook was blown away. "I was just in awe," he said.

Located in Ann Arbor, Michigan, the stadium is an iconic venue in college football and has taken away the breath of many who have seen a game within its walls. For Westbrook, however, this trip, on September 24, 1994, meant a lot more. The Big House, as it is known, is located 45 minutes from Westbrook's hometown of Detroit, and it took him 22 years to get there. "It was like a dream for me because I'm from Detroit and I wanted to play for the University of Michigan," he said.

Growing up, Westbrook never could afford to attend a game at Michigan Stadium. Despite being a standout at Detroit's Chadsey High School, he wasn't wanted by the Wolverines. In fact, there weren't many colleges that did recruit the lanky receiver. Minnesota offered him a chance to walk on, and Colorado offered a scholarship. By the time Westbrook and his CU teammates took the field that day in 1994, he was the best receiver on a talent-rich team that brought a No. 7 national ranking to Ann Arbor.

"To be there in the stadium and playing against them, and the Blue and Gold in the stands and the helmets, I'm just looking at [Michigan] like, 'You should have recruited me. You guys made a big mistake,'" Westbrook said. "I wanted to do something spectacular against them, just for the simple fact that they didn't recruit me."

The Buffaloes and No. 4-ranked Wolverines battled all afternoon, but with six seconds remaining on the clock, the chance for doing something spectacular seemed to be fading away. Colorado

The Buffaloes go crazy and mob Michael Westbrook in the end zone after his improbable catch lifted them to the win over Michigan. (AP Photo / Jon Freilich)

trailed 26–21, had time for only one more play, and stood 64 yards from the end zone. McCartney told quarterback Kordell Stewart to run "Rocket Left."

"When we called it, everybody knew what to do," McCartney said. "We actually practiced that play every Friday, every week. But, it's the only time we ever used it and it worked."

Two decades later, McCartney admitted CU's chances of winning the game in that moment were not good. "It was a pipe dream," he said. "It was the longest of the long shots. But, we knew what we were trying to do. It wasn't inadvertent or something ad-libbing. It was according to script, which is important, because we designed something, we practiced it, and then when we executed it, it worked. I agree it was lucky, but still we had a plan and we worked the plan."

The plan called for Stewart to drop back into the pocket and buy time as the Buffaloes' four receivers—Westbrook, Rae Carruth, Blake Anderson, and James Kidd—raced toward the end zone. The play was designed for Stewart to heave the ball downfield and for Westbrook—the tallest of the bunch—to leap over the crowd and tip the ball to Anderson. "If the ball gets tipped right, one of us will catch it," Westbrook said.

At 6-foot-4 and with great leaping ability, Westbrook was the natural choice to tip the ball. Yet, as he walked to the line of scrimmage, he motioned to Anderson to switch roles. "I wasn't trusting anybody at that time to catch this ball," Westbrook said. "I'm like, 'Switch spots.' It was the first time we ever did that. I don't know what made me do that."

After the snap, Stewart danced around the pocket, Heisman Trophy–winning running back Rashaan Salaam made a key block to buy more time for Stewart, and just as the clock hit all zeroes, Stewart let the ball fly. About 71 yards down the field from where Stewart released the ball, Anderson jumped and got his hand on the ball to tip it. In end zone, just behind the crowd, Westbrook's eyes locked onto the ball.

"It was complete, total slow motion," he said. "You don't hear the crowd anymore, you don't hear anything. You just see the white stripes on the ball going super slow and you start making adjustments accordingly."

Westbrook reached out and snatched the ball, holding on as he fell to the ground with the spectacular moment he dreamed about. Final score: Colorado 27, Michigan 26.

"It was an amazing, amazing, amazing play when you look back at it," said Westbrook, who dealt with cramping during the second half. "It's something that obviously doesn't happen every day."

As the Buffaloes celebrated, legendary ABC-TV announcer Keith Jackson, whose voice has been the soundtrack for so many of college football's great moments, said on the broadcast, "There are no flags on the field; only despair for the Maize and Blue, joy and exaltation for the Buffaloes of Colorado."

Oh, what joy for Westbrook, who once dreamed of displaying his greatness on that field. With more than 50 friends and family in attendance, he fulfilled that dream—just not to the delight of the Wolverines. "I was confused, like, 'What just happened?'" he said of the celebration on the field. "I was excited and confused and crampy and emotional. I really didn't know what to feel and I went into the locker room and I exploded in tears of joy."

While Westbrook never did realize his dream of playing for the Wolverines, he still cherishes his lone visit to The Big House.

"I probably wouldn't have turned out to be the Michael Westbrook I turned out to be if I had gone to Michigan," he said. "The Hail Mary would have never happened. It was an awesome, awesome day that none of us will ever forget."

12 Skiing Dynasty

With a national championship in sight on March 14, 2015, Colorado head skiing coach Richard Rokos was a bundle of nerves as he watched his team go through the final day of competition in Lake Placid, New York. "It was very exhausting mentally," Rokos said.

In the end, Rokos was able to breathe a sigh of relief, as he and his team waved CU flags and hoisted yet another trophy. CU's victory at the NCAA skiing championships was the 20th national title in the sport for the Buffaloes, and eighth for Rokos.

"Obviously it means a lot for me, but I'm more excited on the 20th title for the school, because that's some kind of landmark," Rokos said. "Twenty championships for the school, that's something the school can be proud of, and we are as the skiers. It speaks about the history and tradition of the skiing at the university."

Football is the sport that generates the most revenue and attention at CU, and that's the case at most schools around the country. In terms of success on the national (and international) stage, however, there's no question which sport is king at Colorado. Through 2018, the CU ski team had accounted for 20 of the 29 national championships in the history of the athletic program.

Men's skiing became an NCAA-sponsored sport in 1954. In 1977, women's skiing became a part of the Association for Intercollegiate Athletes for Women (AIAW) and CU won an AIAW national title in 1982. The following year, in 1983, the NCAA sponsored the women for the first time, making the sport co-ed.

From 1954 to 2019, only the University of Denver had won more skiing championships than CU, with 24. Of those, 14 came before 1972. Statistically, CU's success in the sport has been staggering. In addition to the 20 national championships, the Buffs had 13 runner-up finishes (including three in a row from 2016 to '18). Individually, the Buffs had racked up 95 NCAA championships and 510 All-American honors.

"There's a lot of pride," Rokos said of skiing at CU. "The standard has been set a long time ago and we maintain it. It's peer pressure. It goes in the academic area and the athletic area. The expectation is there and no one wants to fail. It's a relatively easy way to maintain it."

The high standard was set around the time Bob Beattie took over as head coach in 1957. He coached the Buffs for nine years and led them to their first two national championships, in 1959 and 1960. Six-time All-American Frank Brown and national champion Dave Butts were among the first stars at CU. Bill Marolt, who won four national titles as a CU skier, coached the Buffs from 1968 to '78 and led them to seven consecutive national titles from 1972 to '78. He later served as CU's athletic director, from 1984 to 1996. Tim Hinderman coached CU after Marolt and led the CU men's team to two national titles and the women's team to one—the AIAW title in 1982. In 1983, he led CU's first NCAA-sponsored co-ed team. In the summer of 1990, Marolt was the athletic director and hired Rokos, a native of Czechoslovakia who had spent three years as an assistant with the Buffs before being promoted. Leading CU to the title in 2015, Rokos passed Marolt for the most championships in school history.

CU's impact in the sport has extended well beyond the collegiate ranks, however. During the second half of his tenure as the Buffs' head coach, Beattie coached the United States ski team's alpine squad. Team USA made history at the 1964 Winter Olympics at Innsbruck, Austria. With Beattie as coach, the U.S. won its first-ever Olympic medals in men's skiing that year: in the slalom, Billy Kidd won silver and Jimmie Heuga won bronze. Both

Sweet 16 of CU Skiing

Colorado has a rich tradition of success with its skiing program. Some of the best to hit the slopes or the Nordic trails for the Buffs:

Frank Brown (1957–59): One of the program's first stars, he earned All-American honors six times, three times in alpine and three in Nordic, and was a key to CU's first team championship, in 1959.

Dave Butts (1959–60): A two-time All-American, he won three national titles, including downhill and jumping.

Maria Grevsgaard (2006–09): A two-time Nordic national champion, she was the program's first eight-time All-American and recorded a school-record 24 wins.

Jimmie Heuga (1963–65): He won the national title in slalom in 1963 and earned All-American honors twice. A two-time Olympian, he won a bronze medal in 1964—the first active CU athlete to win an Olympic medal.

Stephan Hienzsch (1975–78): The first Buff to win the national title in the giant slalom, in 1977, he also won the slalom that year. He was a part of four national championship teams.

Petra Hyncicova (2015–18): A seven-time All-American, she won both Nordic national titles, in classical and freestyle, in 2017. In 2018, she was an Olympian for the Czech Republic.

Bill Marolt (1963–66): Before his exceptional run as coach, he was a rare four-time national champion and three-time All-American as an athlete.

Vidar Nilsgard (1971–74): A star ski jumper (which is now discontinued), he was a two-time national champion, three-time first-team All-American and a key to several national championship teams.

Rune Oedegaard (2012–15): He won a pair of Nordic national titles and earned All-American honors seven times, while also setting a men's school record for career wins (19).

Jana Rehemaa (2003–06): A five-time first-team All-American, she won both Nordic national titles in 2006, while helping CU to a team title.

Joanne Reid (2010–13): A 2013 Nordic national champion, she earned All-American honors seven times and competed in the 2018 Olympics in the biathlon. Her mother was an NCAA champion in cross country in 1983 for Vermont.

Line Selnes (1998): Competed just one year, but she set a school record for wins in a season (11) and consecutive wins (8). Claimed national titles in both Nordic events (classical and freestyle).

John Skajem (1986–1987): A three-time national champion, he swept both alpine events in 1987 and was a four-time All-American.

Mads Stroem (2014–17): The first male to earn eight All-American honors (seven first team), he won three Nordic national titles and 14 races overall.

Buddy Werner (1961–63): A four-time national champion in alpine, he was a two-time All-American and became a three-time Olympian.

Lucie Zikova (2005–08): The first seven-time All-American in CU history, she won three alpine national titles and set a school record, men or women, for alpine wins (16).

were Buffs. Heuga—a two-time All-American—was in the midst of his CU career at the time. Kidd never skied for the Buffs, but was a CU graduate.

"More than half the team [in 1964] was CU skiers," said Curtis Snyder, a member of the CU sports information staff who has worked with the ski team. "It's hard to put enough words behind how significant this program is to its sport. I hesitate to think of any other [collegiate sports] program that had an impact on the culture of the sport within the United States."

Beattie coached Team USA at two Winter Olympics (1964 and 1968), as did Marolt (1980 and 1984). Marolt later became the president of the United States Ski and Snowboard Association. Through 2018, 35 former CU ski team members had competed in the Olympics, including Casey Puckett, who was a five-time Olympian. Another dozen Olympic skiers were former CU students who didn't compete collegiately for the Buffs. Beattie, Marolt, Kidd, and Heuga are among the 12 former Buffs inducted into the U.S. National Ski Hall of Fame.

"It goes back as far as it could go," Rokos said of CU's remarkable tradition in skiing. "It goes on and on and I think the elite level maintains so high throughout the ages."

CU hasn't let up, either. In 2020, Rokos will be in his 30th season as CU's head coach, striving to add to the Buffaloes' list of championships. "Every championship is different and it's always fulfilling," he said. "I don't think you can have enough of it."

13 Nebraska Rivalry

Throughout his eight years as an assistant coach with the Michigan Wolverines, Bill McCartney got an up-close view of one of the greatest rivalries in all of sports. The Michigan vs. Ohio State rivalry in football, dubbed "The Game," is intense and filled with animosity. It's one of those games that can make or break a season. "Our favorite saying was, 'Oh how I hate Ohio State!'" McCartney said.

Hired in 1982 as head coach at Colorado, McCartney asked, "Who is our Ohio State?"

The answer: nobody.

"There was no rival. There was no game to point to," McCartney said.

McCartney fixed that. He looked at CU's schedule and pointed toward the big, bad Nebraska Cornhuskers. Literally circling the game in red, McCartney targeted Big Red as the team to beat for the Buffaloes. "One of the reasons we chose them and not Oklahoma and others is because they're a neighboring state," McCartney said. "They're next door. They can get loud. You've got to shut 'em up. That's how we approached it anyway."

Frankly, it was a bold move. CU was 7–26 in the three years before McCartney arrived. Nebraska was the defending Big Eight champions and hadn't finished lower than 12th in the national rankings in 14 years. On top of all that, CU had lost 14 in a row to the Cornhuskers, including a 59–0 beatdown the year before. It was the Cornhuskers' great success, however, that made them an ideal choice for McCartney. "The teams you want to beat the most are the best teams," he said.

Still, even with McCartney's targeting of the Cornhuskers, this wasn't much of a rivalry in 1982. CU was little more than an annoyance to the Huskers, and in McCartney's first four years, nothing really changed, with Nebraska winning all four meetings by a combined score of 150–47. McCartney's fifth try figured to be more of the same. The Buffs were 2–4 going into the game, on October 25, 1986, at Folsom Field, while Nebraska was 6–0 and ranked No. 3 in the country.

This was not to be Nebraska's day, though. CU's Jeff Campbell scored on a 39-yard reverse to open the scoring. Then, after Nebraska pulled within 10–7 going into the fourth, CU freshman O.C. Oliver threw a 52-yard touchdown pass to Lance Carl on a halfback pass—one of only two passes completed by Oliver during his career. "When they called the play, my eyes got big and my first thought was, 'Me?'" Oliver said after the game. "It made my stomach start growling. We had practiced it, but I had never thrown a pass in my life in a football game."

CU's offense was backed up by a brilliant effort on defense, as the Buffs stuffed the Nebraska rushing attack. As the clock hit zeros, CU had a 20–10 victory and the goalposts came tumbling down in celebration. "It proves you achieve what you emphasize," McCartney said after the game. "You reap what you sow. No, I didn't think it would come this soon. But you have to set your sights on the pacesetter. I think we have a rivalry now."

Throughout the rest of McCartney's tenure, and beyond, the Colorado-Nebraska rivalry became one of the best in the Big Eight/Big 12, and Buff Nation quickly grew to hate not only the Cornhuskers, but the color red.

"To this day, I may not even own a red shirt," Marcus Washington, who played for CU from 1995 to '98, said in 2019. "I don't even wear anything red. It's that serious."

Matt McChesney, who played defensive line for the Buffs from 2000 to '04, grew up in nearby Niwot, Colorado, and came from a family filled with Nebraska fans. Throughout his high school years, the Buffs went 0–4 against Nebraska, losing by a combined 13 points.

Top 5 Wins Over the Huskers

Through 2018, CU had a dismal 19–49–2 all-time record against rival Nebraska, but many of the Buffs' wins were among the biggest wins in program history. Here's a look at five of the biggest victories against Nebraska:

November 3, 1990: Colorado 27, Nebraska 12: Eric Bieniemy scores four fourth-quarter TDs as CU continues march to national title.

November 23, 2001: Colorado 62, Nebraska 36: Led by Chris Brown's six TD runs, the Buffs stunned the No. 2-ranked Huskers.

October 25, 1986: Colorado 20, Nebraska 10: The Buffs snapped an 18-game losing streak to Nebraska by upsetting the third-ranked Huskers.

November 4, 1989: Colorado 27, Nebraska 21: En route to an undefeated regular season, the No. 2 Buffs beat the No. 3 Huskers for their first outright conference title in 28 years.

November 18, 1961: Colorado 7, Nebraska 0: Although not a great Nebraska team, this win helped CU to its only outright conference title from 1948 to 1988.

"For the entirety of my youth and teenage years, we would lose to them on some horse crap call and I would get a phone call with that damn Big Red song," he said. "I was thinking to myself, 'When I get to CU, this is going to change. There's no way I'm going to walk out of this rivalry without an advantage for the rest of my life.' It was a driving force for me. I went to CU to play in this game and beat Nebraska and go play for championships. That's what we did and it's awesome."

The Buffs lost to Nebraska by two in McChesney's redshirt season, in 2000, but CU was 3–1 against the Cornhuskers the next four years. Each of those wins helped CU wrap up the Big 12 North Division title, and the last of those gave Nebraska its first losing season in 43 years and ended a streak of 35 consecutive bowl appearances. "That was a great day," McChesney said.

Every year from 1996 to 2010, the CU-Nebraska game was played on the final weekend of the regular season, and that often meant that the stakes were high for one or both teams. That cranked up the intensity.

"That was the most important game of the year," Washington said. "It was the one of the toughest, if not the toughest, game of the year every year, no matter what our records were. Both teams left that game black and blue because we were physical teams."

Following the 2010 season, CU left the Big 12 for the Pac-12 and Nebraska went to the Big Ten. The rivalry died, but the animosity did not.

"I respect the hell out of them, but I respect them because they're good and they have a great program, historically one of the best programs in college football," McChesney said. "That said, I have a healthy disdain. I don't like them at all and never have."

For McChesney, Washington, McCartney, and many faithful Buffs, there was great satisfaction in 2018, when, on September 8, the two teams renewed the rivalry in Lincoln, Nebraska. CU won, 33–28, after Laviska Shenault caught a 40-yard touchdown pass from Steven Montez with 66 seconds left to play. "I just heard a couple of alums out there say, 'Thank you,'" linebacker Nate Landman said after the win. "That just proves how big this game is; how big it's been in the past, how big it is now—not only for us here, but everyone back in Colorado."

14 Joining the Pac-12

Rumors were swirling in the first half of 2010 that the world of college sports was in for a massive change. Power conferences, such as the Pac-10 and Big Ten, were in serious discussions about expansion, and the Big 12 was in the middle of it all. The Pac-10 had its eye on Colorado and Texas. The Big Ten also liked Texas, while Missouri and Nebraska were looking to move, and other Big 12 teams were exploring options. There were even rumors of the Pac-10 adding six Big 12 teams and becoming the Pac-16.

CU had no interest in waiting around, and on June 10, 2010, took the proactive step to leave the Big 12 and join the Pac-10. The CU board of regents voted unanimously to make the move, which became effective July 1, 2011. The annual Big 12 meetings were held just a week before the Buffs made the official move to the Pac-10, and athletic director Mike Bohn said it became clear in those meetings that CU needed to act.

"When I was there, I was learning about different discussions that institutions were having with other leagues," Bohn said. "This was something I really thought we'd better be on top of. I really had a gut feeling that something was going to happen this summer all along, with the way the TV contracts lined up with the Pac-10 and Big 12, and the opportunities for expansion around the country."

CU's move wasn't a knee-jerk reaction to rumors, though. The Pac-10 had courted CU in 1994 and the school seriously considered a move at that point. However, during that time, CU was one of the leaders in the development of the Big Eight expansion to the Big 12 and felt it was important to see it through. It was enticing enough, however, that the regents were torn, voting 6–3 to stay with the Big 12.

In deciding to move to the Pac-10 in 2010, CU had to forfeit $6.863 million in Big 12 conference distributions—which was much better than the roughly $14 million originally estimated. Although it was a costly move initially, CU believed it was an advantageous move for a lot of reasons.

"Quite simply, the Pac-10 is a great fit for us," chancellor Phil DiStefano said at the press conference announcing the move. "First, we have a strong alumni and student base in California. We have 35,000 more alumni living in the Pac-10 region than in the Big 12 footprint. We are excited about reuniting regularly with our loyal fans that reside within the Pac-10. We also think this will be a great move for our fans. We think the Buffs will be a team that will travel well to Pac-10 destinations. California is our biggest out of state feeder of students, with more than 600 new freshmen joining us from California every year. And, we are excited about the new athletic rivalries this will surely create."

CU's move was the first conference realignment domino to fall in 2010 and others soon followed. Literally the next day, Nebraska announced a move to the Big Ten. A week later, Utah, from the Mountain West Conference, accepted an invitation from the Pac-10, and the conference re-branded itself as the Pac-12.

The shift to the Pac-12 certainly changed the look of CU's annual schedules in athletics. In the Big 12, the Buffs faced Baylor, Iowa State, Kansas, Kansas State, Missouri, Nebraska, Oklahoma, Oklahoma State, Texas, Texas A&M, and Texas Tech. In the Pac-12, the Buffs square off against Arizona, Arizona State,

California, Oregon, Oregon State, Southern California, Stanford, UCLA, Utah, Washington, and Washington State.

After CU and Nebraska left, the Big 12 was down to 10 schools, but decided to stick together, ending the idea of a 16-team super conference out west. In 2011, however, Texas A&M and Missouri announced they were leaving the Big 12 for the Southeastern Conference. To replace them, the Big 12 plucked Texas Christian from the Mountain West Conference and West Virginia from the Big East. While plenty of moves have been made around the country since then, CU was at the forefront and the school has never looked back. The Buffs struggled to compete on the football field in its first few years in the Pac-12, but the move

Buffs Make Move in 1947

CU's move to the Pac-12 in 2010 was its first major conference shift since 1947. On March 1, 1947, CU was announced as a new addition to the Big Six Conference, effective in December of that year. CU had been a longtime member of the Mountain States Conference, which featured Colorado State, Denver, Brigham Young, Utah, Utah State, and Wyoming. Moving to the Big Six, which included Iowa State, Kansas, Kansas State, Missouri, Nebraska, and Oklahoma, was a significant move for CU.

"It was taking another level up in competition and really spreading your wings rather than playing all your games basically in three states," CU sports information director David Plati said. "It was a big time move for us to join those six schools, but also left a bad taste in the mouths of some of the locals."

Despite the area schools being unhappy about CU's move, it started a 63-year connection with the Big Six schools. After CU arrived, the conference became the Big Seven. Oklahoma State was added in 1958 the conference was known as the Big Eight. It remained that way until 1994, when Baylor, Texas, Texas A&M, and Texas Tech accepted invitations to join the Big Eight and leave the soon-to-be dissolved Southwestern Conference. In 1996, the Big Eight became the Big 12.

was considered an overall success, athletically, academically, and financially.

Fundraising increased dramatically after the move and even more so when athletic director Rick George was hired in 2013 to replace Bohn. The success in fundraising allowed CU to undergo a $170 million dollar athletic facility upgrade, which many believe would not have been possible had CU remained in the Big 12.

"We're proud to be in the [Pac-12] Conference," George said. "One of the biggest advantages from an athletic standpoint is the way we're connected with our recruiting areas and with our alumni in California, Arizona, Oregon, and Washington. We have so many alumni on the West Coast, it really connects us."

15 Joe Romig

About three weeks before the 1961 season opener in football, Colorado star senior Joe Romig went down in practice with a knee injury. While it wasn't a devastating, career-threatening injury, it was significant enough to keep most players out for up to six weeks. Romig wasn't most players.

"He was lifting weight with it before the middle of the next week," former CU administrator Fred Casotti wrote in his 1972 book, *Football C.U. Style*. "And I'll never forget the sight of him sitting on a table in the training room raising his leg with the iron boot on it, his eyes closed, teeth gritted and big beads of sweat popping out of his forehead from the pain. The sight of CU's All-American captain fighting back despite the mental and physical miseries he was going through was enough to bring tears to a lot of eyes.... But Joe never wavered in his determination to be ready a lot sooner than everybody said."

Within a couple of weeks, Romig was running, and he missed just one game, returning to the lineup just a month after the injury.

Colorado has had a lot of tough players over the years, but one would be hard pressed to find a tougher man than Romig, a two-way star from 1959 to 1961 and one of the all-time great Buffaloes. "He was probably our last great two-way player," CU sports information director David Plati said of the man who played guard on offense and linebacker on defense.

Romig is one of four players in CU history to have his jersey number (67) retired by the football program. In 1984, he joined Byron White as just the second CU player enshrined in the National Football Foundation's College Football Hall of Fame. Romig has also been inducted into the Colorado Sports Hall of Fame, the Colorado High School Activities Association Hall of Fame and the CU Athletic Hall of Fame.

Listed at 5 feet, 10 inches tall and 199 pounds—and those numbers are said to be slightly exaggerated—Romig played like a much bigger man. "Man has never found a way to weigh the mind or the heart or the stomach—three of the most vital component parts in a great man," Casotti wrote. "If they ever do, Joe Romig would be one of the heaviest men in the history of CU."

Romig's story is one of determination and hard work, despite some trials early in life not of his doing. His parents divorced when he was an infant, and he was raised by his mother, who worked as a nurse in Boulder. During Romig's junior year of high school, his mother passed away. Romig persevered and never stopped working hard to succeed. He became a two-time state wrestling champion and an All-State football player at Colorado's Lakewood High School, all while shining as a student. When he got to Boulder, Romig worked even harder and he had few equals in CU history.

Nearly 60 years after he played, his image—larger than life size—covers part of a wall in CU's Legacy Hall, next to the list of every All-American the Buffs have had. He was one of the greatest on that list. Romig was a two-time consensus first-team All-American, in 1960 and 1961. He was sixth in the Heisman Trophy voting in 1961, while earning United Press International Lineman of the Year honors. With Romig as captain in 1961, the Buffs went 9–2 overall, won the Big Eight Conference with a 7–0 record, and played in the Orange Bowl. From 1945 to 1975, that was the only conference title won by the Buffs.

Undersized for an offensive guard, even for that era, Romig was an excellent blocker, creating space for quarterback Gale Weidner, halfback Ted Woods, fullback Loren Schweninger, and others to do their work with the ball.

"He is the best I've ever seen, and I saw a lot when I was playing and coaching at Michigan State," CU head coach Sonny Grandelius said in 1961 after Romig was named lineman of the year.

At linebacker, he was even better. Newspaper accounts from those years wrote of Romig making half of the tackles on defense. "He is one of the best linebackers I've ever seen," Grandelius said. "I've never seen anyone with an instinct for the ball such as he has. He is where the ball is, and it doesn't matter whether it's a run or a pass into his flat area. He knocked down at least seven passes, which is really unusual for a linebacker who shoots the gap most of the time."

In describing Romig's ability as a linebacker, Casotti wrote, "Romig working his way toward the ball was like an artist at work. It was almost as though the ball was a magnet and Joe was a big chunk of steel."

As a standout player on both sides of the ball, Romig often played nearly the full 60 minutes on game days. Renowned for his great strength, Romig's physical tools were hardly his best asset. "He didn't have enough physical talent to be as great as he was,"

Casotti wrote. "Simply wasn't big enough or fast enough or tall enough or anything enough. His was not a physique that would stand out in a crowd. Romig's greatness was in his mind."

Romig's mind was as sharp as any, and it helped him succeed on the football field while achieving greater success off the field. As he proved with his athletic success, when Romig was interested in something, he attacked it with full force. That included religion, a passion Romig discovered at CU, somewhere in between football and his studying of physics. "Science convinced me there was a God, so I looked into it," he said. One summer, Romig spent nearly two hours per day studying the book of Genesis. He even obtained a Hebrew dictionary, which helped him to fully understand the meaning of words used in the Bible.

As a scholar, Romig earned his undergraduate degree in physics at CU and then was awarded the prestigious Rhodes Scholarship. One of five CU football players to become a Rhodes scholar, Romig never had his eyes on playing professional football. Instead, he left CU and went to Oxford University, where he earned a master's degree in plasma physics. He later returned to CU to earn a doctorate degree in astrogeophysics. During the 1970s, Romig worked in Martin Marietta's advanced planetary programs section that launched NASA's Voyager missions. For decades, he worked in the field of physics and even taught astronomy classes at CU.

Romig is still revered as one of the all-time greats in CU football history, and he credits the sport for helping him become a success in life.

"Football instills a mental toughness and determination that is important in any pursuit," he said in 1984 when he received the first Kodak/AFCA (American Football Coaches Association) All-America Life Achievement Award. "The kinds of pressures we faced on the playing field, and met successfully, have provided confidence to face many of life's challenges."

16 Alfred Williams

Late in the fourth quarter, Colorado's football team was clinging to a 27–22 lead at Darrel K. Royal-Texas Memorial Stadium in Austin, Texas, on September 22, 1990. Ranked No. 20 in the country, the Buffaloes came into the game with a 1–1–1 record and no more room for error if they wanted to make a run at the national title. Two fourth quarter touchdowns by Eric Bieniemy had helped the Buffs rally from a 22–14 deficit against the 22nd-ranked Texas Longhorns, but CU still needed to get a stop on defense. Alfred Williams, the Buffs' All-American outside linebacker, was there to deliver. Williams sacked Longhorns quarterback Peter Gardere in the end zone for a safety, capping CU's 29–22 victory.

"He relished the big games and the big moments," CU head coach Bill McCartney said of Williams years later. "That's when he had that swagger about him. He had an inner confidence. Whenever we would play in the big games on the road, Alfred was always stepping up and taking on the leadership role. He lived for those moments."

Throughout his CU career, from 1987 to 1990, Williams stepped up in a lot of moments. Statistically, Williams compiled 35 quarterback sacks and 59 tackles for loss in his career. Through 2018, he still held the school records in those categories. A consensus first-team All-American in 1989 as a junior, Williams was a unanimous All-American choice in 1990. He was the only CU player, offense or defense, to earn conference player of the year twice, honored by the Big Eight in 1989 and 1990. Williams was also the first Buff to earn a national award. In 1990, he won the Butkus Award, presented to the nation's best linebacker.

Arguably the best linebacker CU has ever had, Williams was a key player to the greatest run of success in program history. He helped the Buffs to the national title in 1990 and they went 22–2–1 during his final two seasons.

In 2010, Williams became the fifth Buff inducted into the College Football Hall of Fame, learning of his induction while doing his sports talk radio show in Denver. "I broke down in tears, I was so happy to represent the University of Colorado," Williams told Buffzone.com in 2010. "This is our 20-year anniversary of our national championship so for me it's been a wonderful year. I've been able to be a part of some great football teams. The men who've coached me over the years have been outstanding and I want to say thank you to all of them. From high school to Colorado, [linebackers coach] Bob Simmons and the great head coach Bill McCartney and all of my coaches in the NFL."

Growing up in Houston, Williams initially never really considered playing at CU. In fact, he wasn't even sure he was going to play football, because he also loved basketball.

"I remember that the University of Colorado wasn't high on my list," he said in 2010. "For me it was a topsy-turvy time with all the teams that were looking at me. CU didn't stack up really high with the programs I was looking at. When I finally got a chance to see Coach Mac, it was really good. But what really changed everything was when I came down to Boulder for a visit. It was just so different than the areas that many of us were raised in. I decided I just wanted to go somewhere totally different than where I was from. My decision was more about the University of Colorado than football."

Williams stood out immediately at Colorado, and not just because he was 6-foot-6 and 240 pounds, with basketball and football ability. (Williams actually made a cameo appearance with the CU basketball team, during the 1989–90 season, suiting up for one game and grabbing a rebound.) He had an outgoing, fun-loving

Dynamic Duo

When Alfred Williams signed with Colorado out of Jesse Jones High School in Houston, he learned that the Buffs had signed another outside linebacker from Houston. Kanavis McGhee, from rival Wheatley High School, didn't know Williams, but they became fast friends. Throughout their careers at CU, McGhee and Williams formed a dominant duo at outside linebacker. The 6-foot-5, 250-pound McGhee had 15 career sacks, earned All-Big Eight honors three times, was a first-team All-American in 1989, a second-team choice in 1988, and an honorable mention in 1990.

"In my estimation, it was pick your poison," said Bob Simmons, CU's outside linebackers coach at the time.

In 1991, McGhee was drafted in the second round by the New York Giants and played 50 games in the league from 1991 to '95. He coached CU's outside linebackers from 2011 to '12.

personality that made him popular on his team and has helped him carve out a long career in sports radio since his playing days.

Darian Hagan, who quarterbacked the Buffs to the national title and came to CU a year after Williams, didn't take long to notice Williams.

"He was a loud mouth, he had these big old glasses on, and I thought he was the ugliest person I'd ever seen," Hagan jokingly told Buffzone.com. "But he was a hell of a player and a good dude.... My true freshman year I couldn't believe the linebackers were that tall and big and athletic. I was a little afraid of them. I was like, 'This dude is going to hit me?' Al was very loud and vocal and intimidating a little bit. But as you get to know him and start practicing with him, you get the feel of how he plays the game. I just tricked him a lot."

Very few quarterbacks could trick Williams, who continued his stellar play in the NFL. In the 1991 NFL Draft, he was selected in the first round (18th overall) by the Cincinnati Bengals. During a nine-year pro career, Williams played for Bengals, San Francisco

49ers, and Denver Broncos. With the Broncos, he was a first-team All-Pro in 1996 and helped them win back-to-back Super Bowls in 1997 and 1998. He totaled 59.5 sacks in his career, 28.5 of those in four years with the Broncos.

Williams has spent most of his post-playing career on the radio, and in 2019, he left 104.3 The Fan after 15 years to join the sports team at KOA Radio.

Through all of his success in the NFL and on the radio, however, Williams has always held CU close to his heart.

"I love my tenure with the Broncos and the Super Bowls were great, but it's nothing like the friendships and family at CU," he said. "If my football career would have ended with my last college game, I would have been all right with that. Our legacy at CU is intact."

17 John Wooten

Following a stellar regular season in 1956—and thanks to a ruling by the Big Seven Conference that prohibited consecutive bowl appearances for its teams—Colorado accepted an invitation to the Orange Bowl. CU went 7–2–1 during the regular season, including 4–1–1 in the conference, finishing second to Oklahoma, which was undefeated for the third year in a row and won the national title. Amid the excitement of CU's first appearance in the Orange Bowl—and first bowl appearance in 18 years—athletic director Harry Carlson received a phone call from the Buffaloes' opponent, Clemson, a top-20 team from South Carolina.

"Clemson took the position that, 'Our state says we can't play teams that have Negroes,'" John Wooten told a Dallas newspaper

John Wooten leads the way for Jim Brown, which he did for years as a member of the Cleveland Browns. (AP Photo / Tony Tomsic)

in 2012. "So our AD told them, 'Then you'd better tell the Orange Bowl committee that you can't play.'"

CU's team in 1956 featured two black players—Wooten, who was an exceptional guard, and Frank Clarke, a talented end who led the team in receiving. Racial segregation was still alive in the United States at that time, particularly in the South, and this was a monumental game for CU in that regard. Clemson was CU's first-ever opponent from the Deep South, and the Orange Bowl, played in Miami, Florida, on January 1, 1957, was to be CU's first trip to the South.

Clemson did play in the game, and so did Clarke, who became CU's first black football player a year earlier, and Wooten, who became the second in 1956. Both men helped CU to a 27–21 victory that day. More satisfying than the win, however, was the bond that experience created for Wooten and his teammates.

Because of the two black players on CU's team, Clemson didn't want to play and the hotel in Miami Beach didn't want them staying there. CU didn't back down, however, and not only did Clemson play, but the hotel eventually allowed Clarke and Wooten to stay in their rooms.

"It was a hectic time," Wooten recalled years later. "I have such great feeling for the stand my white teammates took and for the leadership of [senior center] Jim Uhlir and [sophomore quarterback] Boyd Dowler. Man, what a lesson in human relationship."

For Wooten, it was one of many great moments of his CU career. He was not only a pioneer, but truly one of the best players in program history—regardless of race.

After growing up in Carlsbad, New Mexico, Wooten came to CU in 1955. Freshmen were ineligible for varsity, but he lettered three times, from 1956 to '58 while playing guard on offense and tackle on defense. In 1958, Wooten became just the fifth player in CU history to earn first-team All-American honors and in 2012

Breaking the barrier

In September of 1954, Frank Clarke arrived at CU after spending two seasons playing at Trinidad (Colorado) Junior College. He had to sit out that season because he was a transfer, but in 1955, he made CU history by becoming the first black player ever on the varsity team.

CU ran the run-oriented single-wing offense, but Clarke, a big, 6-foot, 210-pound receiver, made his mark. He caught 13 passes for 407 yards—a whopping 31.3-yard average—and five touchdowns in 1955. He added seven catches for 124 yards and two scores in 1956. A popular man on the CU campus, he was elected "King" at the CU Days festival.

Clarke went on to play 11 seasons in the NFL, with the Cleveland Browns and Dallas Cowboys, catching 291 passes for 5,426 yards and 50 touchdowns. He played in three NFL championship games. Elected to the CU Athletics Hall of Fame in 2008, Clarke passed away in 2018 at the age of 84.

he became the sixth Buff to be inducted into the College Football Hall of Fame.

"After all these years—57 of them since I first stepped on that Colorado campus—somebody, somewhere remembered that I was a pretty decent football player," Wooten said before his Hall induction. "If I scored 20,000 touchdowns, that'd be one thing. But here I was, a pulling guard and a defensive tackle, and somebody thought enough of me to consider me deserving of this. It's a tremendous honor."

Wooten didn't receive the glory that comes with piling up yards and touchdowns, but because of his efforts, several others did. John Bayuk, Howard Cook, Eddie Dove, Dowler, and Bob Stransky were all stars on offense for the Buffs during Wooten's years at CU and they all benefitted from his talent as a blocker. In 1957, CU led the nation in rushing for the first and only time in program history. The Buffaloes averaged 322.4 rushing yards per game. While Stransky (1,097 yards), Dove (620) and Cook (442) led the way in yardage totals, "big John's path-clearing blocking was one of the major reasons" the Buffs led the country, wrote Fred Casotti.

Aside from his excellence on the field, Wooten was "a great guy to have on the team because of his great personality and ability to keep everyone loose," Casotti wrote, while adding, "John was a happy warrior."

Following his time at CU, Wooten was a fifth-round draft choice of the NFL's Cleveland Browns and played 10 years in the league—nine with Cleveland and one with the Washington Redskins. During his first seven years in Cleveland, he was one of the key blockers for Hall of Famer Jim Brown, regarded by some as the greatest running back in pro football history. Wooten was selected to the Pro Bowl twice during his time with the Browns and he helped them win the NFL championship in 1964.

Later, Wooten worked for 17 years in the front office of the Dallas Cowboys before spending time working with the Philadelphia Eagles and Baltimore Ravens. He was instrumental in Super Bowl-winning seasons for the Cowboys in 1977 and the Ravens in 2000. As of 2019, at the age of 82, Wooten was still serving as the chairman of the Fritz Pollard Alliance, which advocates for the hiring and promoting of minorities for coaching, executive and scouting positions in the NFL.

Former CU tight end Jon Embree became CU's first black head coach in 2011. At the time, each of the coaches had their parking spots marked by a legendary name from program history. Embree's choice was Wooten.

"John Wooten is special to me," Embree told the *Boulder Daily Camera* in 2012, prior to Wooten being honored by the school and going into the College Football Hall of Fame. "Obviously what he did allowed opportunities for more African American players to come to Colorado, to have success, to have opportunities. He's a man of great heart, character, and integrity."

18 Herb Orvis

The thought of a second consecutive defeat to Kansas State was too much for Herb Orvis to handle on October 2, 1971. A week earlier at Ohio State, Colorado's senior stellar defensive tackle badly injured his ankle and was expected to miss two games. He didn't play in the first half and Kansas State held a 21–17 lead late in the third quarter at Folsom Field. A year earlier, almost to the day, Kansas State had upset the No. 8-ranked Buffs. Orvis wasn't about to sit there and watch the Wildcats do it again.

"Just when the Wildcats appeared to be getting the upper hand and that the Buffaloes were becoming disheartened, Orvis put himself in the game and his appearance had a dramatic effect on his teammates, who stiffened and held the Wildcats to help turn the game around," Fred Casotti wrote in his 1972 book, *Football C.U. Style*. "A man like Orvis, who makes the big play, has the ability to give a lift to his team just by his presence. Orvis didn't make any big plays against Kansas State in his brief appearance in the game. But the fact that he was on the field rallied the CU defense and that quality is one of the great assets of an outstanding competitor."

The Buffs rallied to win that game, 31–21, as Ken Johnson threw a pair of late touchdown passes. While Orvis didn't make many plays in that game against Kansas State, he made a lot of plays in a lot of other games during his sensational career with the Buffaloes.

CU hasn't had many players as tough or as competitive as the 6-foot-5, 235-pound Orvis, and few have been as accomplished. From 1969 to 1971, Orvis was a dominant defensive end for the Buffs, totaling 193 tackles, 32 tackles for loss, and 20 sacks. He was a first-team All-American in 1971, when he helped CU finish No. 3 in the national polls, and he twice earned first-team All-Big Eight honors. He was named to the 1970s All-Big Eight Decade team. Simply playing the game and being a part of those teams was an honor for Orvis.

"When the band strikes up and the music is blaring; when the whistle blows, it's a real exciting moment," he said years later in recalling his playing days at CU. "Just to be included with this [CU] team, I thought was the epicenter of my whole game. I just felt like Colorado was the right place and we had so many great players—Bobby Anderson, Dick Anderson, Bill Brundige—and fine coaches. When I put that uniform on, Silver and Gold, it was something. I can't near live up to the reputation that precedes me, but we tried our best and I think we enjoyed it quite a bit."

A native of Petoskey, Michigan, Orvis dropped out of school after his junior football season at Flint-Beecher High school. He became a bit of a rebel, locked into a bad crowd of people, and found himself in a lot of fights. Then, at 19 years old, he was drafted by the Army.

"I didn't have any Canadian connections. So, I went into the Army," he recalled a few years later. "Being drafted, that was the best thing that ever happened to me. The Army woke me up. I was taught discipline, I was regimented. The biggest thing I learned was humility."

While stationed in Berlin, Germany, Orvis took tests to get his high school diploma. He spent two years in the Army, and in part of that time, he played football on a brigade team. It was pure luck that Orvis wound up at CU. Missouri head coach Dan Devine was supposed to go on a tour of U.S. army bases in Europe with other coaches in 1967, but when he had to cancel, CU's Eddie Crowder took his place. During the tour, Crowder met Orvis and was impressed. After Crowder's return, he had CU assistant Chet Franklin stay in contact with Orvis.

"I wrote the best letters I ever wrote in my life," Orvis said. "We were 11–0, that Army team, and I thought I could play college football. Well, I wound up at Colorado on a scholarship. For a while there was a lot of doubt I could make it here—a lot of doubt."

Orvis actually thought he'd be joining a few of his Army teammates at CU, but he turned out to be the only one to come to Boulder.

Casotti felt Orvis was one of the toughest and meanest men to ever play at CU—and not just on the field. "Herb was an angry young man," Casotti wrote in 1972. "Angry all the time on the football field. And angry most of the time off it. He wasn't necessarily the most pleasant person to be around when he wasn't in uniform. And he was never pleasant to be around on the field." Casotti also referred to Orvis as "a ferocious competitor who was happy with nothing less than total victory."

That attitude served Orvis well in those years, as he helped CU to a 24–10 record and three bowl games during his three varsity seasons. It was the first time CU had played in bowls in three consecutive seasons. Orvis was then a first-round pick of the NFL's Detroit Lions in 1972 and played 10 seasons professionally with the Lions and Baltimore Colts. In 2014, Orvis was inducted into the CU Athletics Hall of Fame, and in 2016, he became the eighth Buffalo to go into the College Football Hall of Fame.

"It was a total surprise," Orvis said of the honor in 2016. "To receive something like this late in life, you realize you have contributed and it reminds you of the other players that have contributed and probably should deserve this award."

19 The Rise

In the home locker room at Folsom Field, in the moments following a 27–22 victory against Utah in the 2016 regular season finale, Colorado football players bounced and shouted in unison, repeating the lyrics of a Drake song.

> *Started from the bottom, now we're here!*
> *Started from the bottom, now the whole team here!*
> *Started from the bottom, now we're here!*

Those lyrics succinctly described a season that was magical, unexpected and thrilling for a CU program that desperately needed something positive and got it, going 10–4 overall and 8–1 in Pac-12 Conference play. To say that CU's Pac-12 South Division championship in 2016 came out of nowhere would be an understatement. CU came into the year with a streak of 10 consecutive losing seasons and eight consecutive without a bowl game appearance. This wasn't just a team that started at the bottom; it was a team that couldn't get off the bottom. CU joined the Pac-12 Conference in 2011 and finished last in the South Division in each of its first five seasons. The Buffs were once again projected for a last-place finish in 2016, and with good reason.

Head coach Mike MacIntyre was entering his fourth season at CU. The Buffs had shown some progress and were much more competitive in 2015 than they were in previous years, but MacIntyre was 10–27 overall and 2–25 in the Pac-12. Like most coaches in most seasons, MacIntyre went into 2016 with optimism. It was tough for those on the outside to see a dramatic change on the horizon, but MacIntyre had a genuine belief that his team was ready to win.

"I do like this team," he said during August camp. "I like the way they work, I like the attitude they're having. Hopefully they'll respond out there on Saturdays like I think they will."

Even before the season began, the Buffs adopted the slogan "The Rise," although most outside of the program—and even many within the program—could not have projected what would take place over the course of a 12-game regular season in which CU won 10 times.

On opening night, the Buffs stunned local fans with a 44–7 rout of rival Colorado State. Led by senior quarterback Sefo Liufau—the heart and soul of that team who was playing for the first time since a foot injury 10 months earlier—CU overwhelmed the Rams. "It's a surreal feeling to be able to put one of those games out there like that," said Liufau, who threw for 318 yards and a touchdown.

After crushing Idaho State, the Buffs traveled to Michigan to take on the fourth-ranked Wolverines. This was supposed to be a reality check for the Buffs after two easy wins. Instead, the Buffs shocked the 110,000 fans at Michigan Stadium by jumping out to a 14–0 lead. When Liufau connected with Shay Fields for a 70-yard touchdown early in the third quarter, the Buffs led 28–24 and the upset bid was still alive. Michigan wound up scoring the final 21 points to win the game, 45–28, but CU had sent a message that this was, indeed, a different team. CU fans will always wonder how that game would have turned out had Liufau not left early with an injury, however. On the play before his deep touchdown to Fields, Liufau injured his ankle, but gutted it out to throw the scoring pass. He was unable to finish the game, though, and missed the next two. His ankle continued to bother him throughout the season.

Without Liufau, the Buffs weren't given much of a shot at Oregon the next week. Backup Steven Montez had a miserable day off the bench at Michigan and would be making his first career start at Oregon. The Ducks had crushed the Buffs each of the previous five years. Montez, a redshirt freshman, played the game of his life in Oregon's Autzen Stadium. He threw for 333 yards and ran for 135—the first player in CU history to pass for 300 yards and rush for 100 in the same game—and accounted for four touchdowns in a 41–38 upset of the host Ducks. "Pretty much a legendary game for his first one," MacIntyre said.

Although the Buffs would stumble at Southern California, 21–17, two weeks later, the win against Oregon set the tone for their division title. CU would go 8–1 against the Pac-12, a remarkable feat for a team with a 5–40 conference record in the previous five years. Along the way, the Buffs produced some memorable moments:

October 15—Defeated Arizona State, 40–16: CU was 0–7 all-time against the Sun Devils, but physically dominated this game. Running back Phillip Lindsay rushed for 219 yards and three touchdowns, Liufau was masterful in running the offense and scored a touchdown, and linebackers Jimmie Gilbert and Addison Gillam led a powerful effort on defense.

October 22—Defeated Stanford, 10–5: Not pretty, but the Buffs knocked off another team that had destroyed them in recent years, and did it on the road. It was an ugly day on offense, but the defense was sensational. The win secured bowl eligibility for the first time since 2007.

November 3—Defeated UCLA, 20–10: Another underwhelming day on offense, but another dominating effort on defense. Cornerback Isaiah Oliver sealed the win with a 68-yard punt return for a touchdown in the fourth quarter.

November 19—Defeated Washington State, 38–24: The 12th-ranked Buffs knocked off the 20th-ranked Cougars, snapping a 23-game losing streak against ranked foes. Liufau matched Montez's feat from eight weeks earlier by throwing for 345 yards and rushing for 108, while scoring three touchdowns. Lindsay added 144 yards and two touchdowns, and the defense, once again, was stellar.

November 26—Defeated Utah, 27–22: Now up to No. 9 in the rankings, the Buffs secured the South Division title with the win against the No. 21 Utes. Liufau didn't have a great day, but posted 329 yards in total offense and accounted for two touchdowns. Linebacker Kenneth Olugbode came up with the play of the game—and perhaps of the season—when he scooped up a Utah fumble and ran 10 yards for a touchdown and a 27–16 lead with 11 minutes to play.

That season also saw several stars emerge for the Buffs:

CB Chidobe Awuzie: The best overall player on the team, he was a versatile defensive back who did a little of everything, including four sacks, 10 tackles for loss, and 13 pass breakups.

WRs Bryce Bobo, Shay Fields, and Devin Ross: The trio combined for 159 catches for 2,133 yards and 16 touchdowns.

DL Jordan Carrell, Samson Kafovalu and Josh Tupou: In the trenches, this trio was the key to the whole defense, stuffing the run and putting pressure on the quarterback.

OLB Jimmie Gilbert: Wreaked havoc on quarterbacks, with 10.5 sacks and 14 tackles for loss.

RB Phillip Lindsay: A junior, he was one of the most dynamic running backs in the Pac-12, rushing for 1,189 yards and 16 touchdowns, while adding 47 catches for 390 yards and another touchdown.

QB Sefo Liufau: The senior was the face of this team. Although he missed nearly three full games and parts of others with an ankle injury, he was the unquestioned leader. He accounted for 2,667 yards in total offense and 18 touchdowns.

LB Kenneth Olugbode: One of the leaders of the defense, he was sensational all season, piling up 130 tackles, 9.5 tackles for loss, and a pair of interceptions.

S Tedric Thompson: He was around the ball every week, finishing with 75 tackles, seven interceptions and 18 pass breakups.

CB Ahkello Witherspoon: One of the top cover corners in the country in 2016, he had 22 passes defended and was rarely beaten by receivers.

This was Liufau's team, as the senior and primary leader, but the defense made the difference in 2016. Led by second-year coordinator Jim Leavitt, the CU defense ranked top 20 nationally in points and yards allowed. It was a group that grew up together, taking their lumps as freshmen and sophomores in 2013 and 2014 and improving along the way. Throughout the 2016 season, the Buffs leaned on their defense. Routinely, against Stanford, UCLA, Utah, and others, the defense rose to the occasion.

Witherspoon's pick

CU's 2016 season included a lot of great moments, but the signature play came in Week 4, in the closing moments at Oregon. CU led 41–38, but Oregon was in position to take the win. The Ducks had first-and-goal at the CU 7-yard line with about a minute to play. Oregon QB Dakota Prukop took the snap and calmly tossed a fade pass to the back-left corner of the end zone. CU senior cornerback Ahkello Witherspoon was in coverage and he leaped in front of the intended receiver and intercepted the pass with 48 seconds remaining. It was the play CU needed to secure the program's biggest win in years, and the win that would propel the Buffaloes to the Pac-12 South title. "I was just in great coverage and I got the opportunity to look and go for the ball," Witherspoon said. "[Cornerbacks coach Charles] Clark always preaches to become the receiver if you're in position to do so, and that's what I did. It was big. I love playing for my team. Just having them coming over, hugging me and celebrating, that means everything to me. I was actually in the moment shaking my head. That's so much of God's work. I'm thankful He put me in position to make that play." Witherspoon led the country with 21 pass breakups that season, but that was his lone interception.

"We just look at it as a positive thing," linebacker Addison Gillam said. "We like it. We like going out there and being able to get a stop, showing what our defensive is about. It feels good."

Certainly, Liufau, Lindsay and the offense had their great moments, too. The fact that CU could be dangerous on both sides of the ball led them to a remarkable season.

It was a season that ended on a sour note, however. After beating Utah, the Buffs went to Santa Clara, California, for the Pac-12 Championship game and were routed by No. 4 Washington, 41–10. On December 29, the Buffs' reward for a great season was a trip to the Alamo Bowl in San Antonio. That, too, ended in disappointment, with a 38–8 loss to No. 13 Oklahoma State. Even with the tough ending, the Buffs produced the program's first 10-win season since 2001, a No. 17 final ranking in the Associated Press poll, and, at least for a year, a return to glory for CU football.

"We did something special," Liufau said. "We didn't finish with an exclamation point; the wheels on the bus kind of fell off. But I wouldn't trade this season or these teammates for anything."

MacIntyre won several Pac-12 and national coach of the year awards that season, but gave the credit to the players, and the seniors in particular.

"They truly rose this program from the ashes," he said. "Those young men… should be remembered for a long, long time for what they've done for Colorado football."

20 Ralphie

In the moments before kickoff at Folsom Field, the adrenaline starts to flow for those on the field and excitement builds for those in the stands. "Heeeere comes Ralphie!!" yells the public address announcer, just as 1,200 pounds of buffalo explodes out of a cage in the north end zone. With five handlers hanging on, one of the most iconic mascots in college football leads the team onto the field, runs around the Folsom turf, and charges into the back of her trailer.

"Ralphie is just so unique and so special," said John Graves, the Ralphie program manager at CU. "No one else has a live mascot quite like Ralphie. For her, it's just so unique and so special. She brings so much energy and passion to the stadium."

In the mid-1960s, CU had been called the Buffaloes for three decades, but didn't have a live buffalo. A handful of students decided to fix that. The father of freshman Bill Lowery bought and donated a young buffalo to CU. Then, during the summer of 1966, Lowery, Victor Reinking, and fellow sophomores Don Marturano and John McGill started getting to know the young buffalo and working with her. The original CU buffalo was a calf named Ralph—until it was discovered that she was a female.

"The first time we took her for a run, we were all surprised," Reinking said. "It almost overpowered the four of us, even with the harness and hanging on for dear life. We got used to it and it wasn't long before we were out here for the first game and we ran out onto the field and the place just went nuts. We couldn't believe the reaction."

Ralphie's first runs came in 1966, although it wasn't until 1967 that the program was first endorsed by the school. In 2017, CU celebrated the 50th anniversary of the Ralphie program. In its beginning, running with Ralphie was more an experiment than a full program, like it is now. In fact, Reinking and his fellow students figured running with a calf would be no big deal.

"Ignorance is bliss," he said. "The first thing I remember is, 'Whoa, what have we gotten ourselves into here? This thing is going to drag us down. What if we fall down?' We were all running around in cowboy boots. How are [the current handlers] hanging onto a full-grown female buffalo is what I want to know. With a small one, it was all we could do to hang onto that thing. It was surprisingly powerful."

It was no less thrilling than it is today, though.

"It was like no other feeling you could have," Reinking said. "You're going out into a football stadium filled with tens of thousands of people. It was a real high, for sure. It was not like walking a big dog. It was definitely like a wild animal at the end of the leash and you didn't know what was going to happen next. You were just flying out there and then 50,000 people are screaming. It was a treat."

The 2018 season was Ralphie V's 11th, and the thrill is still there for those who handle her—and for Ralphie.

"She enjoys being a buffalo, but man, she loves to run," Graves said. "She loves to run and she does a great job doing it. She's really sweet and we bring her up to Folsom and she's like, 'Okay, I have a job to do, I'm ready to run, let's go.'"

Over the years, it has become a prestigious honor to be one of the handlers. Only about 250 students were handlers during the first 50 years, and becoming a handler requires a tough tryout process. Even then, handlers have to go through a year of training before they can run with Ralphie on game day. The handlers are now a team of their own at CU and they earn varsity letters. When Ralphie does run, five handlers—two on each side and one behind—run with her, holding onto harnesses. Several other

Why a female?

A common misconception about Ralphie is that she is a male. When many opposing players and coaches, or media members, talk about Ralphie, they often believe the animal is a male. Running with a male buffalo would be nearly impossible, however. "Females are just a lot smaller," Graves said. "The males at the hump, they're over 6 feet tall and more than a 1,000 pounds heavier than the female. That's a lot more weight and a lot more strength there. Plus, they're not overly aggressive, but they can be aggressive. The females are a little more mellow."

handlers are positioned around the field, as well. Running with Ralphie requires skill and strength—not to mention some speed.

"We're going 18–20 miles per hour," Graves said. "We can run that fast. It's a matter of running as fast as you can and having her pull you along, as well, while still being in control of your body. It's not fear, but it's nervousness. I still remember the very first time I ever ran with Ralphie, on the Fourth of July in 2007. That was my first time ever I ran with her in public. It was very nerve-wracking."

When Ralphie isn't running, she lives peacefully on a ranch in an undisclosed location. Only the handlers, and a few others, know the location of the ranch, out of safety for Ralphie. A group of Air Force Academy cadets kidnapped Ralphie I in 1970, and CU certainly doesn't want a repeat. Graves said Ralphie is well cared for by the handlers on the ranch. She roams through five different pastures, all of which include scratching posts, tasty cottonwood trees and even some toys. Ralphie loves to flip tires with her horns and play with traffic cones. Those who get the pleasure of working with Ralphie develop a special bond with the animal.

For those players who get the honor of running behind her, it's a feeling they'll never forget.

"Running behind Ralphie to me, it's a feeling you can't really explain," said Devin Ross, a receiver with the Buffs from 2013 to '17. "I feel like no other school has something like that. It's just pretty special. I wish we could do it at all the away games, too. Ralphie is special. It's nothing you can really compare it to."

For Reinking, the feeling is different, but no less special. Five decades after being one of the pioneers of the program, Reinking worked as a professor at Seattle University and marveled at what running with Ralphie has become.

"I'm very proud of it," Reinking said. "It was just this crazy idea that came up and then it actually happened."

21 Eddie Crowder

On October 27, 1951, Colorado head football coach Dal Ward led the Buffaloes into Norman, Oklahoma, with a Big Seven Conference title on his mind. Those hopes were all but lost after Sooners junior quarterback Eddie Crowder carved up the CU defense with four touchdown passes in a 55–14 victory. It was CU's only conference loss that season, and the closest Ward would ever come to winning the Big Seven.

Little did anyone know at the time that Crowder would become one of the most impactful figures in the history of the CU athletic department. Crowder was 31 years old when CU athletic director Harry Carlson hired him as head coach on January 3, 1963, giving him a five-year contract worth $15,000 per year. "I am confident his coming to Colorado will be to the complete mutual advantage of both the school and Crowder," Carlson said.

Crowder more than rewarded that confidence. From 1963 to 1973, he went 67–49–2 as the Buffs' head coach, leading them to five bowl games and a No. 3 national ranking at the end of the 1971 season. After back-to-back 2–8 records in his first two seasons—when CU was still reeling from NCAA sanctions—Crowder would post a winning record in seven of his final nine years.

"What Eddie did was amazing," All-American Bobby Anderson said after Crowder's death in 2008. "In building those first two years, he knew how to keep games close. He maximized every opportunity to win and he minimized the chances to lose. The only thing I regret for him is that he left coaching way too soon. He was a genius on the field."

In addition to his coaching duties, Crowder took over as athletic director on July 1, 1965, after Carlson retired. Crowder would serve as AD until August 3, 1984. He also owned Eddie's Mexican Café in Boulder, a popular eatery that had "killer chips and salsa," according to CU sports information director David Plati.

As athletic director, Crowder hired some of the most iconic coaches in CU history, including Bill Marolt (skiing, 1968); Irv Brown (baseball, 1969); Mark Simpson (men's golf, 1977); Bill McCartney (football, 1982); and Ceal Barry (women's basketball, 1983).

"When we hired Ceal Barry, I remember telling Fred Casotti that I thought it was maybe the best hire that we ever made," Crowder said in a 2001 interview with CUBuffs.com. "She had such a wonderful pedigree in women's basketball, and was the one person in the interview process that had demonstrated the most ideal attitude. And one of the greatest satisfactions was the hiring of Bill McCartney, because of the pressure and the stress with the timing. Chuck Fairbanks left on June 1 and we decided to hire Mac on June 8 or 9, so that was about seven days without sleep. Being available to him with having gone through the same experience, having come here as a new head coach without any previous head coaching experience, that gave me the opportunity to be particularly helpful. It was and remains a great relationship."

Like many long-standing athletic directors, Crowder hit some rough patches, too. He hired Fairbanks as football coach in 1979 and that proved to be a disastrous move for the program. Of course, Crowder made up for that by replacing Fairbanks with McCartney.

"If there were one thing I would do differently, it would be some other choice than the hiring of Chuck Fairbanks, not because he wasn't a capable guy or coach," Crowder said in 2001. "The consequences of the hiring and the legal problems we went through set a difficult tone for the era and it set us back."

During the time Fairbanks was coach, CU athletics struggled financially and in 1980 had a $1 million budget deficit, due in part to trying to remain compliant with Title IX, over-spending in football, and low ticket sales. CU cut seven sports in 1980 to try to balance the budget and university president Arnold Weber disciplined Crowder and took away a month of vacation time. Also during that time, CU was under investigation by the NCAA for infractions that occurred throughout the 1970s. In December of 1980, CU was found guilty of 62 violations and given two years of NCAA probation. CU and Crowder got through that storm, however, and he was credited with helping the athletic program get back on its feet before he retired in 1984. Ultimately, Crowder is remembered and revered as a legendary coach and administrator who had great impact on CU.

"Eddie Crowder held Colorado athletics together," former Big Eight Conference commissioner Chuck Neinas told the *Boulder Daily Camera* in 2008. "Let's be candid—Colorado has never had the resources of an Oklahoma or Nebraska. But, in large part, they've been able to compete with those schools on a fairly regular basis because of the efforts of a guy like Eddie."

22 Hale Irwin

At 45 years old, Hale Irwin had been in a bit of a slump as the 1990 United States Open golf tournament approached. U.S. Open champions earn an automatic 10-year exemption into the event, and while Irwin had won the tournament twice before, it had been 11 years since his second win. Going into the 1990 U.S. Open, Irwin hadn't won any PGA Tour events in five years. Nevertheless, the United States Golf Association (USGA) gave Irwin a special exemption, allowing him to play at the 1990 U.S. Open at Medinah Country Club, near Chicago.

"My goal was not to make this a poor selection for the USGA," he said in looking back at the event 25 years later.

Irwin made the USGA look quite good when he put together a remarkable rally to defeat Mike Donald in a sudden-death playoff and win the tournament. Through 2019, he was still the oldest winner in the history of the U.S. Open, which has been played since 1895. Down six shots heading into the back nine of the final round, Irwin stunned the crowd by forcing the 18-hole playoff with Donald. Down two shots with three holes to go in the extra round, Irwin rallied again, and the two were tied after 18 holes. On the first hole of sudden-death, Irwin rolled a birdie putt into the cup to win the title.

"I was nervous the whole time," Irwin said in recalling his win. "There's a lot of players who take nervousness and turn that into an asset. Jack Nicklaus was the best at it; Tiger Woods. All the great players have taken that tension and become very focused and turned it into an asset for them and make it a plus. That's hopefully what I was doing. The blood was flowing. I was alive. There was work to do."

Irwin's victory in 1990 helped cement his place among the all-time greats in golf. At CU, however, the Boulder High School graduate earned notoriety not only on the links, but on the gridiron—a rare, two-sport combination for a college athlete.

"He was a very good football player, but just an outstanding golfer—and you don't get hit on the golf course," CU sports information director David Plati said. "Hale was extremely talented."

On the football field, Irwin played for the Buffs from 1964 to '66. After beginning his career at quarterback, he became an all-conference safety, earning first-team All-Big Eight honors twice. He intercepted nine passes in his career and, in 1989, was named to CU's All-Century team.

In golf, Irwin was a two-time Big Eight champion and, in 1967 he won the NCAA championship. Through 2018, he was one of just six men—including Nicklaus and Woods—to win an NCAA title and U.S. Open.

Irwin also started a family tradition at CU. His younger brother, Phil, played football for the Buffs and was the first CU athlete on the cover of *Sports Illustrated*. His son, Steve, played golf at CU, and his nephew, Heath, was an All-American football player for the Buffs in 1995.

"He's been a good Buff through the years," Plati said. "He's an icon in the golf world and Hale's been very good to the university when he's asked to come back and do things."

In addition to his three U.S. Open titles, Irwin won 20 events on the PGA Tour. After turning 50 and going to the senior circuit, Irwin won seven majors and 45 tournaments overall and was named Champions Tour player of the year three times. He also made five career appearances in the Ryder Cup, helping the United States to a victory each time.

The Missouri native has been enshrined in the World Golf Hall of Fame, CU Athletics Hall of Fame, Colorado Sports Hall of Fame, and Missouri Sports Hall of Fame.

"All in all, I'd have to say I can't complain," he said, "because I've just gotten to experience so much and meet so many good people and have had such a good run, that it would be ludicrous to complain and say I haven't enjoyed it."

23 Mark Wetmore

Prior to an indoor track and field meet in January of 2019, CU head coach Mark Wetmore stood next to assistant coach Heather Burroughs and watched the Buffaloes' distance runners stretch and prepare for their races. "I said to Heather, 'Aren't we lucky to have good, open-minded kids who are willing to learn toughness and willing to learn courage? Aren't we lucky?'" Wetmore said.

Many of the runners that have come through CU would likely marvel at how lucky they've been to have Wetmore as their coach.

Hired as the head coach for cross country and track and field on November 6, 1995, Wetmore is arguably the greatest distance coach in NCAA history. At CU, only skiing head coaches Bill Marolt and Richard Rokos would be in the conversation with Wetmore for the greatest ever to lead the Buffs.

In the fall of 2018, Wetmore coached the CU women's cross country team to the national title. It was CU's eighth national title in the sport, all under Wetmore's direction. The men have won five national titles (2001, 2004, 2006, 2013, and 2014), while the women have won three (2000, 2004, 2018). Wetmore's cross country teams have dominated regional competition (25 titles between men and women) and conference foes (33 titles). From 1996 to 2007, the CU men won 12 consecutive Big 12 championships.

Individually, Wetmore has coached five national champions in cross country, including three men—Adam Goucher (1998), Jorge Torres (2002), and Dathan Ritzenhein (2003)—and two women—Kara Grgas-Wheeler (2000) and Dani Jones (2018). His runners have earned 135 All-American honors in cross country alone.

CU became just the third school to win the men's and women's titles in the same year in 2004, and Wetmore is the only Division I coach to ever win all four national titles (men's and women's team, and men's and women's individual).

In track and field, Wetmore has won two conference team titles, while his athletes have accounted for 16 NCAA titles, over 100 conference championships and nearly 200 All-American honors.

Throughout his tenure, Wetmore's always had a team-first approach while also producing All-American students.

"He cares about his athletes," said Billy Nelson, a CU assistant coach who was a two-time All-American under Wetmore from 2002 to '03. "He wants his athletes to be successful in the classroom, and he wants his athletes to be successful on the track without running them into the ground. When I was here as a runner we knew it was his job and he did it all day long. But, I think the thought process that really goes into each athlete's individual training on our team... I think that's what I've picked up as a staff member. The amount of effort that goes into each individual person's workout."

The success of the CU program, and the lure of training at high altitude in a city that was seemingly created for runners, is certainly attractive to top-notch recruits, but one of the keys to Wetmore's success as a coach has been his ability to find athletes who have yet to reach their peak and make them stars.

One of the brightest stars of Wetmore's tenure, Emma Coburn, was an eight-time state champion at Crested Butte (Colo.) High School, but coming from a small school, she didn't have the times that one would typically associate with a Division I athlete. She became a three-time NCAA champion in track, a six-time All-American, and, eventually, an Olympic bronze medalist. Coburn and many other runners became significantly better after coming to CU.

"We're aware of that and proud of that history of development of the athletes that come here, both male and female," Wetmore said.

Disciplined, strict, and highly respected, Wetmore is also very unassuming. He's earned national coach of the year honors six times in cross country, with 30 conference coach of the year awards, and yet he prefers to focus on those around him.

"It's no one athlete or no one recruiting class," Wetmore said of the program's success. "The coaches are important, but it takes more than one. Boulder is a great town, but it's also a town where one can be distracted from the disciplines of this trade. It's a confluence of all those factors—the team buying into the culture, the coaches creating the culture, the coaches getting along. The athletes having room for each other's egos in a town that's welcoming to our sport. We're blessed to have them come together."

24 Dave Logan

In preparing for a 1973 game against Air Force, CU head football coach Eddie Crowder wasn't sure if punt returner Steve Haggerty would be available, as the senior was dealing with a shoulder injury. Two days before the game, Crowder had 6-foot-5, 225-pound sophomore receiver Dave Logan try returning punts—something he'd never done in a CU uniform. Then, in the third quarter against Air Force, with CU holding a 7–3 lead, Logan fielded a Falcons' punt and raced 52 yards for a touchdown, busting open the game in what turned out to be a 38–17 rout.

"We picked Logan at game time," Crowder said. "As it turned out, it was a good decision. Logan has good speed, but he also has power. You can't hand-tackle him."

Of course Logan scored a touchdown. One of the greatest all-around athletes in CU history was capable of making an impact seemingly every time he stepped on the football field or basketball court for the Buffaloes.

"Dave's really the last two-sport star we had, when you're talking about football and basketball," CU sports information director David Plati said.

Logan was extremely gifted in several sports, managing the nearly impossible feat of being drafted in the NFL, NBA, and Major League Baseball. He's one of only four people who can make that claim, along with George Carter and Mickey McCarty in the 1960s and baseball Hall of Famer Dave Winfield, who did it three years before Logan. In 1976, Logan was a third-round pick (65th overall) of the NFL's Cleveland Browns and a ninth-round pick of the NBA's Kansas City Kings. In 1972, when he was coming out of Wheat Ridge (Colo.) High School, he was selected in the 30th round of the Major League Baseball draft, by the Cincinnati Reds. "I just like athletics," he said during his senior year at CU. "I enjoy the competition."

While he never played baseball at CU, he crafted a remarkable two-sport career with the Buffaloes from 1972 to '75, played for nearly a decade in the NFL, and has become one of the most recognizable sports figures in the state of Colorado through his long career as a broadcaster and coach.

At CU, Logan played during a time when the Buffs had a run-oriented offense, but he led the team in receiving twice and finished his four-year career with 68 catches for 1,078 yards and four touchdowns. He also returned two punts for touchdowns (adding a second one in 1974) and averaged 35.9 yards on 29 punts. He helped the Buffs get to the Gator Bowl in 1972 and to the Astro-Bluebonnet Bowl in 1975, under first-year coach Bill Mallory. In 1975, Logan was named first-team All-American by the *Sporting News*. On the basketball court, Logan played for coach Sox Walseth and averaged 14.1 points per game for his three-year career (he missed one season with a knee injury). In 1972–73, he averaged 12.4 points, becoming the first CU freshman to average in double figures.

Logan didn't take much time off, either. In the 1975 regular season finale in football, on November 22, Logan caught two passes for 39 yards in a 33–7 win against Kansas State. Seven days later, he had seven points and six rebounds in the basketball season opener against New Mexico. He briefly left basketball in mid-December for football practices, played in the Bluebonnet Bowl (three catches for 20 yards and a touchdown) on December 27 and just two days later was in the starting lineup, scoring nine points, in a basketball game at Kansas.

Eventually, Logan had to pick one sport, and he signed with the Cleveland Browns after the 1976 Draft. In eight seasons with the Browns, he caught 262 passes for 4,247 yards and 24 touchdowns and even landed on the cover of *Sports Illustrated* for the 1980 preview issue. He retired after playing four games with the Denver Broncos in 1984.

Logan, of course, hasn't slowed down in retirement. Shortly after his playing career came to a close, he jumped into broadcasting, doing sports talk radio and play-by-play for some CU television broadcasts. From 1990 to '96, he was the color analyst for KOA radio on Broncos games, and in 1997 he took over the play-by-play duties. In his first two seasons as the Broncos' play-by-play announcer, they won their first two Super Bowl titles. In 2018, he completed his 22nd season as the voice of the Broncos.

In addition to his busy broadcasting schedule, Logan has become one of the most successful high school football coaches in Colorado history. He's the only football coach in Colorado to win state titles at four schools (Arvada West, Chatfield, Mullen, and Cherry Creek). Through 2018, his seven overall championships ranked second in state annals, and he's top five in career wins.

"I'm blessed that I've been offered so many opportunities," he said during a 2015 NFL Films segment. "You look back on what you've accomplished and sometimes you say, 'Wow, did I really do that?' I'm a big believer you appreciate what you have every single day. I've been blessed in many, many ways."

25 Barry's Run of Success

Aside from the fact that she knew basketball and knew how to win, Ceal Barry took a giant leap outside of her comfort zone when she accepted the job to coach the Colorado women's team in April of 1983. Just 28, Barry was a Louisville, Kentucky, native who starred as a player for her home-state Kentucky Wildcats. She then coached the University of Cincinnati women's team for four seasons, compiling an 83–42 record with the Bearcats. Coming to CU was Barry's first venture far from home, and she joined an athletic department that didn't have any other women as coaches or administrators.

"I felt like an outsider," she said. "I was afraid, a little bit scared. I'm out of my comfort zone. But, there's nothing like knowing if you don't win, you're going to lose your job. There's no greater motivator than fear, I think. If you lose, you're done; and I wanted to coach that bad."

The opportunity to coach in a more prestigious conference, the Big Eight, was enough to entice Barry, and she used her fear of failure to sculpt a Hall of Fame career. Barry coached the Buffaloes for 22 seasons, from 1983 to 2005. She posted a 427–242 record (.638 winning percentage), won four regular season conference titles and five conference tournaments. She guided the Buffs to the NCAA Tournament 12 times, reaching the Sweet 16 six times and the Elite Eight three times.

"I think it's incredible," said JR Payne, hired as the women's head coach in 2016. "Everything she accomplished here just speaks for itself. The record and the young women she coached. What those women are out doing in the world—doctors and coaches and teachers and so many incredible things—speaks to the type of program she ran."

It took Barry a while to get rolling, though. Her predecessor, Sox Walseth, retired after a 77–21 record in three seasons. In Barry's first two seasons with the Buffs, they went 16–40. "I didn't have the culture and I'm not sure I had the right staff," she said. "I thought, 'In my time at Cincinnati, I knew I had won, I know how to win. I just have to get the right formula here.' My third year we did much better. We turned it around."

In Barry's third season, 1985–86, the Buffs went 21–9, kicking of a 12-year run of success in which CU never finished below the .500 mark. The tide turned when Barry found success on the recruiting trail, landing stars such as Erin Carson, Crystal Ford, Tracy Tripp, Bridget Turner and others. "Back then, I could out-recruit people and identify [talent] in the '80s," Barry said. "I got a lot of great in-state high school players. We relied on in-state kids to come here. You had to get the best and we did and we could. Our reputation was really, really good."

When the Buffs became a national power in the 1990s, led by Jamillah Lang, Erin Scholz, and Shelley Sheetz, fans flocked to the CU Events Center, creating a raucous atmosphere for home games.

"It was lot of hard work and it was a lot of fun," Barry said of building a winner. "I worked at it along with my assistants. I had great assistants. We were all into it. All of Boulder was into it; all of Colorado was into it. It was fun."

Eventually, the fun ran out. After four consecutive NCAA Tournament appearances, Barry's squad went 9–19 in 2004–05. Adding to that disappointment was that the in-state recruits Barry relied on so much in the early years were no longer choosing to play for CU. "I didn't think I was doing the job at the level the job needed to be done," Barry said of her retirement after the 2004–05 season.

The CU program hasn't been the same since she left. In the 14 seasons after her retirement, the Buffs never came close to a conference title and went to only one NCAA Tournament. Barry, meanwhile, spent her post-coaching years working in the CU athletic department, most recently as senior women's administrator.

"Just an icon here on campus, and not just in the athletic department," CU associate athletic director Lance Carl said. "When I think of Ceal Barry, I think of stability and I think of someone who really genuinely cares for CU and our student athletes and wants to see them be the best that they can be when they leave here."

Barry's competitiveness, passion, and love of her athletes helped to get her inducted into the Women's Basketball Hall of Fame in Knoxville, Tennessee, in 2018.

"It's certainly an honor and it's humbling," she said. "It's nice to be recognized. I think anybody would like to think, 'Maybe I was a small part of pushing it forward. I was just a little segment in there to help push the whole thing.'"

26 The Father of CU Football

In 1895, Fred Folsom was a 21-year-old graduate of Dartmouth College with two enticing opportunities in front of him. Folsom had already planned on attending law school at the University of Michigan when a group of CU students, led by senior football captain William Caley, gave him a different option: coach the football team and attend the CU law school. Having just finished his playing career at Dartmouth, where he led his team to a pair of conference titles, Folsom couldn't pass up the opportunity to remain in the game he loved.

While balancing football and law, Folsom would spend 15 of the next 20 years coaching the CU football team in three different stints: 1895–99, 1901–02, and 1908–15. In all, he coached CU for more seasons than anyone in program history and is known as the "Father of CU Football." Although the schedule was certainly easier in those days, he still has the best winning percentage (.765) of anyone that coached more than one year and only Bill McCartney has more wins than Folsom, who went 77–23–2. Folsom also directed the longest winning streak (21 games from 1908 to 1912) in CU history, won nine conference titles and coached the baseball team for a year.

Folsom left the team after the 1899 season to focus on his law practice, but was drawn back in before the 1901 season. Then, after 1902, he went back to Dartmouth, where he coached for four seasons, going 29–5–4; his .816 winning percentage is the best in Dartmouth history. In 1908, Folsom returned and coached for eight more seasons before retiring for good and devoting his time to his law practice and teaching. He taught in the CU law school until 1943, while also serving as chairman of the athletic board for a time.

In 1924, at the direction of university president George Norlin, Folsom developed the financial plan for a new football stadium. For roughly $70,000, Colorado Stadium was built and opened in October of 1924. After Folsom's death in 1944, the stadium was renamed in his honor and remains the iconic home of the Buffaloes.

Other highlights from the first 30 years of CU football:

- November 15, 1890: CU plays its first game ever, a 20–0 loss to the Denver Athletic Club. Several players get hurt in the game, including quarterback Charles L. Edmundson, a senior from Iowa. He was done for the year and then graduated the next spring from CU's medical department. Thus, CU's first quarterback played just one game. He went on to a long career as a doctor and even served as mayor of Bisbee, Arizona.

- November 22, 1890: The second game still stands as the most lopsided loss in CU history, as the Buffs were crushed by the Colorado Mines, 103–0.

  That first team went 0–4 and was outscored 217–4, but George Darley gets credit for the first touchdown, as he returned a Colorado Mines fumble 65 yards for a score (TDs were worth four points at the time).

- November 26, 1891: After losing its first eight games, CU finally got a win, 24–4, at the Colorado Springs Athletic Association.

- In 1893, quarterback Patrick Carney was named captain for the third year in a row. He was the only player to do that before 2016, when Sefo Liufau matched the honor. In Carney's time, though, the captain was basically the coach.

  CU was a part of the newly formed Colorado Football Association in 1893. The CFA, which lasted until 1908, included Colorado A&M (later CSU), Colorado College, Colorado Mines, and Denver.

- In CU's fifth season, 1894, it finally got a coach, hiring 19-year-old Harry Heller, who was a star at Baker University in Kansas. Heller coached just one year, going 8–1 and winning the CFA with a 5–0 mark. He is credited with helping to make improvements to facilities, instilling some discipline with diet, and getting more students to play. Heller would later play against CU for the Denver Athletic Club and, by the age of 25, was a physician in his home state of Kansas.

- In 1898, the first on-campus football field was built. It was named Gamble Field, in honor of Harry Gamble, who was captain in 1894 and played six seasons at CU.

- On November 17, 1898, CU played an out-of-state team for the first time, losing to Nebraska in Boulder, 23–10.

- In 1910, CU was a part of the new Rocky Mountain Athletic Conference, which included the teams from the CFA, as well as Utah. CU remained in the RMAC through 1937. Over the years, the league added several teams, including Brigham Young and Wyoming.

- Folsom coached 15 of the 25 seasons from 1895 to 1919. In the other 10 seasons, there were six different head coaches: T.C. Mortimer, Dave Cropp, Willis Kleinholz, Frank Castleman, Bob Evans, and Joe Mills.

27 Carroll Hardy

Until the end of time, Carroll Hardy will have his place in baseball history as the answer to one of the game's great trivia questions. The only man to pinch hit for the great Ted Williams? That would be Hardy.

On September 20, 1960, the 6-foot, 185-pound Hardy, who was a journeyman throughout his decade in the major leagues, went to the plate in place of the greatest hitter in baseball history. The 42-year-old Williams was in the final days of his sensational career when, during the first inning at Baltimore, he fouled a pitch off his foot and couldn't continue. "It hurt him so badly that he limped off the field, through the dugout, and up into the clubhouse," Hardy recalled years later. "They said, 'Hardy, get a bat; you're the hitter.' So I grabbed a bat and ran out there and hit into a double play."

While that moment is what has earned Hardy the most attention over the years, he was much more than a footnote in history. At CU, he was one of the greatest multi-sport athletes to play for the Buffaloes. A native of Sturgis, South Dakota, Hardy chose to play at CU over Nebraska and Wyoming because the Buffaloes offered him a better chance to play multiple sports. From 1951 to '55, Hardy earned 10 varsity letters, in football, baseball, and track and field, and he was a star in all three sports.

As a baseball player, Hardy is the Buffs' all-time leader in batting average (.392) and triples (12) and he twice batted over .400 for the season. In track, he ran the 100-yard dash in a blistering 9.8 seconds and set a school record in the broad jump. From 1951 to '54, he excelled on the football field. During his career with the Buffs, he rushed for 1,999 yards and 23 touchdowns, racked up 1,139 yards as a punt/kick returner, intercepted six passes on defense, punted 48 times for 2,074 yards, and even made 14 of 19 extra points as a kicker during his senior year. Hardy's career average of 6.87 yards per rushing attempt remains a CU record. Through 2018, only 10 players in CU history had amassed more all-purpose yards than Hardy's 3,115, despite battling injuries during his career.

Playing for legendary CU coach Dal Ward, who used the single-wing offense, Hardy earned All-Big Seven Conference honors in 1954. He earned All-American honorable mention in 1953 and 1954.

"The single wing was referred to as a 'three yards-and-a-cloud-of-dust' offense," Hardy told *The Denver Post* years later. "But Dal's single wing was capable of big plays. We ran double reverses and some things to keep the opponent guessing."

Hardy never did lead the Buffs in rushing, but teamed with Frank Bernardi, John Bayuk and others to form a stellar attack that helped the Buffs go 26–11–3 during his career. The duo of "Hardy and Bernardi" was famous in Boulder.

The late Fred Casotti, a longtime CU administrator who saw many of CU's greats, wrote in his 1972 book, *Football C.U. Style*, that Hardy was the best tailback he had seen.

"Carroll Hardy could send more sparks of excitement through Folsom Stadium's stands by just coming out of the huddle than a lot of good men produced in their careers," Casotti wrote. "The only other player I've seen at CU who could generate the same kind of excitement by just touching the ball was Clifford Branch."

Hardy was nicknamed "Preacher," by his CU teammates. Casotti said it was because Hardy "preached about the importance of physical conditioning and body care so much."

Hardy capped his football career in style on November 20, 1954. Facing Kansas State at Folsom Field, Hardy rushed for a career-high 238 yards and three touchdowns on only 10 carries. He scored a touchdown on his final play with the Buffs. At the end of that season, Hardy was selected to play in the Hula Bowl, an all-star game for college football. He won MVP honors after rushing for 138 yards on 13 carries in a 33–13 win for his team.

In the 1955 NFL Draft, Hardy was selected in the third round (34th overall) by the San Francisco 49ers. That year, he played in San Francisco with future Hall of Fame quarterback Y.A. Tittle. Before his rookie season with the 49ers, Hardy signed with the Cleveland Indians and spent the summer of 1955 playing minor league baseball. After his season with the 49ers, he returned to baseball and never returned to the gridiron.

Hardy played with a young Roger Maris in Cleveland before going to Boston in 1960. In Boston, he was a part-time player and pinch hit not only for Williams, but for Carl Yastrzemski, who, in 1961, was in the first year of his 23-year Hall of Fame career. Hardy also played for the Houston Colt .45s and Minnesota Twins before retiring after the 1967 season.

After his playing career, Hardy worked for 20 years as an executive with the Denver Broncos, helping to put together three Super Bowl teams. He was with the Broncos when John Elway came in as a rookie in 1983.

"I've had a good life," he said in 2009, more than a decade into retirement.

28 1942 Final Four

Colorado does not have a rich history in men's basketball, but in the early 1940s, the Buffaloes were one of the top teams in the country.

Hired in 1935, head coach Forrest "Frosty" Cox had built a winner in Boulder, including a stellar season in 1940. That year, he led the Buffs to the National Invitation Tournament (NIT) championship and then to the NCAA Tournament for the first time. In 1942, Cox and the Buffaloes climbed to a new level.

Led by All-Americans Robert Doll and Leason "Pete" McCloud, the Buffs reached the Final Four of the NCAA Tournament for the first time in program history. It's a feat that's only been matched once since. Cox's crew gained national attention right away that season with a four-game Eastern road trip. The Buffs opened the season with a 45–29 rout of St. Joseph's (Pa.), and then knocked off St. John's, 39–33, at Madison Square Garden in New York.

"Forrest Cox, the Colorado coach, is nicknamed 'Frosty' because he is so cool under fire, but he has nothing on those cagers of his," sportswriter George E. Coleman wrote after the win against St. John's.

CU started that season 14–0, steamrolling everybody until a 40–39 loss at Wyoming on March 3. Despite that loss, the Buffs won their fourth Mountain States Conference title in five years. At 15–1, CU accepted a spot in the NCAA Tournament. In those days, only eight teams were invited to the tournament—four from the East and four from the West. The tournament took place at Municipal Auditorium in Kansas City, Missouri.

CU's opening game in the tournament was an intriguing matchup against Kansas. The Jayhawks were coached by legendary

Phog Allen, and he and Cox weren't exactly the best of friends. Cox, who grew up in Newton, Kansas, played for Allen's Jayhawks from 1929 to 1931 and was team captain. He earned All-American honors in 1930, twice was named to the All-Big Six Conference team, and led Kansas to the conference title in 1931. He then worked as an assistant for Allen before coming to CU. At some point after Cox left Kansas, the two had a falling out. According to reports at the time, Cox didn't respond when Allen's former players were asked to write testimonials ahead of Allen's 25th anniversary at KU. Cox was listed among Kansas' all-time greats until Allen omitted his name.

In the days leading up to their matchup, Allen threw criticism at Cox, whose CU team was made up of several Kansas natives. "Frosty has a hand-picked team," Allen said. "He has the Kansas boys he wanted while we have a group of players who chose to come to KU for an education. A hand-picked team is likely to win more ball games than a strictly academic group."

CU's roster included seven players from Kansas, including McCloud. Like his head coach, McCloud grew up in Newton. Allen's criticism only fueled the Buffs, who knocked off the Jayhawks, 46–44. McCloud scored 19 points. "I loved it," McCloud said years later. "I remember we played pretty good as a team. With Phog on the bench that was pure joy. That sort of settled the score."

The next night, the Buffs faced Stanford in the national semifinals. The championship quest ended there, however, with a 46–35 loss. A two-time conference scoring champion, McCloud was bottled up by the Stanford defense and he scored just three points.

That would be the last CU basketball game for a while. CU suspended the basketball program for two seasons during World War II. More than 75 years later, however, the 1942 season remains one of the best in CU basketball history.

29 Burdie Leads the Buffs

In the 1950s, Burdette "Burdie" Haldorson dominated the hardwood at CU Fieldhouse (later renamed Balch Fieldhouse).

One of just three men's basketball players in CU history to have his jersey number (22) retired, Haldorson earned All-American honors as a senior in 1955 and was twice named to the All-Big Seven Conference team. At 6-foot-7, 210 pounds, the Austin, Minnesota, native was a force near the basket. From 1952 to '55, he averaged 15.0 points and 9.5 rebounds per game. He still holds CU records for rebounds in a half (21) and a game (31). Haldorson was at his best during his senior season, 1954–55, becoming the first player in CU history to average a double-double, with 21.0 points and 13.8 rebounds per game. His rebounding average is still a single-season school record.

"We'll be just as good as Haldorson," CU head coach H.B. Lee said before the 1954–55 season. "We need the big man to play well for us."

Haldorson wound up being the key player on what is arguably the best team in CU history. With him leading the way, the Buffaloes went 19–6 overall—a school record for wins at the time—won the Big Seven with an 11–1 conference record, and reached the Final Four of the NCAA Tournament for just the second time in school history. Through 2019, CU hadn't been back to the Final Four.

Forward Robert Jeangerard teamed with Haldorson to form a dominating duo. The 6-foot-3 Jeangerard averaged 16.0 points and 6.8 rebounds, was renowned for his defense, and joined Haldorson on the All-Big Seven first team. CU might have been even better

Balch Fieldhouse

For more than 40 years, from 1937 to 1979, CU Fieldhouse—later renamed in honor of longtime athletic department member Roland E. Balch—was home to the Buffaloes' basketball team. Built in 1937 at a cost of $174,500, the fieldhouse was home to many of the great moments in basketball history, until a new arena was built in 1979. At Balch, the men's basketball team went 298–115 (.718 winning percentage) and the women's basketball team played its first five seasons there. Over the years, the building has also hosted women's volleyball, gymnastics, wrestling, and indoor track and field. Balch is located on the west side of Folsom Field, is attached to the six-level press box, and is still in use for football game days, summer camps, and other athletics activities.

that year had Art Bunte finished his career with the Buffs. As a sophomore in 1952–53, Bunte led the Buffs with 19.1 points and 8.5 rebounds per game. The next fall, however, the Denver native, who didn't get along with Lee, transferred to Utah. He would have been a senior with the Buffs in 1954–55.

Even without Bunte, Lee and the Buffs did just fine, winning back-to-back Big Seven titles after he left. Heading into the postseason in 1955, the Buffs were on a roll, having won 13 of their last 14 regular season games.

At the time, just 24 teams played in the NCAA Tournament, and the Buffs got a first-round bye. In the regionals, the Buffs opened the tournament with a 69–59 victory against Tulsa, led by Haldorson's 28 points and Jeangerard's stellar defense.

In the regional finals against Bradley—a team that beat the Buffs in the NCAA Tournament the previous year—Jeangerard had 29 points and Haldorson 23 in a 93–81 win. That victory propelled the Buffs into the Final Four against one of the greatest players and teams in college basketball history.

On March 19, CU faced the University of San Francisco and their All-American center, Bill Russell. From 1954 to '56, the Dons went 57–1 and captured back-to-back national titles, led by Russell and another future Hall of Famer, K.C. Jones. Russell was a two-time All-American at San Francisco and went on to become one of the greatest players in NBA history, winning five MVP awards and helping the Boston Celtics to 11 championships.

Despite the daunting task, Lee was confident. "We're going to win that game against San Francisco," he said. "A lot of people are going to get quite a surprise."

Russell and the Dons were too good for the Buffs—and everyone else—however. Russell scored 24 points, Haldorson was held to nine and San Francisco rolled to a 62–50 victory. The Dons won the championship the next day against La Salle, while CU knocked off Iowa, 75–54, in the third-place game.

Lee coached the Buffs for six seasons, from 1950 to '56, going 63–74 and winning two conference titles before becoming the athletic director at Kansas State.

Following their CU careers, Haldorson and Jeangerard were teammates—along with Russell and Jones—on the 1956 U.S. Olympic team that captured the gold medal in Melbourne, Australia.

Haldorson was also a member of the 1960 Olympic team, which won gold in Rome and, in 2010, was inducted into the Naismith Memorial Basketball Hall of Fame. In addition to the Olympics, Haldorson starred for the Phillips 66ers—based out of Oklahoma—in the National Industrial Basketball League.

30 Falling Short in 1994

Ranked No. 2 in the country, the Colorado football team went into Lincoln, Nebraska, on October 29, 1994, with a tremendous amount of confidence. The Buffaloes had won 11 games in a row and they were off to a 7–0 start that season. CU had already knocked off five Top 25 opponents, including the Hail Mary win at No. 4 Michigan. Third-ranked Nebraska was the last major hurdle in CU's path to an undefeated regular season.

"The national championship is our ultimate goal, and Nebraska is in our way," CU receiver Michael Westbrook said before the game.

CU won its only national championship in 1990. The 1989 team came up one win short and the 1923 team, which went 9–0, was possibly the most dominant. The 1994 squad, however, may have been the best team ever assembled in Boulder.

Head coach Bill McCartney's final team was loaded. From that roster, 28 players became NFL draft picks and 32 played in the league. It featured Heisman Trophy–winner Rashaan Salaam, Thorpe Award–winner Chris Hudson, future Pro Bowl quarterback Kordell Stewart, and two first-round draft picks at receiver in Westbrook and Rae Carruth. All five starting offensive linemen and nine defensive starters were NFL draft picks.

"That was probably one of the greatest teams ever at Colorado," said Tony Berti, the Buffs' left tackle. "That showed through in our season and how we played."

CU was on a championship mission all season and hadn't lost since 364 days earlier, when Nebraska came to Boulder and left with a 21–17 win. Stewart had perhaps the worst day of his career

Rashaan Salaam stands with the Heisman Trophy after being named the 60th winner of the award at the Downtown Athletic Club in New York on December 10, 1994. (Getty Images / Jed Jacobsohn / Staff)

in that game, including an interception with 1 minute, 21 seconds to play that ended hope of a comeback.

Heading into the rematch in 1994, Colorado had revenge on the mind, but Nebraska was loaded, too. The Cornhuskers were 8–0 and eyeing a championship of their own, and despite all the talent on the CU roster, the Buffs left Lincoln with a devastating 24–7 loss.

Nebraska led 24–0 at one point before Salaam scored a touchdown late in the third quarter. Stewart's career-long struggle against Nebraska continued, and the CU defense was not as dominant as usual.

"Other than Nebraska's fine play, I don't have any explanation for why we didn't play better," McCartney said. "You have to give credit to the Cornhuskers."

Following the loss, CU rolled past Oklahoma State, Kansas, and Iowa State. Then they dominated Notre Dame in the Fiesta Bowl and finished 11–1 and No. 3 in the Associated Press poll. Only the 1990 championship team had a better finish.

Some still argue the 1994 team was the best in CU history. Twenty years after that season, Salaam had no doubt.

"It was a powerhouse," Salaam said in 2014. "We were putting guys in the league. It was a special time. [The 1990 team] has got the rings, they've got their name in the stadium and I respect it. Those guys from that team brought me here; they were the reason I came to Colorado. But, if we played against those guys, head up, we would beat them."

Salaam knew, however, that it was a team that didn't complete its mission. Making matters worse, Nebraska finished 13–0 and won the national title.

"That still stings," Salaam said of the loss in Lincoln. "To go into Nebraska and not pull that win out, that really puts a damper on the season, because that's what it was all geared for."

31 Neuheisel Takes Over

Buff Nation was stunned when McCartney announced his retirement on November 19, 1994.

CU and its fans were in for another surprise nine days later when 33-year-old Rick Neuheisel was hired as McCartney's replacement. Athletic director Bill Marolt kept his coaching search internal, with defensive coordinator Mike Hankwitz, offensive coordinator Elliot Uzelac, defensive line/assistant head coach Bob Simmons, and Neuheisel the top candidates. Neuheisel, hired by McCartney earlier that year as quarterbacks/receivers coach, got the job despite being the least experienced of the bunch.

"It was a shock to a number of us that Rick Neuheisel was the chosen person for the job," said cornerback Marcus Washington, who was a true freshman in 1994. "A lot of us thought Bob Simmons was going to get the job. Nobody saw Rick Neuheisel being the guy."

Taking over a CU team that went 11–1 in 1994, Neuheisel had the pieces in place to keep the train rolling and Marolt liked the fact that Neuheisel was a younger coach. After all, Marolt was only 26 when he took over as CU's skiing coach years earlier.

"The thing I really like about Rick Neuheisel is he's energetic, he's full of enthusiasm, and the youth of our country need to look to leaders who are full of life and have that spark to make the difference," Marolt said at the time.

A former UCLA quarterback who spent two seasons playing in the United States Football League, Neuheisel was certainly energetic and he related to his players. With guitar in hand and plenty of laughs, Neuheisel appealed to a lot of people around the program.

"We had fun playing for Rick," Washington said. "What you saw from the outside is exactly what it was in the inside. Rick was very charismatic. He was fun. He was full of energy. He was very positive. Even when we lost, Rick seemed to find the silver lining in the situations. He was a players' coach."

Neuheisel didn't often have to look for the silver lining. During his four seasons as the Buffaloes' head coach, from 1995 to '98, he went 33–14 with three bowl game appearances. Although a disappointing 1997 season ended a 10-year run of winning seasons,

Neuheisel kept the Buffs rolling—even if he wasn't the expected choice to take the job.

"Honestly, I think it was kind of a smooth transition to Rick because we had a number of leaders on the team already," Washington said. "We had already had a leadership base on the team. We already had a lot of established roles on the team for players when Rick took over."

Neuheisel had another surprise in store for CU and its fans, however. After a solid regular season in 1998, Neuheisel led the Buffs to a victory against Oregon in the Aloha Bowl on Christmas Day at Aloha Stadium in Honolulu. Later that night, in the same stadium, Air Force rolled past Washington in the Oahu Bowl.

Washington athletic director Barbara Hedges, who fired Huskies coach Jim Lambright after the Oahu Bowl loss, was impressed with

Rick Neuheisel is carried off the field after the Buffaloes beat the Oregon Ducks 38–6 in the '96 Cotton Bowl. (AP Photo / Boulder Camera / Cliff Grassmick)

Neuheisel in Hawaii. Initially, Neuheisel rejected Washington's interest, but Hedges offered him one of the richest contracts in college football at the time, a seven-year deal worth more than $1 million annually. At CU, Neuheisel made about $650,000 annually and, per state legislation, was limited to a one-year contract.

"There were a lot of reasons for me to say yes," Neuheisel said. "Washington is a program with great prestige and tradition. I currently had a job with great prestige and tradition, which is what made this so difficult. I think in the long term, for my career and my family, this is the best decision."

Athletic director Dick Tharp, CU players, and fans weren't happy with the decision.

"That was a big slap in the face to a lot of players," Washington said of Neuheisel's departure. "When he left, a lot of people felt betrayed."

Neuheisel had a rocky ride at Washington. On the field, he compiled a 33–16 record in four seasons, but off the field issues caught up with him. In the fall of 2002, CU was given two years probation because of 53 NCAA violations, 51 of them coming when Neuheisel was coach. Washington banned him from off-campus recruiting for several months. Then, in February of 2003, Neuheisel interviewed for the head coaching job with the NFL's San Francisco 49ers, but lied to Hedges about that interview. In June of 2003, he was fired by Washington after he broke NCAA rules by betting on the NCAA basketball tournament and lying to school officials and investigators about it.

He would go on to spend three years (2005–07) as an assistant with the NFL's Baltimore Ravens and four years (2008–11) as head coach at UCLA before beginning a career in broadcasting.

32 Barnett's Rise and Fall

Following the fairly sudden departure of Rick Neuheisel as head coach following the 1998 season, CU turned to a familiar face to lead the football program. Gary Barnett, who had been an assistant coach with the Buffs from 1984 to 1991, playing a key role in their rise to national prominence, had directed a remarkable resurgence at Northwestern University and was lured away by CU athletic director Dick Tharp.

Barnett was Tharp's first choice, but contract negotiations hit a snag. Denver Broncos offensive coordinator Gary Kubiak was targeted, but he turned down the job, so Tharp went after Barnett again and got him. Barnett led moribund Northwestern to the Big Ten title in 1995, going 10–2 and playing in the Rose Bowl. He followed that with a 9–3 season in 1996. After turning down other opportunities to leave the Wildcats, Barnett called Colorado "home."

Hired on January 20, 1999, Barnett immediately coined the slogan, "RTD—return to dominance." He delivered—sort of. From 1999 to 2005, he went 49–38 with five bowl appearances and four Big 12 North titles.

The Buffs hit their peak under Barnett in 2001, going 9–2 in the regular season, then knocking off Texas in the Big 12 title game. At 10–2, the Buffs were ranked No. 3, one spot shy of playing for the national title. They finished 10–3 after a loss to Oregon in the Fiesta Bowl.

Off the field, Barnett's tenure began to turn sour in December of 2001. As the Buffs prepared for the Fiesta Bowl, a female student alleged that she was sexually assaulted by players and recruits at a party.

Over the next few years, the recruiting scandal rocked the university and the football program and sullied the reputation of Barnett.

Two female students filed a lawsuit alleging they were raped by players and recruits at that off-campus party on December 7, 2001. Boulder County district attorney Mary Keenan accused Barnett and the football program of using sex and alcohol at parties to lure top recruits to CU. In all, nine women between 2001 and 2004 came forward with allegations of sexual assault by players or recruits. One of the accusers was former walk-on kicker Katie Hnida, the only female player in CU history. Hnida later transferred to New Mexico, where she became the first female to score in a Division I game.

While at New Mexico, Hnida made her allegations public in a *Sports Illustrated* article in February of 2004. Barnett said that was the first he had heard of those allegations. During that press conference, he was asked about Hnida as a player and responded by saying, "It was obvious Katie was not very good. She was awful. Katie was not only a girl, she was terrible. Okay? There's no other way to say it."

The fact that Barnett was responding to a direct question about Hnida's talent didn't matter. In light of the allegations by Hnida and others, CU president Elizabeth Hoffman said Barnett's comments were "extremely inappropriate and insensitive" and placed him on administrative leave.

No charges for sexual assault were ever filed against CU players. However, in 2007, CU settled a lawsuit with two of the women, with one receiving $2.5 million and the other $350,000.

The scandal also led to tighter restrictions on recruiting at CU and it contributed to a massive change in university leadership. Tharp resigned under pressure in November of 2004. The next month, chancellor Richard Byyny retired. In March of 2005, Hoffman resigned.

Barnett's reputation was damaged, but he kept his job. He led the Buffs to another North Division title in 2004—while being named Big 12 coach of the year—and again in 2005. The 2005 season ended with a thud, however. The Buffs were routed by Nebraska, 30–3, in the regular season finale, but backed into the Big 12 title game, where they were embarrassed by Texas, 70–3. The scandal couldn't take Barnett down, but those losses did. He was fired by new athletic director Mike Bohn.

More than a decade later, Barnett said he believes the loss to Texas, "provided an excuse for someone to make a decision that they wanted to make. I think there were a lot of things in the works at that time and that game just created the opportunity for someone to go in a different direction. We had survived all the other stuff, and we had been told that our contracts were going to be extended."

After being fired, Barnett had opportunities to become an assistant coach, but only wanted to be on the sidelines as a head coach. He got into radio and television broadcasting to stay close to the game and keep his name in the coaching circle. Despite never being proven guilty of doing anything wrong during the "scandal," however, Barnett couldn't get a school to hire him. "About the fourth or fifth year, you start realizing that maybe this wasn't going to happen," he said. "It was a huge disappointment."

Time has healed a lot of the wounds, Bohn and others who had a hand in Barnett's firing moved on, and in 2016, Barnett joined the KOA radio broadcasts of CU games as color analyst. Working alongside play-by-play announcer Mark Johnson, Barnett was once again involved with CU football.

"I think it's a little difficult to come back and be the color broadcaster for the team you used to coach, and the team you got fired from," he said before the 2016 season. "It's awkward, but life is too short to worry about that stuff. You never really know how it's going to be accepted, and it's just been really tremendous to hear so many people actually say they're looking forward to me being a part of it. That's made it very easy, and made it a little more exciting for me."

33 Football Facilities

Gary Barnett spent eight years as an assistant football coach at CU, seven more as head coach, and many other years as a broadcaster or visitor. After all those years, Barnett still gets a special feeling when he walks into Folsom Field.

"It's home," he said. "It has everything that, moving out here, I grew to love. It's home. I don't know what else to say. You're at home here. I'm at home in Folsom."

Folsom Field has been home to hundreds of Buffs since 1924, when it was dedicated as one of the grandest stadiums in the western United States. For around $70,000, Colorado Stadium—as it was known then—was constructed to accommodate the growing interest in football. CU's program was nearly 35 years old at that time and it had outgrown Gamble Field and its roughly 9,000 seats. When first built, Folsom had a capacity of 26,000.

Over the years, Folsom Field has gone through several changes. Stadium expansion increased capacity to 45,000 in 1956. In 1967, the quarter-mile track that surrounded the football field was removed to make room for 6,000 more seats.

More changes, including a six-level press box and new bleachers changed the look and capacity over the years. Then, in 1991, came a massive change. On the north end of the stadium, the Dal Ward Center—a state-of-the-art facility for the football team—was built, along with new bleacher seats behind the end zone.

Another major addition came in 2003, when $45.2 million was spent to renovate the east side of the stadium, adding 1,900 club seats and 41 suites and creating a space that is year-round for events. The most impressive change, however, has come in recent years. Hired in the summer of 2013, athletic director Rick George saw the need for CU to upgrade its football facilities to keep up with the competition, and he immediately started an aggressive fund-raising campaign. His efforts led to what has become one of the finest football facilities in the country.

In May of 2014, ground was broken on a $160 million project that included a remodeling of the northeast corner of Folsom Field, the construction of the Champions Center and the building of a permanent indoor practice facility.

The Champions Center is a 212,000-square-foot facility attached to Folsom Field in the northeast corner. The building includes new offices for football coaches, athletic administrators, and coaches in most other sports on campus. It also includes dynamic strength and conditioning facilities, hydrotherapy pools, and an impressive football locker room. Not only for the athletes, the Champions Center also includes a rooftop terrace, which is often rented out for weddings and other events, and the CU Sports Medicine and Performance Center, which is open to the public.

"I think this building has been everything we thought it would be," George said.

What started off as a $70,000 stadium in 1924 has gone through more than $200 million in upgrades and now stands as the iconic home of the Buffaloes—and a place that coaches and players will never forget.

"It's a special place to play," safety Afolabi Laguda said after his final game at Folsom in 2017. "So much history here; you can feel it when you play."

34 Bill Marolt

When the 2006 class of the CU Athletics Hall of Fame included Bill Marolt, it wasn't much of a surprise. After all, of the many men and women who have been inducted, very few have been as deserving.

Had Marolt been just an athlete at CU, that would have been enough to get him in. As a skier, he was a four-time national champion, three-time All-American and competed with the U.S. Olympic team while still a student in Boulder.

Had Marolt been just a coach at CU, that would have been enough to get him in. He directed the Buffs' ski team from 1968 to 1978 and won seven consecutive national championships.

Had Marolt been just an athletic director at CU, even that might have been enough to get him in to the Hall of Fame. He was the AD from 1984 to 1996, helping the department recover financially, overseeing the construction of the Dal Ward Center and adding three women's sports—golf, soccer and volleyball. During his time as AD, the football and women's basketball programs rose to national prominence

Hired about a year before Marolt came in as athletic director, former women's basketball coach Ceal Barry lists Marolt among the three most influential people in her career.

"I think Bill gave me a lot of confidence," Barry said. "Bill could relate to a coach who was coaching a non-revenue sport. I think that helped me to report to someone who was a Coloradoan and gone to school here, had coached here, and had coached a non-revenue sport."

Marolt not only gave Barry confidence; he showed faith in struggling football coach Bill McCartney, surprising many by giving him a contract extension during a 1–10 season in 1984. A year later, McCartney led CU to the first of nine bowl games in 10 years.

"He had the foresight to extend McCartney and then he put together a good plan to raise the money for the Dal Ward Center after we won the national championship [in 1990]," CU sports information director David Plati said. "He also hired good coaches pretty much up and down the line."

Among Marolt's hires was Richard Rokos, who has won eight national titles in skiing, and Mark Wetmore, who has won eight national titles in cross country. Marolt, Rokos, and Wetmore and have combined for 23 of CU's 29 national titles.

Outside of his accomplishments at CU, Marolt has been one of the most influential figures in U.S. Ski Team history. Prior to being hired as CU athletic director, Marolt coached the U.S. at the 1984 Olympics, helping them to five medals. He later served as president and CEO of the U.S. Ski and Snowboard Association, vice president of the International Ski Federation, and on the United States Olympic Committee board of directors.

In addition to the CU Athletics Hall of Fame, he's a member of the Colorado Sports Hall of Fame and the U.S. Ski Hall of Fame. In 2014, Marolt finally stepped away from athletics and into retirement.

"I've been involved in athletics one way or another since I was a kid," he said at that time. "It's really been my whole life. So to step away from something you're really passionate about, something that you know a lot about and had success with, yeah, it's hard to step away from that. There are certain things that you get tired of and are not going to miss, but what you will miss are the events, watching the athletes perform at the highest levels."

Many athletes—and coaches—performed at high levels, in part, because of Marolt.

35 Buffs Upset the Nittany Lions

When head coach Joe Paterno led his Penn State Nittany Lions into Folsom Field for the first—and only—time on September 26, 1970, he brought one of the finest college football teams in the nation to Boulder.

Entering the game, Penn State was ranked No. 4 in the country, and the Nittany Lions had the nation's longest winning streak (23 games) and longest unbeaten streak (31 games).

Colorado didn't quite have the star power of Penn State, but the 18th-ranked Buffaloes had home-field advantage and a bitter taste from a 27–3 loss to the Nittany Lions the year before.

CU had clawed past Indiana, 16–9, the week earlier, but head coach Eddie Crowder believed his Buffs were looking past the Hoosiers and ahead to Penn State a bit. If they were, it was certainly understandable. This was a Penn State team that featured the running back tandem of Franco Harris and Lydell Mitchell—who would later combine for 18,654 yards and 12 Pro Bowl appearances in 22 NFL seasons—and it was a group that had dominated CU in 1969.

"Penn State is a better team than last year," Crowder said before the game. "They're better even though they don't have a super play producer. We'll have to play the best game we're capable of playing."

The game was big enough to be broadcast on national TV. It was just the fifth national TV appearance ever for CU, with the first four being bowl games. It was the first time a national audience would watch a game being played in Boulder. It was also the first time that a big-time national power from the East was coming to Folsom Field.

To the Buffs, this game was a huge deal, although Boulder didn't quite treat it that way. *Sports Illustrated's* Dan Jenkins highlighted in his account of the game how Boulder didn't quite have the same fervor that other college towns would for a big game.

"Ironically, the town seemed as if it sort of hated to think about it during the week," Jenkins wrote. "This was the school, then, that was expected to have the best chance of ending Penn State's run: a school noted for its inconsistency and indifference, its sophistication and diversions, a school half stocked with long-haired fun types discussing new mountain crags to start a commune on, and half stocked with the other kind, those afraid even to drive past The Hill for fear that some fleas might leap off the hippie cloaks and sandals and jam the engines of their Maseratis."

Okay, so maybe Boulder didn't possess the same passion for football that was present in State College, Pennsylvania; Lincoln, Nebraska; or Norman, Oklahoma. The Buffs had a pretty good football team, though, and they proved it that day against the Nittany Lions.

On the first play of the game, CU safety Pat Murphy intercepted a Nittany Lion pass. Five plays later, running back John Tarver scored on a one-yard touchdown run. CU led 13–0 after the first quarter and 20–7 at halftime. After intermission, the Buffs' Cliff Branch took the second half kickoff and raced 97 yards for a touchdown. By the end, CU had racked up 406 yards in total offense, forced five turnovers, and controlled the dynamic Penn State running back duo. The Buffs' 41–13 victory was such a thorough beating that many of the 42,850 fans in attendance had left by the fourth quarter.

At the time, the No. 4 Nittany Lions were the highest-ranked team CU had ever defeated, making it one of the greatest wins in the program's history.

"I would have to say this was our big one," said Crowder, in his eighth season at CU. "The boys felt we could win this, but I had no idea it would be by as big a margin as all that."

The victory landed CU on the cover of *Sports Illustrated* for the first time, with a picture of linebacker Phil Irwin tackling a Penn State runner. It also gave the Buffs a measure of national respect, even though they didn't back it up, losing four of their next five and finishing that season at 6–5.

Paterno made no excuses for his team getting whipped.

"We were outcoached, outplayed, out hit, and outscored," he said. "It's as simple as that. The trip wasn't a total loss, though. My wife got to see the Rockies. Sue had never been out of Western Pennsylvania. She woke me up this morning pointing and said, 'Have you seen those mountains?'"

Yes, the mountains are impressive. On that day, however, so were the Buffaloes.

36 Reaching 10 Wins

Although the 1970 season produced what was arguably the greatest win in program history to that point, against Penn State, the overall result of that campaign was a disappointment. The following year, however, was to be a monumental one for the Buffaloes.

CU came into the 1971 season unranked and figured to stay that way with a brutal early-season schedule. Coming off a 6–5 season, CU had to play at No. 9 LSU in the opener, and then two weeks later pay a visit to Ohio State, which came into the year ranked No. 11.

Charlie Davis

A key to Colorado's success in 1971 was the emergence of sophomore tailback Charlie Davis, who put together one of the best seasons ever for a CU runner. At the time, freshmen were not eligible to play varsity, so the 5-foot-11, 200-pound Davis, from West Columbia, Texas, had to wait a year to take his turn. He didn't take long to explode, topping the 100-yard mark in each of his first three games and seven times that season. In 1971, Davis broke school records for rushing yards in a game (342, vs. Oklahoma State) and a season (1,386). Through 2018, he still had the single-game record and the fifth-best season total. Davis played for the Buffs from 1971 to '73 and left CU as the school's all-time rushing leader, with 2,958 yards (through 2018, he was sixth) and 24 touchdowns. Adding bowl games—which don't count in CU's career totals—he totaled 3,172 yards. In the 1974 NFL Draft, Davis was a second-round pick of the Cincinnati Bengals, but had a short, injury-plagued career with the Bengals and Tampa Bay Buccaneers.

Coach Eddie Crowder had a good team in 1971, but nobody really knew how good it could be. Stars such as Herb Orvis, Cliff Branch, John Stearns, and others were back, but CU had 49 sophomores that would be playing varsity for the first time. The Buffs had a new group of offensive linemen, a new starter at quarterback and plenty of youngsters that had to step up. Crowder, however, carried optimism into the opening game in Baton Rouge, Louisiana. "I believe we're going to win," Crowder said. "I've got a gut feeling."

Crowder's confidence stemmed from watching his team in preseason workouts and seeing the talent on the field.

"This team has the greatest potential of any team we have had in our tenure at Colorado," said Crowder, who was in his ninth season leading the Buffs. "If there is one flaw right now before the season opens, it is a lack of competitive maturity. You know the team has the basic elements and that at some point in the season it's going to be a football team. You're hopeful it's this Saturday night."

CU gained some competitive maturity in Death Valley, shocking the sellout crowd at LSU's Tiger Stadium for a 31–21 win. Charlie Davis rushed for 174 yards and two touchdowns in his first game as a Buff, Branch returned a punt 75 yards for a touchdown and the defense shut down the Tigers.

Two weeks later, the Buffs were 2–0 and ranked No. 10 when they visited Ohio State, which had vaulted to No. 6. Branch returned another punt for a touchdown, quarterback Ken Johnson ran for two touchdowns and was masterful with the triple option, and the defense stuffed the Buckeyes on three possessions inside the 10-yard line to pull off the 20–14 stunner.

"From a coaching standpoint, all wins are big ones," Crowder said. "This one was very satisfying."

Although the Buffs were out-classed by national powers and Big Eight Conference rivals Oklahoma and Nebraska later in the season, they used the momentum of those two early upsets to go 9–2 in the regular season and earn a trip to the Astro-Bluebonnet Bowl in Houston.

Against Houston in the bowl game, Davis was sensational (202 yards, two touchdowns), the defense forced three turnovers, and the Buffs earned a 29–17 win.

CU had its first-ever 10-win season and became part of a rare piece of college football history. In the final Associated Press rankings, Nebraska (13–0) was No. 1, Oklahoma (11–1) was No. 2, and Colorado (10–2) was No. 3. It's the only time that three teams from the same conference finished 1-2-3 in the polls.

Orvis and Branch were both first-team All-Americans, while defensive lineman Bud Mangrum earned third-team honors, and Davis honorable mention.

37 Dal Ward

Under the direction of Bernie Bierman, the University of Minnesota had the finest college football team in the nation during the 1930s and early 1940s. Between 1934 and 1941, Bierman led the Gophers to five national championships, including the first one ever awarded by the Associated Press, in 1936.

One of Bierman's top assistants was a former Oregon State star by the name of Dallas "Dal" Ward. With CU leaving the Mountain States Conference and entering the "big time" of the Big Six, it needed a coach with big-time experience, and Ward was hired on February 3, 1948. He signed a three-year contract worth $8,500 per year—making him one of the highest paid coaches in the west.

Ward's job was not easy, taking a young, inexperienced team into a new, tougher conference, but he expressed some optimism before the 1948 season, saying, "We'll give our opponents, and the customers, an interesting afternoon all this fall."

The 1948 season went about as expected, with the Buffs going 3–6. They went 3–7 the next season. In Ward's 11 seasons as head coach, those would be the only two that ended with a losing record.

Overall, Ward posted a 63–41–6 record with the Buffs, with nine consecutive winning seasons, two second-place finishes in the Big Seven Conference and four third-place finishes. He also led CU to its first appearance in the Orange Bowl in 1956. That season, the Buffs went 8–2–1, with a No. 20 national ranking and a 27–21 win against Clemson in the bowl game. Ward was named the Big Eight coach of the year in 1956.

In Ward's single-wing offense, the duo of "Hardy and Bernardi"—Carroll Hardy and Frank Bernardi—became stars.

Many others, including John Bayuk, Don Branby, Howard Cook, Ralph Curtis, Eddie Dove, Boyd Dowler, Merwin Hodel, Zack Jordan, Bob Stransky, and Emerson Wilson, were exceptional skill players in Ward's offense. Under Ward, 13 different players earned All-American honors and it was during his tenure that the color barrier was broken, with CU's first two black players, Frank Clarke and John Wooten.

Ward had done what he was hired to do by leading CU through a time of transition and into big-time football. He had taken CU to the Orange Bowl, and won it. He had delivered winning seasons. It was not enough to satisfy the CU Board of Regents, however.

Nearly two months after the 1958 season, on January 22, 1959, Ward received a phone call from university president Quigg Newton just before midnight. That night, the regents voted 5–1 to fire Ward. Newton gave Ward a choice: resign or be fired. A statement from the regents simply said Ward's dismissal was in the "best interests of the university."

In a statement issued by Ward, he said, "The request to step down as football coach came as a complete surprise to me. I am stunned. I have not talked with any member of the Board of Regents since the Orange Bowl game in Miami two years ago."

Players, fans, and even some of the media covering the team were upset, but the decision was not to be reversed. With his wife and five children happy in Boulder, Ward never looked for another coaching job. Instead, he continued teaching physical education at CU and returned to coaching briefly, in 1962, when he served as defensive coordinator for coach Bud Davis—who lasted just one year. In 1963, Ward became an assistant athletic director with the Buffs, and held that position until he retired in 1975.

Despite the stunning end to his head coaching tenure, Ward remains a revered figured in CU history. In 1991, when CU's new, $14 million athletic complex opened on the north side of Folsom

Field, it was named in his honor. The Dal Ward Center is still used daily by CU athletes.

A plaque inside the building reads, "This impressive athletic center is a tribute to the man who took the University of Colorado from relative obscurity into national prominence with a bone-crushing brand of single wing football that earned him recognition as one of the most respected coaches in the nation."

38 Cliff Meely

Oklahoma had no answer for CU's Cliff Meely on the night of February 13, 1971. The Buffaloes' senior dazzled the home crowd at CU Fieldhouse with a Big Eight Conference record 47 points and an eye-popping 25 rebounds during a 99–69 rout of the Sooners.

"He had springs in his knees, mercury in his sneakers, and a computer in his right arm. And the scorekeepers had as much trouble keeping up with him as Oklahoma did," *Daily Oklahoman* reporter Bob Hurt wrote of the performance. "Who's he? He's Cliff Meely, a 6'8" scoring machine in human clothing."

Much of Meely's CU career could have been described the same way. In the pre-Chauncy Billups years (before 1995), Meely was arguably the most exciting player to hit the hardwood at CU.

"Cliff Meely was really, to me, one of the pioneers of Colorado basketball," said Tad Boyle, who would become the coach of the Buffs nearly 40 years after Meely's career.

Meely grew up in Chicago and played his freshman year at Northeastern Junior College in Sterling, Colorado. As a sophomore

The Top 15 Scorers in CU Men's Basketball History, through 2019:

Rank	Player (years)	Career points
1.t	Cory Higgins (2007–11)	2,001
1.t	Richard Roby (2004–08)	2,001
3.	Donnie Boyce (1991–95)	1,995
4.	Cliff Meely (1968–71)	1,940
5.	Shaun Vandiver (1988–91)	1,876
6.	Askia Booker (2011–15)	1,740
7.	Stevie Wise (1987–91)	1,727
8.	Josh Scott (2012–16)	1,709
9.	Emmett Lewis (1975–80)	1,680
10.	Randy Downs (1982–86)	1,566
11.	Xavier Johnson (2012–17)	1,463
12.	Michel Morandais (2000–04)	1,428
13.	Stephane Pelle (1999–03)	1,367
14.	Scott Wilke (1984–88)	1,366
15.	Ken Charlton (1960–63)	1,352

in 1968, he transferred to CU and spent the next three years dominating the Big Eight and rewriting the CU record book. Meely was named the Big Eight player of the year twice, earned All-Conference honors three times, and several All-American honors during his senior year.

"He is the most complete player I have ever coached," said Sox Walseth, whose 20-year career at CU included Meely's three seasons.

Through 2019, Meely still held several CU records, including:

Career scoring average: 24.3

Career rebounding average: 12.1

Single-season scoring average: 28.0 in 1970–71 (his 23.8 average in 1968–69 is second)

Single-game point total: 47, vs. Oklahoma

Meely topped the 40-mark five times, while every other player in CU history has combined to do it just four times, and he owns three of the top seven single-season rebounding averages in program history.

"He was a heck of a player and a guy who probably doesn't get enough credit for what he did while he was here," Boyle said. "If you just look at the numbers he put up, they're incredible."

In the 1971 NBA Draft, Meely was selected seventh overall and he played 318 career games with the Houston Rockets and Los Angeles Lakers.

Following his playing career, Meely lived in Boulder until his death in 2013. He was a longtime CU season ticket holder and became close with Boyle late in his life.

"Cliff was obviously a terrific player, but for a guy that grew up in Chicago and matriculated to Boulder and ended up living here for most of his adult life is a testament to what college athletics can do for people in terms of changing their lives," Boyle said. "I'd have him come speak to our teams. When you heard him speak about what this community and what this university meant to him, it was deeply changing in his life.

"What I'll never forget is going to his funeral and the stories that were told by members of the community, by former teammates, and friends of his. Cliff was a special, special guy in the history of Colorado basketball."

39 Seven Sports Get the Axe

For a number of reasons, CU found itself in a financial crisis in 1980, leading to one of the toughest years ever faced by the athletic department.

CU was one of a number of schools around the country that took a financial hit with the implementation of Title IX. The federal law passed in the 1970s mandated equal spending for men's and women's sports and that meant devoting more money to several non-revenue programs. With very little return on the investment, many schools responded by cutting varsity sports just to balance their budgets. Among the cuts in 1980, Kansas dropped gymnastics, UCLA dropped wrestling, Southern Methodist eliminated baseball, and Colorado State dropped three sports.

An astonishing seven sports were cut by CU in 1980—baseball, wrestling, men's swimming, women's swimming, diving, men's gymnastics, and women's gymnastics. That left the athletic department with just eight varsity sports, the minimum allowed by the NCAA to maintain Division I status. "These have been the most difficult decisions I have been involved in during my 16 years as athletic director," Eddie Crowder said at the time.

CU's cuts went much deeper than most schools because the financial problems went well beyond Title IX. At the time, CU had an athletic budget of just under $5 million (by comparison, the budget was near $90 million by 2019), but projected a deficit of nearly $1 million for the 1980–81 school year.

Also, fund-raising for the brand-new CU Events Center wasn't going well, leaving the department with an annual $350,000 debt payment. The department also had excessive spending, to the tune of $420,000 over budget, with the football program; and ticket sales for football came in more than $250,000 short of budget for the 1979 season.

Football coach Chuck Fairbanks, hired in 1979, was criticized as a free spender, including thousands of dollars (over budget) for renovations to his office and football facilities. The fact that the football program was failing miserably on the field hurt matters even more.

University president Arnold Weber called the situation "a source of public embarrassment to the university," and he was right. CU's financial woes were so significant that *Sports Illustrated* wrote an article about the precarious situation of the department. Author Douglas Looney, a CU graduate, wrote: "The Buffaloes' once proud athletic program, with its national-championship-contending football team, is in near ruins, the result of un-monitored, unplanned, and uncontrolled spending."

On top of all the financial woes, CU's football program was being investigated by the NCAA and, in late 1980, slapped with two years' probation for 62 rules violations.

To fix the financial problems, CU not only cut sports—which angered those involved, of course—but asked staff members to curb their spending. Fairbanks even donated two months of his salary, which was about $7,500, to keep football recruiting afloat. The athletic department also implemented a $10-per semester athletic fee for students to help get more money into the program; that, of course, did not go over well with students and faculty.

It was a dark time for CU athletics, perhaps the darkest time in its history. Eventually, the tide would turn. By the mid-1980s, football and women's basketball began to win, and CU actually started adding sports. The seven cut have never returned, but women's volleyball (added in 1986), women's golf (1994), women's soccer (1996), and women's lacrosse (2014) have all been added and been very competitive teams for CU.

40 Sox

As the Colorado athletic department was going through great financial turmoil in 1980, the Buffaloes suddenly found themselves in need of a women's basketball coach.

Rene Portland, who had coached the Buffs for two seasons, left CU to take the head coaching job at Penn State (where she spent the next 27 years). Athletic director Eddie Crowder asked administrator Russell "Sox" Walseth to take over. A longtime Buff who had previously coached the men's basketball team for two decades, Walseth accepted the assignment and promptly took the women's team to new heights, going 77–21 in three seasons. Walseth's three-year run with the women's team was part of his legendary, 38-year career at CU.

A native of Aberdeen, South Dakota, Walseth came to CU as a student-athlete in the mid-1940s and earned six letters in basketball and baseball. After graduating in 1948, Walseth coached the CU freshmen basketball team for five years and then went back to South Dakota for three years.

In 1956, he was hired as head coach of the CU men's basketball team. In 20 seasons, he went 261–245 with three conference titles and five Big Eight coach of the year awards. He was also very popular among his players.

"One of the major reasons I came to CU was Sox standing by me when I injured my knee as a senior in high school," Cliff Meely, who played for Walseth from 1968 to 1971, said after Walseth's death in 2004. "A lot of other schools that were recruiting me backed off, but Sox was there for me. And once I was here, he was just a great man to play for and learn from. He wasn't just interested in us playing basketball, he wanted us to get our degrees.

"He also had a great sense of humor. He would make us laugh. Whenever I would see him, including the last time I saw him, he'd always say, 'How ya doing, kid?' His wife, Ellie, too. When you played for Sox you were part of his family. He'll always be with us. The things he taught us in sports, the things he taught us in life. He will always be a part of who I am, who we are."

Walseth's men's team struggled in his final two years and he was fired, but CU immediately hired him for an administrative role. Then he took on the challenge of leading the women's team.

"I've enjoyed the last three years a great deal," he said after retiring from that job in 1983. "I think this is a great time to retire because the program is in excellent shape."

Walseth led the women to three consecutive 20-win seasons, including back-to-back 28-win campaigns.

"It's hard to describe what that man meant," Lisa Van Goor, the star of Walseth's three women's teams, said after his death. "He's been a constant in my life for the last 23 years. We always knew his door was always open to all of us. The percentage of his players that stayed in touch with him is a testament to what he was to everybody."

In 1996, he was honored at the CU Events Center, and the basketball teams now play home games on Sox Walseth Court.

41 Rocky Mountain Showdown

Growing up in El Paso, Texas, quarterback Steven Montez didn't know much about the rivalry between CU and Colorado State. It didn't take long for him to realize it wasn't like other games, especially since it was played at the 76,125-seat Broncos Stadium at Mile High—the home of the NFL's Denver Broncos.

"I was definitely shocked the first time," Montez said prior to the 2018 edition of the Rocky Mountain Showdown. "When I first got on campus and we went to that game, the atmosphere is nuts. Half the stadium is Rams, half the stadium is Buffs. They get that, 'It sucks to be a CSU Ram!'—they get that going on our side and it gets pretty live. It's always a pretty good game, evenly matched."

CU first met CSU (then known as Colorado A&M) on the gridiron on February 11, 1893, taking a 70–6 win in Fort Collins. From 1906 to 1958, they met every year, except during World War II (1944–45). They were rivals in the Rocky Mountain Athletic Conference (RMAC) and then the Mountain States Conference through 1947 and then kept the rivalry going for a while after CU left for the Big Seven.

Prior to the 1958 meeting, CU had decided to drop the Rams from its future schedule because it wanted to play "big time" opponents. The Buffs were in a major conference, the Big Eight, while the Rams were in a lesser conference, the Skyline League.

That basic sentiment has never really changed at CU. Since joining the Big Seven in 1947, CU has always been in what is now referred to as "Power 5 conferences," while the Rams have always been in lesser conferences. Thus, the Buffs and their fans have often viewed CSU as their "little brother."

Even when the series resumed in 1983, it was done with reluctance on the part of CU. A newspaper report in 1983 said CU athletic director Eddie Crowder "and other CU officials complained that CU, considered by many to be the more prestigious institution and the possessor of the better football program, had nothing to win and everything to lose by scheduling CSU."

Nevertheless, the teams played off and on from 1983 to 1992. Beginning in 1995, the rivalry became an annual affair once again, but is set to end after the 2020 meeting. Once again, CU's desire to play "big time" opponents will take the Rams off the schedule in 2021 and 2022. From 1998 to 2019, the Buffs and Rams played all but three of their 22 meetings in Denver.

While CU has always had a "big brother" mentality, that attitude, combined with the close proximity of the campuses and the school pride of the players and fans—who often are neighbors—has all kept some energy in the rivalry. Before the 2018 tilt, Montez said it's "just another game" for the players, but added, "I know CSU doesn't like us. I don't think we like them any more than they like us."

The 2018 game—a 45–13 CU victory—was the 90th meeting between the Buffs and Rams. CU won 66 of those games and there have been some memorable moments between the in-state rivals located only about an hour apart.

November 29, 1923—CU 6, Colorado A&M 3: Going in, the winner would be crowned RMAC champion. Art Quinlan kicked two field goals, including the game-winner in the fourth quarter, to not only take the game, but win the conference title and finish off a perfect 9–0 season.

November 22, 1958—CSU 15, CU 14: In Boulder, CU led 14–7 until the Rams scored a touchdown—and two-point conversion—with 4:29 to play. That was the first year of the two-point conversion in college football. It was also a loss that contributed to coach Dal Ward being fired at season's end and the last time these teams would play for 25 years, giving the Rams years of bragging rights.

September 5, 1998—CU 42, CSU 14: During the first meeting in Denver, CSU took a 14–13 lead in the third quarter before quarterback Mike Moschetti threw two touchdown passes during a 29-point surge to finish the game.

August 30, 2003—CU 42, CSU 35: Arguably the most disliked Ram, at least in recent years, was quarterback Bradlee Van Pelt. In 2002, he scored on a game-winning 23-yard touchdown run in the fourth quarter and then promptly threw the ball into the face of CU safety Roderick Sneed. Leading up to the 2003 game, Van Pelt did plenty of trash talking and backed it up with 416 yards of total offense. The Buffs got their revenge, however, when Joel Klatt threw for 402 yards and four touchdowns and running back Bobby Purify scored the game-winning touchdown with 40 seconds left.

September 2, 2016—CU 44, CSU 7: This was a stunner, as CU had been dreadful for several years, but wound up with the most lopsided victory in the series since 1956. Quarterback Sefo Liufau and Denver-native running back Phillip Lindsay sparked the Buffs, who took a 31–0 lead at the half. The victory set the tone for a resurgent, 10-win season.

42 Jeremy Bloom

Jeremy Bloom's much-anticipated college football debut finally became a reality on the afternoon of August 31, 2002, when the Buffaloes faced in-state rival Colorado State at Mile High Stadium in Denver.

On the first play of the fourth quarter, the Buffs trailed 13–0 when Bloom stood near his own 25-yard-line to field a CSU punt. With the ball in his hands for the first time as a Buff, Bloom took off to the right, followed his wall of blockers, juked a couple defenders, and sprinted to the end zone for a 75-yard touchdown.

"I was lucky enough to watch him when he was here and he was the fastest guy on the field," said Curtis Snyder of the CU sports information department. "Every time he touched the ball, whether it was on a punt return or as a slot receiver, he was exciting to watch."

Just 5-feet, 9-inches tall and 175 pounds, Bloom was explosive and had four plays of 75 yards or more in his career at CU, tying him with legendary Byron "Whizzer" White for the second most in program history. Bloom returned two punts and one kickoff for touchdowns. He also began emerging at receiver, with 24 catches for 458 yards and two touchdowns. Bloom's first touchdown catch, a 94-yarder from Robert Hodge against Kansas State on October 5, 2002, was the longest passing play in CU history, through 2018. His second touchdown catch, in 2003, covered 81 yards.

The former Loveland High School star, who earned All-State honors as a senior, had an exhilarating but frustratingly brief career with the Buffaloes. A casualty of the NCAA's rules on amateurism, Bloom played just two seasons with the Buffs and was done with college football just as he was starting to take off.

While stellar at football, he was world class as a moguls skier. At just 16 years old, he began competing for the United States Freestyle Ski Team. Then, in 2001, he finished third in the moguls at the USA Championships, and that result helped him land a spot on the U.S. Ski Team for the 2002 Winter Olympics in Salt Lake City.

Bloom delayed his college football career to train for the Olympics, where he finished ninth. A month after the Olympics, he won the World Cup moguls title in Ruka, Finland.

Following his freshman season with the football team, in 2002, Bloom went back to training for skiing, but he also began a two-year battle with the NCAA. For him to keep his dream of taking aim at the 2006 Winter Olympics, he had to continue skiing professionally, and the only way he could afford to do that was by earning money from endorsements. The NCAA, however, ruled that accepting endorsements would make him ineligible for collegiate athletics.

Jeremy Bloom returns a punt 80 yards for a touchdown against Oklahoma in the 2002 Big 12 Championship game. (AP Photo / Brett Coomer)

"I knew I was fighting an uphill battle, but I felt like what [the NCAA] was trying to make me do wasn't right, it wasn't fair. So I wanted to challenge that," Bloom told *The Denver Post* in 2014.

Bloom's argument had plenty of merit. There were numerous examples of the NCAA allowing players such as Drew Henson or Ricky Williams to get paid to play minor league baseball while still being eligible to play football. Bloom's situation was viewed in a different light, however, and in the summer of 2004, his final appeal was denied. Bloom continued to pursue his skiing career, giving up his final two years with the Buffaloes.

"What he could have done [in football], I think, is off the charts," Snyder said. "The sky is the limit for what he could have done and I think it's unfortunate that he wasn't even trying to make money. He was just trying to break even and pay for his skiing with his endorsements during that four-year time and it wasn't able to happen."

During the 2004–05 ski season, Bloom broke the world record with six consecutive victories and earned the World Cup moguls championships. He went on to finish sixth in the moguls at the 2006 Olympics in Turin, Italy. In 2013, he was inducted into the U.S. Ski and Snowboard Hall of Fame.

About two months after the 2006 Olympics, Bloom jumped back into football, as he was selected in the fifth round of the NFL Draft by the Philadelphia Eagles. He spent time with the Eagles and Pittsburgh Steelers, but never appeared in a regular season game.

Following his athletic career, Bloom made a name for himself as an entrepreneur and philanthropist, while also working in broadcasting for ESPN, Fox, NBC, and the Pac-12 Network.

While his battle with the NCAA didn't go as hoped, Bloom doesn't regret it.

"I stood up for what I believed was right," he said. "I'm proud of that, and I learned a great deal throughout the process. I would have loved to have played my junior and senior years at Colorado. I feel like those years were taken from me. But it's hard for me to look back on my athletic career with anything but a smile and think, 'Gosh, I was so lucky.' To be able to accomplish and experience the things that I did in two sports—how could I ever complain about that?"

43 Kordell Stewart

Colorado was still running the wishbone offense in 1991 when it signed 6-foot-3, 210-pound Kordell Stewart out of John Ehret High School in New Orleans.

Stewart had all the physical tools to be an exceptional option quarterback, which is why Nebraska and Oklahoma were on his list during the recruiting process. By the end of 1991, however, CU head coach Bill McCartney had made the decision to give his offense an overhaul, ditching the wishbone attack that led the Buffs to national prominence and installing a pass-oriented, pro-style attack. Stewart, who had a rocket arm to go with his tremendous athleticism, won the starting job.

"I was really excited," Stewart said when he was named the starter over Koy Detmer and Vance Joseph. "I feel like I've improved in everything—the drops, throwing the ball, reading defenses, understanding the plays."

Stewart had a sensational debut, throwing for a school-record 409 yards and four touchdowns in a 37–17 victory against Colorado State. That was the start of a brilliant three-year run for Stewart.

A true dual-threat at quarterback, Stewart threw for 6,481 yards and 33 touchdowns and ran for 1,289 yards and 15 touchdowns during his three seasons as the starter. He started his final 28 games as a Buff—the second-longest starting streak ever for a CU quarterback, through 2018.

Stewart's most famous moment in a CU uniform came in 1994, when he threw a 64-yard touchdown pass to Michael Westbrook on the final play of the game to beat No. 4 Michigan, 27–26. Stewart threw the ball about 72 yards in the air.

"You had athletes down there and you had the quarterback at the other end that could make that happen," Westbrook said of the magical play. "The boy could throw."

Kordell Stewart heaves the 64-yard Hail Mary against Michigan.
(AP Photo / Jon Freilich)

Yes, he could. While the throw at Michigan was Stewart's signature moment, his career filled a highlight reel. He went 27–5–1 as a starter and helped the Buffs reach three bowl games. Stewart was second-team All-American and first-team All-Big Eight in 1994. At the time of his graduation, he was CU's all-time leading passer. As offenses have become more pass-oriented in recent years, Stewart has slipped to fifth on the list. Despite coming to CU as option quarterback, he was really the first prolific passer in program history. In 2018, he was inducted into the CU Athletics Hall of Fame.

"It's beyond me," Stewart said of the honor. "You never thought that the work you put in and the things that you do because you love it so much, you never even really care so much about getting to a hall of fame, but more or less trying to win a championship with the guys around you."

In 1995, Stewart was selected in the second round of the NFL Draft by the Pittsburgh Steelers and was nicknamed "Slash" because he played both quarterback and receiver during his 11-year pro career. Playing for the Steelers, Chicago Bears, and Baltimore Ravens, Stewart finished his NFL career with 14,746 passing yards, 2,874 rushing yards, and 658 receiving yards. He was Pittsburgh's primary starting quarterback for five years and was named to the Pro Bowl in 2001. He quarterbacked the Steelers to two AFC Championship games, in 1997 and 2001.

44 62–36

At the conclusion of the first quarter, Colorado sophomore defensive lineman Matt McChesney sat next to linebacker Sean Tufts and glanced at the scoreboard.

"I remember looking at Sean and going, 'Dude, we're doing it. We're beating the hell out of the No. 1 team in the country, who happens to be Nebraska, in our backyard to go to the Big 12 title game,'" McChesney said. "It was a surreal moment and something I'll remember for the rest of my life."

Very few Buffs or their fans have forgotten that day, with "62–36" being a very recognizable phrase nearly 20 years later.

On November 23, 2001, the 14th-ranked Buffaloes, who were 8–2, hosted rival Nebraska at Folsom Field. The undefeated Cornhuskers came into Boulder ranked No. 1 in the Bowl Championship Series (BCS) standings and they were favored by 10 points. In its nearly 130-year history of playing football, CU has won more than 700 games on the gridiron. Very few have been as satisfying as the 62–36 domination of the Cornhuskers on that day in 2001.

Asked in 2018 about his favorite memory of Folsom Field, Gary Barnett joked, "Oh, let me think... November 2001!" The head coach of the Buffs in 2001, he directed the Buffs to that remarkable win, which secured the Big 12 North division title.

"You never think it will go like this, obviously," Barnett said after the game. "But every once in a while, it all works."

CU stunned the college football world with a 28–3 first quarter lead. Less than three minutes into the second quarter, it was 35–3. Nebraska pulled within 42–30 after three quarters, but CU running back Chris Brown scored on three touchdown runs in the first five minutes, 19 seconds of the fourth quarter to extend the lead to 62–30.

"They came back in that game. They played us tough and tried to make it a ball game, but there was a 10-year build up," said McChesney, referring to CU's nine-game losing streak to the Cornhuskers, the last five by a combined 15 points. "On top of that, it was five years of losing to them in unspeakable ways that rip your heart out. It was personal that day, and it's still personal."

Brown rushed for 198 yards and a school-record six touchdowns. Bobby Purify added 154 yards and a touchdown. Bobby Pesavento threw for 202 yards and a touchdown and ran for a score. Tight end Daniel Graham caught four passes for 112 yards and a touchdown. The defense forced four turnovers and completely dominated early to help the Buffs get out to their big lead. In the end, the 62 points were the most ever allowed by Nebraska at the time.

CU went on to beat Texas, 39–37, the next week in the Big 12 championship game, but was slapped with disappointment when it finished No. 3 in the final BCS standings. The top two played for the national championship and the Cornhuskers, despite their blowout loss to CU and not even winning their division, were slotted at No. 2. Nebraska played for the title, but got thumped again, this time by Miami (Florida), 37–14.

Disappointed about being left out of the title game, the Buffs were routed by Oregon, 38–16, in the Fiesta Bowl, finishing 10–3 and ranked No. 9. It wasn't the final result the Buffs wanted, but it didn't take away the pure joy of that day in November when they destroyed their rivals. It's also not lost on CU fans that the Cornhuskers haven't been the same since.

From 1981 to 2001, Nebraska won three national titles, 12 conference titles, finished with a top-10 ranking 16 times, and had 15 seasons with 10-plus wins. The Cornhuskers hadn't finished a season unranked since 1968. In the 17 years after its humbling defeat in Boulder, from 2002 to 2018, Nebraska was never in national title contention, had zero conference titles or top-10 rankings, produced just four 10-win seasons, and finished unranked 11 times.

"They've fallen off since we smashed their face in on national TV," McChesney said. "It's extremely satisfying."

45 Sefo Liufau

Badly limping after being tackled during the third quarter, Sefo Liufau lined up for the next play at Michigan Stadium on September 17, 2016.

Center Alex Kelley turned around to see if his quarterback was OK and Liufau nodded his head. Running back Phillip Lindsay stood next to Liufau and asked if he was OK. The quarterback waved him off and said he was fine.

Moments later, Liufau took the snap, dropped back to pass and heaved a 70-yard touchdown pass to Shay Fields. While teammates celebrated, Liufau went to the ground in pain from a badly sprained ankle. "It was all arm," Liufau said of that throw. "I couldn't push off of (the ankle)."

Well, arm and heart. Liufau had injured his ankle on the previous play—an injury that would knock him out of the next two games and bother him the rest of the year—but wasn't about to come out of the game if he didn't have to.

"I'm always impressed with Sefo," Fields said. "That's why he's one of our leaders."

That play epitomized the career of Liufau, who, from 2013–16 put his body on the line every Saturday in his quest to make the Buffaloes a winner.

Liufau wrapped up his career as CU's all-time leader in passing yards (9,568) and total offense (10,509), two of the 99 school records he set or tied with the Buffs. He will forever be remembered, however, as a gritty competitor, uncompromising leader, and the face of CU's remarkable run to the Pac-12 South title in 2016.

"He's just an amazing guy overall," receiver Devin Ross said. "You want to be around him and you want to make plays for him and be a teammate for him. He leads you. Every day he has the right mindset; never late for anything. Just the ideal teammate, the ideal person you want to play under and play for and just have his back all the time."

Liufau, who grew up in Tacoma, Washington, came to CU at a time when the Buffs were at a low point. The Buffs were coming off a 1–11 season and the coach he committed to—Jon Embree—had been fired. Liufau stuck with CU, and new Buffs' head coach Mike MacIntyre stuck with him. In 2013, CU had hoped to redshirt Liufau, as Connor Wood began the year as the starter. Five games into the season, though, the struggling Buffs made a change and put Liufau in the lineup. Wood threw just eight more passes as a Buff, and Liufau spent the next four seasons rewriting the record book.

Not that life was easy; far from it, in fact. CU was in full-fledged rebuilding mode through much of Liufau's career, and they didn't win much. From 2013–15, the Buffs went 10–27 overall, 8–21 in Liufau's starts.

Liufau battled through a back injury during his freshman year, as the Buffs struggled. Statistically, he had his best year as a sophomore in 2014, throwing for 3,200 yards and 28 touchdowns—breaking school records in both categories. Although some of his 15 interceptions that year came at bad times, his sophomore performance provided plenty of optimism for the future. Throughout his final two years at CU, however, Liufau took a physical beating.

During the third game of 2015, he separated the AC joint in his throwing shoulder. He had the shoulder popped back into place, missed one play and took pain pills to remain in the lineup. His wrist was banged up that year, too, and then, in the 11th game of the season, he suffered a Lisfranc injury to his left foot. Not only was his junior season over, but there were doubts about whether he'd be ready for 2016.

After months of rehabilitation, Liufau got himself ready for the 2016 season. There was a percentage of fans ready to move on from him because of his win-loss record, but MacIntyre never wavered in his support.

"I think he should have one of those years where everybody talks about Sefo in a positive stretch," MacIntyre said that summer. "I'm excited about seeing it. I'm very confident in Sefo and looking for him to have an excellent year because I think the team has caught up to him."

Liufau was sensational in the first three games of the 2016 season, including his three-touchdown performance at Michigan. Although his ankle injury sent him to the bench for a few weeks, Liufau returned to lead the Buffs to a remarkable season. During CU's six-game winning streak to close the regular season, the 6-foot-4, 230-pound Liufau was as much of a running threat as a passing threat. But, more than anything, he was a leader and became the first CU player since Pat Carney in the 1890s to be named a captain three years in a row.

Liufau's final game at Folsom Field, on November 26, 2016, concluded with him taking a knee to run out the clock, as a sellout crowd—the first packed house in Boulder in eight years—poured onto the field to celebrate a 27–22 victory against Utah that clinched the Pac-12 South division title.

"My freshman year, when I was hurting and things weren't going very well at all, I told my mom, told my dad, told my girl-friend, 'By the time I'm done here, I want to fill out the stands.

I want to pack Folsom. I want to lead them to a championship,'" Liufau said.

He came up one win short of winning the conference, falling to Washington in the Pac-12 title game, but Liufau did help to engineer the best season CU had seen in 15 years.

"It took a little longer than I wanted, but to be able to turn the program around with this team and to be able to have meaningful November games and everything, that ultimately was the best I could ever ask for," he said.

While Liufau's career included many bumps along the way, he left on a high note, not only with a host of records, but as a winner.

"I think when people look back at Sefo here, they'll say his warrior mentality, his toughness, his mental toughness, his character is what embodied bringing Colorado football back," MacIntyre said. "He'll be long remembered."

46 Holidays in Hawaii

There have been a lot of great teams in Colorado history, but there may not have been one more dominant than the 1924 squad.

Led by head coach Myron Witham and quarterback Hatfield Chilson, CU was the only team in the country to go through the regular season without allowing a single point—an unheard of feat then and now. After defeating Colorado State, 36–0, on November 22, to wrap another Rocky Mountain Athletic Conference (RMAC) title, CU was 7–0–1 and had outscored the opposition 194–0. It was really a remarkable two-year run for Witham and the "Silver & Gold"—it would be another decade before CU adopted the nickname "Buffaloes"—which posted a 9–0 record in 1923.

The 1924 season will forever be remembered as the inaugural campaign at Folsom Field, which was named Colorado Stadium at the time. Another first occurred in 1924, as CU played its first-ever postseason games—although they were scheduled before the season began. A group of fans in Hawaii raised funds for CU's football team to spend the holidays in Honolulu. The Silver & Gold was scheduled to play two games in Hawaii—on Christmas Day against a group of Hawaii-Navy All-Stars and on New Year's Day against Hawaii University.

Witham's squad—18 players, plus coaches—left Boulder on December 10 and made its way to San Francisco. On December 13, the team set sail for Hawaii, arriving December 19.

On Christmas Day, the Silver & Gold dazzled the local crowd with a 43–0 victory against the Pearl Harbor Navy team. Writer Mike Jay of the *Honolulu Star-Bulletin* wrote it was "an exhibition of football that proved an eye-opener to island fans."

Chilson, the star of the Silver & Gold, was impressive in the win. Jay wrote:

> *Little "Chilly" Chilson, quarterback of the visiting eleven, was the outstanding player for the Silver and Gold. He ran interference, he tossed passes and he smashed right through that heavy Navy line. And the rest of the Colorado team followed his lead. They all starred but tiny Chilson stood head and shoulders over the others. Not since Oregon university visited here some years ago have Hawaiian football fans seen such a high brand of gridiron science.*

At 5-foot-8, 142 pounds, Chilson was described in the *Star-Bulletin* as "a little shrimp of a fellow." The little shrimp completed five of 11 passes for over 100 yards and two touchdowns to lead the way.

A week later, on New Year's Day, CU closed its season against Hawaii. For the first time in more than two years, Witham's squad walked off the field with a defeat, falling 13–0.

"…over Manoa valley shone not only one but several brilliant rainbows, the kahuna rainbows that signal victory for the island team," wrote the *Star-Bulletin*.

It was a monumental win for Hawaii, toppling a CU team viewed as one of the best from the mainland. CU had seven passes intercepted and could only tip its cap to the Deans.

While the trip produced CU's first loss in more than two years, ending a streak of 19 consecutive games without a loss (18–0–1), it was a highly successful venture that led to both sides showing respect for the other.

"I can only say that we are going away disappointed at not winning but with a warm spot in our hearts for Hawaii," Witham said in the *Star-Bulletin*. "Not a single complaint to make. We lost simply because Hawaii outplayed us and the local team should be given credit for that. We've been treated splendidly and appreciate that very much. We made mistakes in the game but we can accept defeat in as good spirit as victory. Aloha to Hawaii."

Another local paper, *The Honolulu Advertiser*, wrote this upon CU's departure from the island on January 3:

> We hope that the Silver and Gold men carry back with them the same Aloha for Hawaii which all good sports, and particularly the Navy and Hawaii teams, hold for them. The University of Colorado can well be proud of its team; it played good, hard football to the best of its ability, and Hawaii is glad of the opportunity of meeting and knowing such clean sportsmen. As we bade them welcome two weeks ago, so do we bid them Aloha and success for the future today.

For Witham, the remarkable run during 1923 and 1924, was the highlight of his 12-year tenure as head coach. In CU history, only two men have had longer runs as head coach: Fred Folsom for 15 years and Bill McCartney for 13. Witham posted a 63–26–7 record as CU's head coach, from 1920 to 1931. He won two RMAC titles and had just two losing seasons. Dismal results against rival Utah caught up to Witham, though. He lost his last seven to Utah, including by a combined score of 106–0 in the last three. CU regents voted not to renew his contract after the 1931 season. William Saunders was hired and coached the Buffs for three years, going 15–7–2.

47 Chilly Chilson

Long before Tim Tebow used the jump pass in his arsenal during his legendary career at the University of Florida, a small, but tough quarterback from Colorado gained national attention for utilizing a new style of moving the football down the field.

Olin Hatfield "Chilly" Chilson quarterbacked the Silver and Gold from 1923 to '25 and became known as one of the first—if not the first—to utilize the jump pass. From a 1925 newspaper account, published around the country with a picture of Chilson throwing the ball:

> *Followers of that institution believe they have the most accurate and dangerous forward passer in the country. Chilson has a style all his own. He dashes out toward the wings, leaps into the air in full stride, and turns with an acrobatic twist, flipping his passes while at the top of his leap. The altitude he*

achieves, added to his six feet of height, gives him a bird's-eye view of his objective. His flip lays the ball easily and accurately into the receiver's hands.

While there was no question Chilson's passing was a weapon for CU, that account exaggerated his stature. Chilson, from Pueblo Centennial High School in southern Colorado, stood just 5 feet, 8 inches tall and he weighed in at around 140 pounds.

Despite being one of the smallest quarterbacks to play at CU, Chilson had exceptional accomplishments on the field and a lasting legacy off the field.

"In my eyes, he was a giant of a man and he was only 5 foot, 8 inches tall," his son, John, said in 2018 during a video for his father's induction into the Rocky Mountain Athletic Conference Hall of Fame.

In addition to the RMAC Hall of Fame, Chilson was also inducted into the CU Athletics Hall of Fame in 2018. While both honors came 27 years after his death—and 93 years after he completed his career at CU—they were the culmination of an athletic career in which Chilson beat the odds against him.

Chilson had a tough childhood, as his brother and father both passed away while he was young. Growing up in southern Colorado, he was forced to mature a bit sooner than some and learned the value of hard work as a youth.

"He was a self-made man," John said. "He came out of great poverty. He started working when he was about 12 years old to help the family make it financially and he was the hardest working man I think I probably ever knew."

With that background, simply getting to college was a difficult task, but Chilson made his way to Boulder in 1922 on a rotary scholarship. He worked different jobs to put himself through school, while also playing football, baseball, and basketball. Chilson earned 11 total letters at CU and was captain of the football and basketball teams, while serving as vice-captain for the baseball team. It was football that first gave him national fame, however.

At the time, freshmen were not allowed to play varsity, so Chilson had to wait until 1923 to play. That season, CU was led by veteran quarterback Art Quinlan, who was an All-Conference performer in 1922. Quinlan was exceptional in 1923, as well, helping the Buffs to wins in each of the first six games. During that sixth game, a 47–0 win against Colorado Mines, Quinlan broke his right hand. A senior, Quinlan played the rest of the year as kicker, but he could not continue at quarterback. Coach Myron Witham moved Chilson to quarterback and the next week he threw for 183 yards in a 17–7 win against Utah.

With Chilson at quarterback—and Quinlan handling kicking duties—the Buffs finished off a 9–0 season in 1923. Quinlan actually was the hero in the final game, kicking two field goals in a 6–3 win against Colorado State.

Chilson still had two seasons to play, but nearly didn't get that chance. On May 29, 1924, Chilson and three other students were trapped on the third floor of the Alpha Tau Omega fraternity house when it caught fire. A newspaper account of the incident said Chilson and the others "escaped by making a sheet ladder of bed clothing and sliding three floors to safety."

With that close call behind him, Chilson went on to play two more sensational seasons. In 1924 and 1925, it was Chilson who guided CU to a 14–4–1 record. Chilson was named first-team All-RMAC in 1924 after he led what has become known as the "Wonder Team." That season, CU went 7–0–1 in the regular season and was not only unbeaten but unscored upon. They finished 8–1–1 after losing to Hawaii in a New Year's Day game in Honolulu.

In addition to his 2018 hall of fame honors, Chilson was inducted in the Colorado Sports Hall of Fame in 1985. Chilson's legacy went well beyond athletics, though.

After he graduated from the CU law school in 1927, Chilson practiced law for decades in Colorado. He was the city attorney in Estes Park for 28 years and in Loveland for five years. He was also district attorney for Colorado's Eighth Judicial District for eight years in the 1940s.

Chilson spent years in soil and water conservation and became known as a specialist for water litigation. Chilson even served on the Loveland school board for 10 years. Since 1987, the Hatfield Chilson Recreation Center has been enjoyed by residents in Loveland.

In 1956, U.S. President Dwight D. Eisenhower appointed Chilson to be the assistant secretary of the Department of the Interior. In 1957, Eisenhower appointed Chilson as the Undersecretary of the Department of the Interior, where he played a role in Hawaii's statehood. Chilson later became judge of the U.S. District Court for the District of Colorado.

From humble beginnings, Chilson carved out an amazing life that included his greatness on the gridiron and his achievements off the field. In 1960, he told the *Boulder Daily Camera*, "If anyone had predicted all the good things that would happen to me in my life, I would have thought he was out of his mind."

48 Brock Brothers

Growing up in Beaverton, Oregon, just outside of Portland, Pete Brock was a high school All-American in 1972 and recruited by a lot of schools, including Notre Dame and nearby Oregon State. When he took a recruiting visit to CU, however, he was sold.

"I saw nothing but a lot of growth potential, and wanting to be a part of an up and coming program had appeal to me," Brock said in 2018 before his induction to the CU Athletics Hall of Fame. "It's the outdoors that really sold me on it. During part of my recruiting trip, I went skiing at Eldora and went fly fishing on the South Platte."

With that, a pipeline from Beaverton to Boulder was opened, as Brock was the first of three brothers to play for the Buffs in the 1970s. Pete played for CU from 1972 to '75, while Willie played from 1975 to '77 and Stan from 1976 to '79. All three were offensive linemen and all three were exceptional players.

"I guess Willie and Stan went to Colorado because they came to watch my games when I was there and got to like the school," Pete said years later.

They were also close as a family and the chance to play together was appealing (Pete and Stan never played together, but both played at CU with Willie). Their father, Len, was a football player at the University of Portland and saw potential in the boys when they were young and larger than most boys their size. "When we got to seventh grade, dad would start taking us out to the back pasture and have us start running wind sprints," Pete said. 'We didn't play Pop Warner football or anything like that because we were all too big. I weighed 170 pounds when I was in the seventh grade and my brothers were all big."

Their size may have been a problem for youth football, but it served them well in high school, college and the NFL. Pete played center and was a first-team All-American by the *Sporting News* in 1975 and selected to CU's All-Century team in 1989. Stan was CU's left tackle, earning first-team All-American by the *Sporting News* in 1979, as well as All-Big Eight honors. Willie was a key backup during his CU career, playing center.

There were two other brothers, as well. Joe was younger than Stan and wasn't able to play football because of a disability, and

Ray, the youngest, went on to play offensive line at LSU. Ray's position coach at LSU was George Belu, who coached Pete, Willie and Stan at CU.

Following their careers at CU, Pete, Willie and Stan all went to the NFL. Pete was the 12th overall pick, by New England, in the 1976 NFL Draft and played his entire 12-year career with the Patriots. Stan matched his brother by becoming the 12th overall pick in the 1980 draft, by New Orleans. He played 13 seasons with the Saints and three more with the San Diego Chargers. Willie was selected in the 12th round of the 1978 draft by the Kansas City Chiefs and wound up playing four games with the Detroit Lions before a knee injury ended his career.

Stan was inducted to the CU Athletics Hall of Fame in 2017— one year ahead of his brother. All the brothers spent just a few years in Boulder, but none of them forgot the impact that Boulder had on them.

"I was born and raised in Portland, Oregon," Stan said at his 2017 Hall of Fame induction, "but I'm very proud that behind my name through the 16 years in the National Football League, it always said, 'Stan Brock, University of Colorado.'"

49 Jenny Simpson

At the start of the indoor track season in 2009, Jenny Barringer (who later became Jenny Simpson after marriage) was already a star for the Colorado Buffaloes, but the senior was on the verge of scaling new heights.

On January 31 of that year, she broke the school record in the 3,000 meters. Two weeks later, she recorded the fastest indoor 5K in NCAA history. Two weeks after that, she smashed the NCAA indoor record in the mile.

"I would say nothing blew my mind until the winter of '09," CU track and cross country head coach Mark Wetmore said. "She made the Olympic team in '08, but when she started that series of indoor races and outdoor races where she took the lead and led wire to wire, setting records, that's when I said, 'Yikes, this woman is really special.'"

CU has featured dozens of stellar track and field and cross country athletes over the years—many of them coached by Wetmore—but it's difficult to put anyone ahead of Simpson.

"Jenny's the best track athlete that's ever been here," Wetmore said. "She's very talented, she's courageous."

Wetmore added that Simpson, a three-time Olympian, is remarkable at bouncing back from adversity.

"Stuff happens—she has a bad day, a bad workout, a bad race—and two days later she's back to full power again," he said. "She just recovers from disappointments or setbacks. She's the best I've ever seen at that."

Like all runners and athletes, Simpson had her share of bad days, but there aren't many women in the history of the sport that had have as many good days.

At Oviedo High School in Florida, she won three state titles in cross country and five more in track (three in the mile, two in the two-mile). As of 2018, she still held the Florida high school records for the 1,600 meters (4:48.90) and the 5K in cross country (16:55).

During her time at CU, Simpson was a four-time NCAA champion and seven-time All-American. She broke seven CU records and six NCAA records, while becoming the American record holder in the 3,000-meter steeplechase (9:12.50). In cross country, she was NCAA runner-up twice, in 2006 and 2007, and won a conference title. On the track, she won three national titles in the steeplechase and one in the indoor 3,000 meters.

Going into 2019, she still held NCAA records for the indoor mile run (4:25.91) and the outdoor 1,500 meters (3:59.90) and 5K (15:07.64) and owned three of the six fastest steeplechase times in NCAA history.

Outside of her CU career, Simpson has been one of the most accomplished middle distance runners in American history. She won the USA steeplechase championship in 2007 and 2009 and broke the American record while finishing fifth at the 2009 World Championships. She was the USA indoor champion in the mile and 3K in both 2011 and 2012; the outdoor 5K champion in 2013; and a three-time USA champion in the 1,500 meters (2014, 2015 and 2017). At the IAAF World Championships, she won gold in the 1,500 meters in 2011 and silver in that event in 2013 and 2017.

Simpson qualified for the 2008 Olympics in Beijing for the steeplechase. For the 2012 Olympics in London and the 2016 games in Rio de Janeiro, she ran the 1,500. At Rio de Janeiro, she won a bronze medal, crossing the line in 4:10.53 and becoming the first American woman to medal in the 1,500.

"It just feels incredible," she said after winning her bronze medal. "I want to be somebody that this country can be really proud to cheer for. I wanted to be that person eight years ago. This has been a long ride of highs and lows. Hopefully every American watching my race tonight, I want each of them to feel like they can take a small piece of ownership in this medal."

As Wetmore continues coaching and recruiting athletes to his stellar program, he acknowledges that many high school runners don't know about Simpson. But, they will find out when they get to CU, because Simpson still trains at CU and has been a volunteer coach since 2014.

"She is a big sister to the women on the team," he said.

50 Frank Potts

A fortuitous visit to a sporting goods store in 1927 changed the life of Frank Potts and made a long-lasting impact on CU athletics. An All-Conference football player and NCAA pole vault national champion at the University of Oklahoma, Potts was nearing graduation when he went to the store.

"A sporting goods salesman told me in the winter of my senior year at Oklahoma that there would be a track job open at Colorado, but when I checked into it, they told me they wanted the track coach to also coach wrestling," Potts said years later. "Since I didn't know the first thing about wrestling and wasn't very willing to start learning, I forgot about the job. Then, shortly after that, a staff member died and they shuffled some assignments and began looking for a track coach who could help out with football, so I got the job."

Hired in 1927, Potts would spend the next 41 years coaching the CU track and field team, retiring in 1968 after what is still the longest tenure of any CU coach or administrator.

During his 41 years coaching the Buffs, Potts led them to 10 Rocky Mountain Conference championships. He coached six NCAA champions, 19 All-Americans and more than 50 conference champions. He also coached three Olympians, including Bill Toomey, who won the gold medal in the decathlon at the 1968 Olympics in Mexico City.

Under Potts' tutelage, Gil Cruter won back-to-back national titles in the high jump in 1937 and 1938. Don Meyers also won two national titles under Potts, in the long jump (1961) and pole vault (1962). Potts picked Meyers as his successor when he retired.

"I'd say his greatest quality as a coach was his ability to rec-ognize potential and develop it," Meyers said after Potts' death in 1990. "He was a student of track and field, one of the best in the country."

Meyers was one of three pole vault national champions coached by Potts, who fell in love with the event as a kid in Oklahoma, when he first saw some high school students vaulting.

"I went home from that meet and built some standards," he said. "Then I went to the furniture store and got a wooden pole that was used as a rug pole. That cost me a whole quarter and that was my equipment."

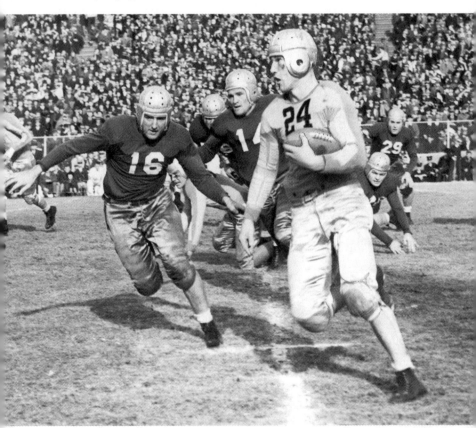

Potts is still remembered for helping get Byron "Whizzer" White (shown above running with the ball) to Colorado. (AP Photo)

From that point, Potts never stopped working to excel, whether as an athlete or as a coach. In addition to his 41 years coaching the CU track team, Potts spent 21 seasons, from 1927 to 1947, with the football team.

In 18 of Potts' 21 seasons with the football team, he was an assistant, but he did take the reins of head coach for three years. In 1940, the Buffs were in transition after Bunny Oakes quit, and Potts coached the team to a 5–3–1 record. He then served as head coach for two seasons during the days of World War II, from 1944 to '45. The Buffs went 11–5 in those two seasons.

Potts' greatest contribution to the football program came in the early 1930s, when he played a key role in recruiting Byron "Whizzer" White—arguably the greatest player in CU history—to Boulder.

After retirement, Potts was inducted into the Colorado Sports Hall of Fame and CU Athletics Hall of Fame. In 1984, CU's track was officially dedicated and renamed Potts Field. It has served as CU's outdoor track for more than 50 years.

All the honors were well deserved for a man who gave so much to the university and the athletic department. By the time 1968 rolled around, however, Potts knew it was time to move on. Plenty had changed in the world of college athletics and, at 65 years old, he passed the baton to Meyers.

"Coaching a track team at a major university has become just too big a job for a man my age," he said at the time. "It's a year-round job, and you put in plenty of 18-hour days.

"Ever since I was big enough to ride a bicycle, I worked at odd jobs and went to school, then got into coaching. I've never known what it's like just to forget everything and loaf. I'm going to give it a try for a while."

Perhaps more than anyone in CU history, Potts earned the break.

51 Roll Tad

At the time that Tad Boyle was hired as the CU men's basketball coach in April of 2010, he said it was his "dream job." It sounded good, but he certainly wasn't the first coach in sports history to make that declaration. Many of those other coaches moved on after a better opportunity came along.

"Here's the thing: I mean it," Boyle said in 2019, while in his ninth season leading the Buffaloes. "A lot of coaches say those things at press conferences, but I don't know how many of them mean it. To be the head coach at the flagship university in your home state is a dream come true."

Boyle has turned that dream into one of the most successful eras of CU basketball.

Born in Pueblo, Colorado, Boyle was a star at Greeley Central High School, leading the Wildcats to a state title in 1981 while being named the state player of the year. He went on to become a captain at Kansas, where he was a part of two NCAA Tournament teams, and then began a career as a financial broker. For several years, Boyle coached in high school before leaving the brokerage business to work his way up the college coaching ladder. He worked as an assistant at Oregon, Tennessee, Jacksonville State, and Wichita State before spending five years (2006–10) as the head coach at Northern Colorado, located in his hometown.

After the sudden departure of Jeff Bzdelik, who left the Buffs to take the head coaching job at Wake Forest, CU looked north for a replacement. Hiring Boyle has been a significant boost for a school not always known for its hoops.

Through the 2018–19 season, Boyle ranked second at CU in all-time wins (189) and third in winning percentage (.606). He also had four NCAA Tournament appearances and three trips to the NIT.

CU joined the Pac-12 before Boyle's second season, and that year he led the Buffs to the conference tournament championship. The No. 6 seed, CU won a stunning four games in four days to claim the only conference tournament title in program history.

In Boyle's first season, 2010–11, the Buffs were surprisingly snubbed by the NCAA Tournament selection committee, but made it to The Dance in four of the next five seasons. Before that run, CU had made just two tournament appearances in the previous 47 seasons. Boyle's success led fans to coin the slogan, "Roll Tad," a play on the University of Alabama rally cry, "Roll Tide."

"One of the things I've tried to do is bring enthusiasm into Colorado basketball and a belief that this program can be great, that it can compete for a championship," Boyle said.

Booker sinks the Jayhawks

When CU welcomed former Big 12 rival Kansas to Boulder for a non-conference basketball game on December 7, 2013, the Buffs and their fans had years of pent-up frustration. CU had lost 19 in a row to the Jayhawks and owned a dreadful 1–46 record against them in the previous 22 years. With 2.9 seconds to play and the score tied at 72–72, the crowd of 11,113 was on its feet and eager to see a change in fortune. Nearly 75 feet from the basket, CU's Xavier Johnson inbounded the ball to Askia Booker, who dribbled two times and Euro-stepped past KU defender Frank Mason. With 0.8 on the clock, Booker launched a 30-foot shot. The buzzer sounded, the ball slipped through the hoop and the fans spilled onto the court in celebration of a thrilling 75–72 upset of the sixth-ranked Jayhawks.

It was the most memorable win of the Boyle era and the highlight of the sensational—yet sometimes frustrating—career of Booker, who would graduate as the sixth-leading scorer in program history. "I guarantee you, whoever was in here is not going to forget about that night," Booker said. "That's something you take pride in."

While CU isn't a basketball blueblood, such as Duke, Kansas, Kentucky, and North Carolina, Boyle is motivated by seeing schools like Butler, George Mason, Loyola-Chicago, Virginia Commonwealth, and Wichita State reach the Final Four in recent years. "It drives me to strive for that and try to get this program to that point some day," he said.

Striving for that success has helped Boyle and the Buffs produce several NBA players, including first-round draft picks Alec Burks (2011), Andre Roberson (2013), and Derrick White (2017), and second-round picks Spencer Dinwiddie (2014) and George King (2018). Other players from the Boyle era, including Askia Booker, Carlon Brown, Wesley Gordon, Cory Higgins, Xavier Johnson, and Josh Scott have played in the NBA G League or overseas.

In addition to his pursuit of championships, Boyle has made a habit of holding reunion weekends each season, honoring different eras of CU basketball.

"I've really tried to tie all the eras of Colorado basketball together and to make every former player feel like they're a part of this program and I want our current players to feel ownership in this program," he said. "If I can hopefully do one thing before I leave Colorado, it's to galvanize all the former players and the fans to appreciate all the hard work that people have put into this program and to hopefully bring it to national prominence."

52 Bolder Boulder

In the late 1970s, Steve Bosley had visions of creating a track meet in the city of Boulder. Olympic gold medalist Frank Shorter, who lived in Boulder, had another idea.

"He said, 'Why don't you do a road race?'" Bosley said.

There were already a few annual races in the area, but Bosley thought it was a good idea and, in 1979, the Bolder Boulder made its debut with about 2,700 runners registered. "I was disappointed with 2,700," said Bosley, who was the longtime president of The Bank of Boulder. A CU alum, he later served two six-year terms on the school's Board of Regents.

Four decades after its inception, the Bolder Boulder has become one of the largest road races in the United States and an annual attraction for hard-core runners, weekend warriors and weight loss goal-setters. In 2018, there were 51,407 people registered for the 40th annual 10-kilometer race. In 2019, the Bolder Boulder surpassed the 1.5 million mark for all-time registrations.

For many in the elite running community, the Bolder Boulder is a bucket list type of race, as it draws many of the top distance runners in the country and the world each year. In addition to the citizen's race, the Bolder Boulder hosts a pro team challenge, with some of the best male and female distance runners from Eritrea, Ethiopia, Japan, Kenya, Mexico, the United States and other countries. For many citizens in the area, the Bolder Boulder has become an event to point towards in reaching a fitness goal. Race organizers have heard countless stories of people who ran their first 10K at this event as the conclusion of a long process of weight loss; or those who battled cancer and other illnesses and used the Bolder Boulder as motivation.

"The stories that we hear that come to us ... some of them are real earth shattering stories of changing lives," Bosley said. "Eighty-some percent do more training and prepare more fitness because of the Bolder Boulder. To know that you are doing something that's affecting so many hundreds of thousands of lives is a very humbling feeling."

While the top of the pack of the citizen's race is led by the elite runners, the event is a top attraction each year because of its family-friendly nature. Numerous families and sets of friends run, jog, or walk the course together—many in honor of loved ones who may have passed away or are currently battling serious illnesses. As the event takes place on Memorial Day, many participants also honor veterans and current military personnel.

The course is also filled with entertainment along the way—including live bands, a Slip 'n' Slide, a bacon station, and more. The participants themselves are often the entertainment, as thousands dress in costume.

Since 1981, the Bolder Boulder has finished inside Folsom Field, and as the morning goes along, the stands fill up. By the time the final runners cross the line, it's a nearly packed house. It's chaotic, but thrilling for the participants and the thousands in attendance.

What truly sets the Bolder Boulder apart, however, is the patriotic atmosphere of the Memorial Day tribute. After all the runners cross the finish line, thousands remain in the Folsom Field stands for what has become one of the largest Memorial Day celebrations in the country. The first Bolder Boulder wasn't held on Memorial Day, but as time went on, it moved to the holiday and the tribute grew larger and larger. It now includes a presentation of the colors, a 21-gun salute, a mass enlistment ceremony, a military flyover, and military sky divers carrying flags from each branch of the military as they land in the stadium. In addition, the Bolder Boulder each year honors a couple of veterans—a list that has included medics from Vietnam and soldiers who fought at Iwo Jima in World War II.

"We have an obligation now and that is not a negative; that is not a duty," Bosley said. "We have an obligation to do this and do it right, but the opportunity to have the obligation is overwhelming. I was concerned about people perceiving we were commercializing Memorial Day, but that's the furthest thing from my mind. That happens to be my favorite holiday. The Memorial Day tribute as a whole is spectacular to me."

To pull off an event this big, it takes year-round work and hundreds of workers and volunteers. For Bosley and his son, Cliff, who has taken over as race director, the Bolder Boulder is hard work, but it's a labor of love.

"You're so intent day by day, week by week, month by month of the hundreds of things that have to come together on that day, it's tough to step back away from it and see what it is," Steve Bosley said. "I started many years ago… at some point during the day, you have to go into the stadium and you have to sit for 15 minutes and watch the race and look at what we produced. Because if you don't, it's gone and all you've done is look at the job you've done. You have to step away from it and say, 'Holy cow, how does everybody else look at this?' We sneak up into the stadium, take off your orange (workers) jacket and meld into the crowd and just sit and watch, and I cry."

53 Michael Westbrook

Lightly recruited when he was a senior at Chadsey High School in Michigan, Michael Westbrook didn't come to Colorado with visions of posting monster numbers as a receiver.

"I signed with Colorado because I liked the coaches and the players," he said during his sophomore year in 1992. "I felt comfortable here."

Truth is, when Westbrook came to CU in 1991, there weren't a lot of numbers to be had for a receiver, even one with Westbrook's size and skill. At 6-foot-4, 210 pounds, Westbrook was a big target and one of the most talented receivers to ever come through CU, but the Buffs had a run-oriented wishbone attack on offense.

As a freshman in 1991, Westbrook led the team in receiving yards, but had just 309. He also led the team in touchdown receptions (five) and was second in catches (22). In preparation for the Blockbuster Bowl that year, however, head coach Bill McCartney made the bold decision to scrap the wishbone for a more pass-oriented offense. Leading up to the 1992 season, the Buffs were all in on their new offense. Westbrook—along with Charles E. Johnson, who was a year older—were the ideal targets at receiver for the new offense.

In 1992, Westbrook and Johnson both became the first receivers in program history to post a 1,000-yard season. Westbrook set a team record with 76 catches that season—a record that would last for more than a decade.

"I'm not really concerned about my statistics at all," he said during that season. "I just want to win football games."

With Westbrook as one of the leaders of the offense, the Buffs did just that. During his four-year career at CU, from 1991 to '94, he caught 167 passes for 2,548 yards and 19 touchdowns. All three numbers were program records at the time of his graduation. A quarter century after his CU career ended, he still ranked third in yards and fourth in catches. Most important to Westbrook was that the Buffs won, going 36–9–3 during his career.

Of all the catches he made for the Buffs, there's one that stands out above the rest. On September 24, 1994, he caught the Hail Mary pass from Kordell Stewart on the final play of the game to beat Michigan, 27–26. He will forever be remembered for the Miracle in Michigan.

Michael Westbrook running free during a 57–38 victory over the Baylor Bears in 1992. (Getty Images / Joe Patronite / Stringer)

"If that didn't happen, people would still remember Michael Westbrook as being a great receiver at Colorado, but because that happened, they truly remember that as me being that guy," he said.

Westbrook earned All-American and All-Big Eight honors twice and he earned MVP honors at the 1995 East-West Shrine Game.

In the spring of 1995, he was the No. 4 overall selection in the NFL Draft, by the Washington Redskins. Only one other player in CU history—Bo Matthews in 1974—was drafted higher. Westbrook played eight seasons in the NFL—seven with Washington and one with the Cincinnati Bengals—catching 285 passes for 4,374 yards and 26 touchdowns during his career. In 2016, he was inducted into the CU Athletics Hall of Fame.

54 Kayo Lam

Very few players in CU football history could match the rhythm that William "Kayo" Lam had on the field. Perhaps nobody could match the rhythm he had off the field.

Lam had a brilliant football career at CU from 1933 to '35, but he also made a name for himself as a wrestler, boxer, track and field athlete, and as a crooner and tap dancer. Just 5-feet, 9-inches tall and 160 pounds, Lam was small even for his day, but the Glenrock, Wyoming, native had remarkable moves on the field, and he attributed some of his skills to his talent as a dancer.

"Tap dancing has helped greatly with my football," he said during his senior year in 1935. "It makes me lighter and shiftier on my feet. Footwork and change of pace mean a lot in open field running. It would improve the play of any backfield man. Skipping rope also helps toughen the leg muscles, and I often tap dance while I'm listening to the radio and keep the muscles in my legs loose and supple."

It's hard to argue with that logic when seeing Lam's success on the field. During his three seasons as the Buffs' quarterback, he rushed for 2,140 yards and 18 touchdowns, averaging 6.8 yards per carry, and helping CU to an 18–7–2 record. In 1935, Lam rushed for 1,043 yards, becoming the first known Buff to top the 1,000-yard mark. According to newspaper reports at the time, he set a collegiate record for single-season rushing yards (a record which wouldn't last long, as his own teammate, Byron White, rushed for 1,121 yards two years later).

Lam led the country in rushing in 1934 (906 yards) and 1935—still the only CU player to ever lead the nation in a statistical category in back-to-back years. As a senior, he also led the nation with 2,225 all-around yards (1,043 rushing, 364 passing, 530 on punt returns and 288 on kickoff returns).

He was never one to take too much credit for his success, however. "No back can get very far unless the other fellows go out there and knock 'em down in front," he said.

And, when told he was closing in on the rushing yards record, he said, "I don't think that's very important. As long as we win games, that's what counts."

Outside of football, Lam lettered twice each in track and wrestling, where he was a conference champion. He was also an accomplished boxer and rode broncos at the family ranch in Wyoming.

While all of that was fun, Lam, known as the "Crooning Quarterback," paid his way through college with his musical talent. He played six different instruments and conducted a college dance orchestra, where the performances included his singing. He was featured on local radio stations, as well, and he continued to lead orchestras after graduation.

After leaving CU, Lam was a lieutenant in the Navy during World War II. He then spent 36 years working at CU, including two years as assistant football coach, three years as head wrestling coach and 30 years as the athletic department business manager.

In 1989, Lam as named to CU's All-Century team and in 1999, he was inducted into the CU Athletics Hall of Fame.

55 Buffs Finally Go Bowling

Featuring one of the nation's brightest stars in 1937, the Colorado football team was a prime target for bowl game executives.

Quarterback/halfback Byron "Whizzer" White was an All-American and he led the Buffaloes to an 8–0 record during the regular season in 1937. CU dominated everyone in its path that season, cruising to the Rocky Mountain Athletic Conference (RMAC) title.

Bowl games were still a fairly new concept in the late 1930s. Prior to 1934, the Rose Bowl was the only postseason game played annually in college football. In 1934, the Sugar, Orange, and Sun bowls were added to the postseason schedule, and in 1936, the Cotton Bowl came into existence. In 1937, there were only five bowl games—all played on New Year's Day. It was an exclusive group that got invited, although not every top team got or accepted bowl invites. The Big Ten, for example, didn't allow its teams to play in bowls. Top-ranked Pittsburgh didn't play in a bowl that year, despite an invitation to the Rose. It was reported that the Pittsburgh players made demands of "pocket money" between $100 and $200 and for two weeks of vacation, and those demands were not accepted.

Still, receiving a bowl invitation was a big deal, and for the first time ever in 1937, the Buffs got one. They were invited to play in one of the New Year's Day main events, facing Rice in the Cotton Bowl on January 1, 1938. Cotton Bowl president J. Curtis Sanford sent the invitation via telegraph to CU athletic director Walter B. Franklin. The telegraph read: "The high scholastic requirements and the fine code of good sportsmanship in your athletics and the very excellent record attained by the University of Colorado team this year convinces the Cotton Bowl athletic association committee that your school has the nation's outstanding team for our New Year's Day classic. It is with pleasure that we hereby extend to the University of Colorado our invitation to play the representative team of the Southwest Conference in Dallas New Year's Day."

CU was also wanted for the Sun Bowl, but elected to play in the Cotton Bowl. A CU faculty executive council met and approved the invitation, making the Buffs the first RMAC school to play in a bowl. CU's fans were excited, with about 10,000 expected to make the trip to Dallas.

"Why, up in those mountains we celebrated Christmas this year only because it was printed in red on the calendar," Francis W. Reich, secretary of the Boulder chamber of commerce, said a few days before the game. "The real event is this game. It's the biggest thing up there since gold was discovered."

CU head coach Bunny Oakes felt good about his team's chances after scouting Rice. "If we play our best football, I think we've got a chance," he said.

Rice, which won the Southwest Conference title, was a bigger team and featured star sophomore Ernie Lain. The Buffs, however, had White, who led the nation in rushing (1,121 yards) and scoring (122 points). White ran the ball, threw the ball, returned punts and kickoffs, punted, and starred on defense. With his athletic and academic prowess—he earned the Rhodes scholarship in the weeks

181

Bowl History
Colorado's bowl game history, through the 2018 season:

Date	Bowl	Result
January 1, 1938	Cotton	Rice 28, CU 14
January 1, 1957	Orange	CU 27, Clemson 21
January 1, 1962	Orange	Louisiana State 25, CU 7
December 23, 1967	Bluebonnet	CU 31, Miami (Fla.) 21
December 13, 1969	Liberty	CU 47, Alabama 33
December 12, 1970	Liberty	Tulane 17, CU 3
December 31, 1971	Bluebonnet	CU 29, Houston 17
December 30, 1972	Gator	Auburn 24, CU 3
December 27, 1975	Bluebonnet	Texas 38, CU 21
January 1, 1977	Orange	Ohio State 27, CU 10
December 30, 1985	Freedom	Washington 20, CU 17
December 31, 1986	Bluebonnet	Baylor 21, CU 9
December 29, 1988	Freedom	Brigham Young 20, CU 17
January 1, 1990	Orange	Notre Dame 21, CU 6
January 1, 1991	Orange	CU 10, Notre Dame 9
December 28, 1991	Blockbuster	Alabama 30, CU 25
January 1, 1993	Fiesta	Syracuse 26, CU 22
December 25, 1993	Aloha	CU 41, Fresno State 30
January 2, 1995	Fiesta	CU 41, Notre Dame 24
January 1, 1996	Cotton	CU 38, Oregon 6
December 30, 1996	Holiday	CU 33, Washington 21
December 25, 1998	Aloha	CU 51, Oregon 43
December 31, 1999	Insight.com	CU 62, Boston College 28
January 1, 2002	Fiesta	Oregon 38, CU 16
December 28, 2002	Alamo	Wisconsin 31, CU 28 (OT)
December 29, 2004	Houston	CU 33, UTEP 28
December 27, 2005	Champs Sports	Clemson 19, CU 10
December 30, 2007	Independence	Alabama 30, CU 24
December 29, 2016	Alamo	Oklahoma State 38, CU 8

leading up to the Cotton Bowl—White was well known around the country and a star attraction.

Although rain had hit the Dallas area hard in the days leading up to the game, there were clear skies for the contest. Early in the game, White certainly lived up to his billing, leading the Buffs to a 14–0 lead in the first quarter. He threw an 8-yard touchdown pass to Joe Antonio for the first touchdown. Then, he intercepted a Lain pass and returned it 47 yards for a second touchdown. Lain and the Owls took over from there, scoring three second-quarter touchdowns en route to a 28–14 upset. Lain threw three touchdown passes and ran for another.

White impressed those who watched the game, but he didn't have much help. Rice's depth overpowered the Buffs, outgaining them 412–55.

The game didn't turn out like CU had hoped, and it would be 19 years before the Buffs would return to a bowl game, but it was a monumental achievement for the program. It was also the highlight of a solid five-year run for Oakes as coach. From 1935 to '39, he went 25–15–1.

56 Deon Figures

Notre Dame quarterback Rick Mirer took the snap with 13 seconds on the clock in the Orange Bowl, stepped up in the collapsing pocket and delivered an off-balance pass down the field.

"Intercepted by Colorado… Deon Figures!" NBC Sports' Dick Enberg said on the national broadcast. "And Figures runs out the clock! And the figures may be No. 1 for Colorado!"

The interception by the CU sophomore secured the Buffaloes' only football national championship on January 1, 1991, and was the signature play in a stellar career for Figures. It was also a moment of sweet redemption for the cornerback from Compton, California Voted the Big Eight Conference newcomer of the year by coaches in 1988 when he was a true freshman, Figures ran into trouble after that season. Twice he was involved in fights in Boulder bars. Head coach Bill McCartney had a policy that two offenses warranted a season-long suspension. Although Figures had not been arrested after the second fight, McCartney held firm on his rule. Figures sat the entire 1989 season, watching as CU went 11–0 in the regular season and then lost the Orange Bowl to Notre Dame.

"I had to deal with it like a man and make the best of it," Figures said toward the end of the 1989 season. "I've learned to deal with situations I wouldn't have in my freshman year."

When Figures returned from his suspension, he played three more exceptional seasons and became one of the best corners to ever play at CU. In the fifth game of the 1990 season, Figures had two interceptions, including one in the end zone with 59 seconds left to secure a 20–14 win against Washington. Then, he capped the season with that pick against Notre Dame.

"Once I caught it, I can't describe the feeling," Figures said after the win against the Irish. "I knew then we had won the whole thing. It was great."

Figures continued to get better as his career went along and took his game to a new level as a senior, in 1992. That season, he won the Thorpe Award as the nation's top defensive back, was a consensus first-team All-American and the Big Eight defensive player of the year. That season, he had a career-best six interceptions and gave up just 12 completions to receivers he was covering. By the end of his senior year, Figures was being compared to star corners in the NFL.

"Athletically, he's everything you look for," CU secondary coach Greg Brown said as the Buffs' prepared for the Fiesta Bowl game at the end of the 1992 season. "Footwork is a cornerback's bread and butter, his livelihood. Deon has the best footwork of any player I've ever coached."

In the spring of 1993, Figures was selected in the first round of the NFL Draft (23rd overall) by the Pittsburgh Steelers. He played four seasons with the Steelers and two with the Jacksonville Jaguars before retiring. Figures returned to Boulder in 2014 for induction to the CU Athletics Hall of Fame.

"I want to thank the University of Colorado for even coming to Compton, to even look at a young kid like me, 17–18 years-old; to even give me the opportunity," he said during his induction speech.

57 Joel Klatt

Had Joel Klatt stuck with his original plans, he'd be a former minor league baseball player with a career in real estate. Klatt's ability to adjust, however, made him a star on the gridiron and, now, a household name in the world of college football.

A three-sport star at Pomona High School in Arvada, Colorado, Klatt was coached in football by his father, Gary, and had scholarship offers in baseball and football. When the San Diego Padres selected him in the 11th round of the 2000 baseball draft, he signed a contract.

Less than two years later, he was a struggling third baseman with a .209 batting average and his hopes of reaching the majors were fading as quickly as his passion for the game. "There was

Joel Klatt throws a pass during the second quarter of a 2004 game against UTEP in the Houston Bowl in which he passed for 333 yards and two touchdowns in a 33–28 win. (AP Photo / David J. Phillip)

nothing about professional baseball I loved anymore," he said in 2003.

Because he signed out of high school and skipped college, Klatt's contract with the Padres included a $45,000 tuition bonus for whenever he wanted to return to school. In 2002, he quit baseball and walked on to the CU football team.

Klatt earned the starting quarterback job going into the 2003 season and exploded in his first start. During the 2003 opener, Klatt threw for 402 yards and four touchdowns and led the Buffs to a game-winning touchdown in the final minute of a 42–35 win against rival Colorado State.

"Joel didn't come here expecting to be the starter and I certainly didn't plan on it, either," CU head coach Gary Barnett said during the 2003 season—shortly after Klatt led the Buffs to a come-from-behind overtime win against Kansas. "But everything about Joel Klatt is surprising."

Klatt remained in the starting lineup for three seasons, through 2005, leading the Buffs to a 19–15 record and two Big 12 North division titles. He set 44 school records, graduating as CU's all-time leader in passing yards (7,375) and touchdown passes (44).

After his time with the Buffs, Klatt set out for a job in the "real world."

"I was an economics major at the University of Colorado and was fully planning on one of two or three options," he said. "I was going to get involved with some sort of real estate company."

Klatt was working his day job when Fox Sports Rocky Mountain asked him one day if he'd do color analysis for a high school football broadcast.

"I feel in love with it that night, realized I had a little bit of a feel for it and then was just really blessed with not only opportunities but with great people around me," he said.

With a high football IQ and charisma, Klatt rapidly moved up the broadcasting ladder. In 2015, Fox Sports made him their lead analyst on college football games and paired him with one of the best play-by-play announcers in broadcasting, Gus Johnson. Klatt and Johnson team up for Fox's top game each week. Klatt has become known as one of the top college football analysts in the country.

"To say that I love my job is an understatement," he said after his first season with Johnson. "I pinch myself every day. It's been fantastic. I couldn't be happier and I couldn't imagine doing anything else with my life right now."

Klatt is one of several CU alums that have made a name for themselves in sports media, including Emmy Award-winner Jim Gray, ESPN college football icon Chris Fowler and longtime voice of the Denver Broncos, Dave Logan. The list also includes Jeremy Bloom, Christian Fauria, Charles Johnson, Kordell Stewart, Solomon Wilcots, Alfred Williams, and former women's basketball player Kate Fagan.

58 Chris Hudson

It was obvious to Chris Hudson early in his career at CU that there were high expectations for anyone playing cornerback. When Hudson was a sophomore, teammate Deon Figures won the Thorpe Award. Figures and Ronnie Bradford were both seniors that year who wound up being taken in the NFL draft.

"Those guys really influenced me, as far as seeing their work habits," Hudson said near the end of his senior year in 1994. "I felt I had good work habits, but seeing them made me go to a higher work ethic. So I would take my game to a higher level."

CU has had a long tradition of great cornerbacks, and Hudson is near the top of the list. As a senior, he joined Figures as a Thorpe Award winner, capping a remarkable career with the Buffs. The Houston native, who played safety early in his career, earned All-Big Eight honors three times, was a third-team All-American as a junior, and a consensus All-American as a senior.

"He's special because he studies the game of football," Chuck Heater, CU's defensive backs coach in 1994, said that year. "He wants to be a great football player. He's gonna do whatever you ask him to do. All he wants to do is find out how to do it and how you can help him do it. He's just a work-ethic guy, and there aren't many of those guys anymore. He's a throwback. He studies film on his own. He's a student of the game. He has great anticipation. He makes plays."

Perhaps most remarkable about Hudson's senior year was that he played most of the campaign with a painful toe injury. "Every other kid I've coached would have sat down," Heater said. "He played every week."

During his career, Hudson had 141 tackles and 15 interceptions—still the second-best career total in CU history. He also returned punts, averaging 9.7 yards per return. Hudson was also a part of a great run of success for the team. The Buffs went 36–9–3 during his career with four bowl appearances.

Like Mark Haynes, Figures, Bradford and others before him, Hudson made his mark as an elite cornerback at CU. After leaving CU, he followed Figures and Bradford to the NFL, getting selected in the third round (71st overall) by the Jacksonville Jaguars in 1995. He played 77 career games with the Jaguars, Chicago Bears, and Atlanta Falcons.

59 Tasmanian Devil

Football scouts have always had a particular mold they use in trying to find the best players at each position.

Phillip Lindsay didn't fit the mold of a major Division I college football running back when he arrived at CU in the fall of 2013, standing just 5-feet, 8-inches tall and weighing 160 pounds. Despite those physical limitations, Lindsay made his presence known immediately.

"He was on the scout field and two to three times a week, you just hear Phil's voice on the other side of the field getting in someone's face," center Alex Kelley said in recalling Lindsay's true freshman season.

Lindsay didn't back down from anyone, and even got into a practice altercation with a 6-foot-3, 325-pound defensive lineman.

"I was in all kind of fights on the field," Lindsay said. "Coach [Mike MacIntyre] had to put me in time out. He had his own time out room for me. That's just who I was. I always was aggressive, I was always a dog."

By the time he finished his career at CU in 2017, he was one of the top dogs in program history. A proud Colorado native who came to CU after a stellar career at Denver South High School, Lindsay left the Buffaloes' program among the all-time leaders in numerous categories:

1st in all-purpose yards (5,760)
1st in yards from scrimmage (4,683)
2nd in rushing yards (3,707)
2nd in rushing touchdowns (36)
1st in receptions by a running back (110)
4th in total points scored (234)

Lindsay became the first player in CU history with back-to-back 1,000-yard rushing seasons, in 2016 and 2017, and the first running back to record 100 or more receptions. Of the top-10 single-season rushing totals in CU history, Lindsay owns two of them. And, in 2017, he set CU records for rushing attempts in a game (41) and season (301). In all, he set 24 school records and became one of the most popular players to ever suit up for the Buffaloes—not only among the fans, but in the locker room.

Phillip Lindsay celebrates a first quarter touchdown against the Arizona State Sun Devils at Sun Devil Stadium on October 10, 2015. (Getty Images / Chris Coduto)

"He's an all-around good guy," said Darian Hagan, former CU quarterback and Lindsay's position coach with the Buffs. "He's a great football player, great person, great teammate, great son. He's a guy you love to be around because he's infectious."

Lindsay came from an athletic and ultra-competitive family. His father, Troy, played at Colorado State. His two older sisters both played college sports and his two younger brothers both played running back in college. He had an uncle play at Utah and two cousins play at Oklahoma State.

While at Denver South, Lindsay broke the Denver Prep League record for career rushing yards. The record was previously held by his father. Both of his brothers joined him in becoming Denver Prep League MVPs. Lindsay broke the DPL record in the first game of his senior year, but in that game he injured his left knee. It wasn't until two weeks later—after he rushed for 139 yards in the first quarter and tweaked the knee again—that it was discovered he tore the anterior cruciate ligament (ACL). He missed the rest of his senior season, and college recruiters shied away from him.

Already committed to CU, Lindsay was worried when the coach who recruited him, Jon Embree, was fired. MacIntyre was hired and honored the commitment, although he was unsure where Lindsay would play. It didn't take long in 2013 to realize Lindsay was going to make his mark as a feisty running back.

"We knew he was undersized and had to put some weight on, but the thing you didn't really understand was his toughness, his heart," Hagan said. "When I saw that, I knew that he had a chance to be really, really special. As soon as he gets on the field, he turns into a different animal. That's why coach Mac nicknamed him the 'Tasmanian Devil'—just seeing his heart and his passion for the game."

After redshirting in 2013, Lindsay shared the load in 2014 and 2015. He flashed his talent, but coaches worried about his durability to be the featured back. He averaged just 8.8 carries per game in those two seasons. In 2016, he proved he could handle the heavy lifting and became a focal point of the offense in his final two seasons.

"If you give him the ball over and over and over again, he's special," Hagan said.

Despite taking on a heavy load, Lindsay was relentless in his efforts to take care of his body, and it paid off. After missing most of his senior year at South, he played in all 51 of CU's games from 2014–17.

Beginning with those early practices as a freshman, when his "dog" mentality would come out, Lindsay became highly respected by his peers because he wasn't just a great player; he was a great teammate. Following a 2016 game against Arizona State, when he rushed for 219 yards and three touchdowns in a victory, Lindsay brought his entire offensive line to the postgame press conference and made sure they got attention for their work in that game. Throughout his career, Lindsay often made it a point to praise his linemen and his teammates for his own success.

"I never wanted it to be just about me," he said. "I just wanted my presence to be known that I'm here for my teammates. What I am is real. I don't just do it for the show. This is who I am. I'm always thinking about other people."

Deeply loyal to his close-knit family, his friends, CU, and his home state, Lindsay was one of the most passionate players to ever compete at Folsom Field, and he left everything on the field for the Buffs.

"It's been a long road, fun journey," he said as his CU career came to a close. "It's been tough, sad, happy—all the emotions. But, overall it helped me grow as a man and helped me see things in different perspectives and I'll go into my life with different reasoning, different ways of thinking, and different ways of acting and being more patient with people and with myself."

Following his time at CU, Lindsay prepared for the NFL, but, at only 5–8, 190 pounds, he again didn't fit the mold. Despite being one of the nation's top running backs during his final two seasons with the Buffs, Lindsay wasn't invited to the NFL Combine and he wasn't selected in the NFL Draft. The hometown Denver Broncos signed him as an undrafted rookie, and once again he had to fight—this time just to make the team. He made the roster and began the year as a backup. By season's end, he was the starting running back and led the team with 1,037 rushing yards and nine touchdowns. He became the first undrafted rookie offensive player in NFL history to be named to the Pro Bowl. Lindsay was proud of his Pro Bowl moment, but, of course, was thinking of others as he enjoyed his success with the Broncos.

"It's a great story for kids coming up that feel like they can't do anything, or they don't have a chance," he said. "You've got to keep pushing, you just never know. You've got to keep the faith no matter what. Everybody can take anything from you, but they can't take your faith. That's what you've got to rely on. You've got to go for your dreams."

60 Mike Pritchard

CU's 1990 national championship team featured dynamic quarterback Darian Hagan and Big Eight Conference players of the year Eric Bieniemy (offense) and Alfred Williams (defense). When it came time to vote for the team's Most Valuable Player, however, the Buffs selected receiver Mike Pritchard.

"He's an inspiration... and not a bad athlete at all," defensive lineman Joel Steed said in December of 1990. "You wonder, 'If you've got all these talents, why not be cocky?' He's far from that. That's why everybody enjoys his presence and voted him MVP."

The team MVP award was a testament to the all-around talent and selfless attitude of Pritchard, a 5-foot-11, 180-pound athlete who came to CU from Las Vegas. Pritchard had one of the most dynamic seasons in school history in 1990. He caught 28 passes for what was at the time a school-record 733 yards and six touchdowns. His 26.2-yards-per-catch average is still a single-season school record (minimum 20 catches). He also rushed for 445 yards and five touchdowns and racked up 331 yards in kickoff returns.

During Pritchard's first three seasons, from 1987 to '89, he was a halfback and wingback in the Buffs' I-bone attack and was used primarily as a blocker and receiver. In the spring of 1990, Pritchard asked head coach Bill McCartney if he could play wide receiver.

"We had trained him for two years to be the wingback, and now we were moving him to another position," McCartney said as the Buffs prepared for the Orange Bowl that season. "That wouldn't have been my first choice. Now that it's unfolded, I'm glad he asked."

After the switch to receiver, Pritchard's 1990 season began with him playing tailback. McCartney had suspended Bieniemy for the season opener against Tennessee and gave the starting nod to Pritchard. He lost a fumble and overcame a slow first half to post 217 rushing yards that day, including touchdown runs of 55 and 78 yards.

From there, he took off as a receiver, posting two 100-yard games, including a 151-yard, two-touchdown performance in a win against Oklahoma State.

Going into the Orange Bowl, there was a lot of attention on Notre Dame superstar Raghib "Rocket" Ismail, an all-purpose play-maker who was runner-up for the Heisman Trophy. National media viewed Pritchard as CU's "Rocket."

"I know we're both big-play people, but I wouldn't try to compare or contrast me to Rocket," Pritchard said. "He is, in my opinion, the Heisman Trophy winner because he is the best player in college football. We're used totally different in our offenses. I'm not embarrassed but flattered to be compared to him. But, he's an all-purpose player and I'm a receiver."

Despite his modesty, Pritchard was much more just a receiver for the Buffs. He is the only player in CU history with at least 400 rushing and 700 receiving yards in the same season. He closed his career with 47 catches for 1,241 yards and 10 touchdowns, while adding 585 rushing yards. Of the nearly 100 players in CU history with 30-plus catches, nobody comes close to Pritchard's career average of 26.4 yards per catch.

After leaving CU, Pritchard was a first-round pick (No. 13 overall) by the Atlanta Falcons in 1991. He played nine years in the NFL with the Falcons, Denver Broncos, and Seattle Seahawks, catching 422 passes for 5,187 yards and 26 touchdowns.

Like many other Buffs, Pritchard has had a career in broadcasting after his playing days and, as of 2019, was a co-host of a sports talk radio show in Denver.

61 Jon Embree

It may have been too short to be considered an "era," but the Jon Embree years as head football coach at CU were rather forgettable. Two seasons with a 4–21 record and an embarrassing amount of blowout losses was hardly what he and CU envisioned when he was hired before the 2011 season. Regardless, Embree will always be remembered as a beloved and loyal Buff.

A graduate of Denver's Cherry Creek High School, Embree was a talented tight end who was a part of head coach Bill McCartney's first recruiting class, signing with the Buffs in 1983. Embree would go on to play an integral role in CU's rebuilding. In 1984, when the Buffs were still running more of a pro-style offense, he led the team in receiving, with 51 catches for 680 yards and three touchdowns. In his final two years, the Buffs switched to the run-heavy wishbone offense and his numbers decreased dramatically. He still led the team in receiving in 1985, but with only nine catches for 140 yards. For his career, from 1983 to '86, Embree caught 80 passes for 1,166 yards and five touchdowns. He's still second in CU history (behind Daniel Graham) for receiving yards by a tight end. He also helped the Buffs reach a bowl game in 1985—their first in nine years—and again in 1986.

Selected by the Los Angeles Rams in the sixth round of the 1987 draft, Embree played two seasons in the NFL (his father, John, also played two years in the NFL, with the Denver Broncos).

McCartney then gave him his start in coaching, as a graduate assistant at CU. Embree spent 10 seasons (1993–2002) as a full-time assistant with the Buffs, working with three different head coaches: McCartney, Rick Neuheisel, and Gary Barnett. Coaching stops at UCLA and in the NFL with the Kansas City Chiefs and Washington Redskins set him for his dream job. On December 6, 2010, Embree was named the Buffs' head coach—the first black head coach in school history and the first former CU player to take the reins since Bud Davis in 1962.

"I never doubted in my mind that I would be standing here one day," he said at his introductory press conference. "I know where this place can go. I'm more excited about that than what has happened the last couple of years. It's going to be a great run and a great ride."

Initially, Embree brought energy and enthusiasm back to the program and the fans, but that quickly disappeared as his teams simply couldn't compete in the Pac-12. They went 3–15 in conference games, with 13 of those losses by at least 25 points.

Although fired after the 2012 season, with three years left on his contract, Embree has remained loyal to the program. He returned to coaching in the NFL, but has been involved with the program as a founding member of Buffs4Life, an organization designed to help CU alumni in need.

"It's reunited guys and got guys reconnected," Embree said of Buffs4Life. "When you leave and go a bunch of different directions and start having kids and families, sometimes you lose contact. This has been a way for a lot of guys to come back and reconnect. We're just trying to find ways to continue to grow it so we can keep helping people. I've always been a Buff and always will continue to be and I'll do anything I can to help."

62 MacIntyre Years

It's standard that a press conference to introduce a new head coach comes with a blanket of optimism, and it was no different when Mike MacIntyre was named the Buffaloes' head coach on December 10, 2012. Given the state of the program at the time, however, there was a measure of despair, as well.

MacIntyre took over what was arguably the worst major conference team in the country. During the previous two years—CU's first two years in the Pac-12—the Buffs went 4–21 and were routinely routed by conference foes. CU had not been to a bowl game since 2007 and had not posted a winning season since 2005.

CU hoped MacIntyre was the man to turn the tide. Prior to CU, MacIntyre had turned around San Jose State. The Spartans were 1–12 in his first year and 10–2 in his third and final season. CU hoped for the same type of results.

"My slogan is: 'No excuses, no regrets.' Find a way," MacIntyre said during his introductory press conference. "We'll win a lot of football games but at the same time these young men are going to learn a lot of life lessons, and I want them to walk out of here men that will be great fathers, great leaders, great businessmen, and great husbands, and you can do all of that in college football. That is why I coach college football. That is why I enjoy it. I enjoy mentoring young people and I'm excited about what we have ahead of us. Yes, we have a long way to go, but I've been there before and I know what to do."

MacIntyre's first three years in Boulder were rough, as the Buffs extended their bowl drought to eight seasons. They were 10–27 from 2013–15, including a dreadful 2–25 record in Pac-12 games. But, the signs of progress were evident. The freshmen and sophomores MacIntyre played early in his tenure grew up. Slowly, the Buffs became more competitive, eliminating many of the blowout losses. In 2015, CU went 4–9, but had five one-score losses.

Finally, in 2016, the Buffs broke through, and they did it in a big way. CU went 10–4 in 2016, including 8–1 in the Pac-12 to claim the South Division title. The Buffs were fueled by a talented and driven senior class that had fully bought into MacIntyre.

"He's a great coach, but he's also a great man and a great mentor to us and he teaches us a lot about life," defensive tackle Jordan Carrell, a senior in 2016, said that year. "It's not just about football. Like he said this whole year: Welcome to the fight. Life is a fight, and that's going to be with me for the rest of my life."

MacIntyre was emotionally fueled by the memory of his late father. George MacIntyre passed away January 5, 2016, and that was extremely difficult for Mike, who was very close to his father. George was not only a father, but a mentor who inspired his son to get into coaching. George was a longtime coach who led Vanderbilt to a resurgent season in 1982. George earned the Bobby Dodd national coach of the year award in 1982.

In December of 2016, less than a year after George passed, Mike won numerous national coach of the year awards, including the Dodd Trophy. The sensational 2016 season earned MacIntyre a hefty raise and contract extension, but that year would prove to be his peak in Boulder.

Just a week after the 2016 Pac-12 championship game, the ex-girlfriend of then-assistant coach Joe Tumpkin informed MacIntyre that Tumpkin had violently abused her for the previous two years. Because there were no charges, MacIntyre allowed Tumpkin to call the defense for the Alamo Bowl just a few weeks later.

Tumpkin was eventually suspended and then fired. CU then commissioned an outside agency to investigate how MacIntyre, athletic director Rick George and chancellor Phil DiStefano handled the allegations. Ultimately, CU president Bruce Benson and CU's Board of Regents gave DiStefano a 10-day suspension and ordered George and MacIntyre each to pay $100,000 in fines to a domestic violence organization. It was a slap on the wrist, but it took the shine off of MacIntyre's rebuilding job with the Buffs.

The shine wore off on the field, too. The Buffs went 5–7 in 2017, losing their last three. In 2018, they started 5–0 and vaulted to No. 19 in the national rankings, but MacIntyre couldn't find another win. After six straight losses dropped the Buffs to 5–6, MacIntyre was fired with one game to play.

"What this came down to was I wanted to see more consistency with winning seasons," George said. "Mike had an amazing 2016 season and we really hoped that kind of achievement would be continuous, but unfortunately that didn't happen."

MacIntyre posted a 30–44 record during his six-year tenure, mixing the magical 2016 season with five last-place finishes. Ultimately, it wasn't what CU had in mind when it hired MacIntyre, but he did leave the program in better condition than he found it. In addition to the 2016 season, he made them much more competitive and led the Buffs to a memorable 33–28 win against longtime rival Nebraska in 2018.

MacIntyre also got to share much of his tenure with his son, Jay, who was a slot receiver for the Buffs from 2014–18. Jay was a starter during his last three seasons, finishing his career with 86 catches for 1,035 yards and six touchdowns. Jay played the final game of his career without his father, though, and it resulted in another loss, as they finished 5–7 again. For the MacIntyres, it was a difficult finish, but a remarkable opportunity to share five years together.

"We're going to leave here happy with what we accomplished and all the relationships we made, all the people we influenced and all the people that influenced us," Jay said. "I think that's bigger than football. We're not really going to let these last couple of weeks define what we know this place to be. That's life. It doesn't always go the way you want it to."

After Mike MacIntyre's dismissal, CU hired Georgia defensive coordinator Mel Tucker to lead the Buffs in 2019.

63 Mason Crosby

Football coaches would almost always rather put seven points on the board with a touchdown than settle for a field goal. From 2003–06, however, there were plenty of times when a field goal didn't seem so bad for Colorado because it meant Mason Crosby got a chance to show off his leg.

"You were almost rooting for the offense to stall around the 50 so he could try a 60-yard field goal," longtime CU sports information director David Plati said. "With Mason, you wanted to see him trot out there and try a long one."

CU has produced a bunch of good kickers and punters over the years, but nobody was as good—or as entertaining—as Crosby, a highly decorated place-kicker who came to the Buffaloes in the fall of 2003 from Georgetown, Texas. Crosby did actually hit a 60-yarder in a game once, as a sophomore in 2004 against Iowa State. As of 2018, it remained the longest field goal in CU history.

CU's all-time leading scorer, with 307 points, Crosby holds numerous school records, including field goals made (66) and attempted (88), and field goal percentage (.750). He was 54-of-64 (84.4 percent) inside 50 yards.

"He would regularly boot them from 60–65 yards in practice," Plati said. "He had a strong leg and he was accurate. He could also punt, but we had great punters when he was here, too, so he didn't need to punt."

Crosby became just the seventh two-time All-American from CU and the seventh Buff to earn first-team All-Conference honors three times. Through 2018, he was the only kicker in CU history to make at least 19 field goals in a season, and he did it three times, including a school-record 21 in 2005. Crosby was a consensus All-American in 2005, a year in which he was runner-up for the Lou Groza Award, given to the nation's top kicker. He was also the Big 12 special teams player of the year in 2005.

Shortly after his career at CU came to a close, his No. 16 jersey was honored by the university and is one of several recognized inside Folsom Field.

"It's awesome, it's unbelievable," he said of having his jersey honored in 2007. "This is something I've always dreamed about. When I first came into this stadium I looked up there [at the other honored jerseys] and thought it would be awesome; a goal and a dream to be up there with all those great names. All the guys that are on this wall, and now I'm going to be a part of it. I could never compare myself, but it is obviously a great honor. It's a culmination of a whole career, everything I've accomplished and everything I have done. Those guys [already honored] are unbelievable players and it is definitely something I wanted to be a part of."

Following his time at CU, Crosby was selected in the sixth round of the 2007 NFL Draft by the Green Bay Packers and he led the National Football League in scoring with 141 points as a rookie. In 2010, he helped the Packers to a victory in Super Bowl

Mason Crosby is mobbed by fans and media after he kicked a game-winning field goal against Colorado State. (AP Photo / Jack Dempsey)

Happy Feet

Mason Crosby isn't the only great kicker to come through Boulder. CU has had a long tradition of standout punters and kickers. Some of the best:

PK Jeremy Aldrich (1996–99): An honorable mention All-American in 1998, he led the Buffs in scoring three times. Through 2018, he ranked third in CU history in kicking points (231) and field goals made (48).

P/PK Mitch Berger (1991–93): First-team All-American as a punter in 1992. Punted three years and scored 111 points as a placekicker. Punted for 14 years in the NFL, going to two Pro Bowls and winning a Super Bowl with the Pittsburgh Steelers.

P Keith English (1987–88): He was CU's primary punter for just one season, in 1988, but he was a first-team All-American and led the country in punting average (45.04).

PK Tom Field (1979–83): Led CU in scoring three times during his career. Through 2018, he still ranked fourth in CU history for career points (190) by a kicker.

P Barry Helton (1984–87): Arguably the best punter in CU history, he was a two-time first-team All-American and three-time first-team All-Big Eight. He played four seasons in the NFL, winning two Super Bowl rings with the San Francisco 49ers.

P Mark Mariscal (2000–02): CU's only winner of the Ray Guy Award, established in 2000 to honor the nation's best punter. He won the award as a senior in 2002, while also earning first-team All-American honors.

PK Will Oliver (2011–13): A semifinalist for the Lou Groza Award, he closed his career as the second-leading scorer in CU history and one of only two (along with Crosby) to make 50 field goals.

P Tom Rouen (1989–90): A transfer from Colorado State, he was first-team All-American in 1989 and honorable mention in 1990. Played 13 years in the NFL, including 10 with the Denver Broncos, helping them win two Super Bowls.

P John Torp (2002–05): A second-team All-American in 2005, he was runner-up for the Ray Guy Award that season.

XLV. Through the 2018 season, his 13th with the Packers, he was the all-time leading scorer in Green Bay franchise history and ranked among the top 30 in NFL history in field goals made.

"It's been fun to follow his career, especially when a guy stays with one team his whole career," Plati said. "It's cool to see what he's meant to that franchise."

64 Matt Russell

Colorado linebackers coach Brian Cabral wasn't sure what to expect from Matt Russell when he showed up to the college football awards banquet in Orlando, Florida, on December 14, 1996.

"I didn't know if he'd show up with a new hairdo or what," Cabral said at the banquet. "Or, he said he might wear a sleeveless tuxedo."

Russell arrived in traditional attire, but throughout his CU career, from 1993 to '96, there was no telling what he'd actually do off the field. Head coach Rick Neuheisel described Russell in 1996 as, "Eddie Haskell meets Arnold Schwarzenegger." Years later, former teammate Marcus Washington wouldn't disagree.

"Matt Russell has a funny personality," Washington said. "He is a comedian. He is a practical joker. Matt was always doing something silly, off the wall, off the cuff, that would make people laugh."

Where he was less unpredictable was on the football field. Russell, from Fairview Heights, Illinois, was arguably the best inside linebacker in CU history. Through 2019, he ranked second all-time in tackles (446), fourth in tackles for loss (44) and perhaps first in bone-crushing hits.

Linebacker Matt Russell (16) and safety Ryan Black celebrate against Michigan.
(Getty Images / Jed Jacobsohn /Allsport)

"I don't remember Matt Russell missing a tackle," Washington said. "Not only was he a hitter, he was a tackler. Matt did both. Matt didn't miss tackles and he would knock the snot out of you. He had a nose for the football and he was a nasty beast. He never played dirty, but he would knock you flat on your behind like you would not believe."

Russell earned first-team All-Conference honors twice and was a third-team All-American as a junior in 1995. During his senior year, in 1996, Russell had 137 tackles, 13 tackles for loss and three sacks. He was a consensus first-team All-American and then, in Orlando, won the Butkus Award as the nation's best linebacker.

"My heart's about to explode," Russell said when Dick Butkus, arguably the best and hardest-hitting linebacker in history, presented him with the award. "This is without a doubt the greatest moment of my life. It's certainly something I'll remember forever and savor very much. I guess I've drawn some comparisons to Dick Butkus. But he was the most feared player ever."

Russell, who said hitting was a "thrill," struck fear in opponents, as well, and his passion for the game—and for playing linebacker—was evident every time he hit the field.

"Matt enjoys life to the fullest and loves the game of football; everything from the smells of the locker room to the rigors of the weight room," Cabral said in 1996. "He wells up with emotion, energy and pride, and pours it all out on the field."

In the spring of 1997, Russell was selected by the Detroit Lions in the fourth round of the NFL Draft, but injuries limited him to just 14 career games. Shortly after his playing career came to a close, Russell became a scout with the New England Patriots and Philadelphia Eagles. Since 2009, he has worked in the front office of the Denver Broncos, helping them to a victory in Super Bowl 50.

65 Nelson Spruce

Michael Westbrook may have been the most physically impressive receiver to ever come through Colorado. Rae Carruth, Shay Fields, Mike Pritchard, and Paul Richardson were among the most talented. Cliff Branch turned out to be the best of the bunch professionally. None of them could touch the numbers Nelson Spruce compiled during his four seasons with the Buffaloes, however.

Of course, Spruce benefitted from playing during a pass-happy era, but from 2012–15, he posted eye-popping numbers. Spruce racked up 294 catches for 3,347 yards and 23 touchdowns—all school records—during his career. At the time of his graduation, he had 79 more catches and 799 more yards than any receiver in CU history. During his four seasons, Spruce led the Buffs in receiving three times.

"I feel like I was under-recruited, but I've always been confident in myself," Spruce said as he wrapped up his career in 2015. "I knew there was no question I could be a playmaker at this level. The amount of records I was able to set, that was surprising."

Spruce was the first player in CU history with 100-plus catches in a season, hauling in 106 in 2014. He was just the third to post two 1,000-yard seasons. He also set a single-season record for touchdown receptions (12 in 2014) and caught a single-game record 19 passes in a double-overtime loss to California in 2014. No player in CU history had ever caught more than 11 passes in a game before his arrival, but he had 13 or more catches three times. In all, Spruce set 41 records at CU and he played in each of CU's 49 games from 2012–15, catching at least one pass in his final 38. He was named second-team All-Pac-12 twice.

"He can play in any style of offense and excel," his head coach, Mike MacIntyre, said. "He's also had a great work ethic. He's always been prepared to play every game. He keeps showing up every day and that's a credit to his toughness, his mental toughness and the way he takes care of his body."

Spruce, who graduated as the Pac-12's all-time leader in receptions (a record held for only a year), gained a reputation for running precise routes and catching just about everything thrown his way.

"I trust him a lot," quarterback Sefo Liufau said in 2015. "He's like a security blanket. He's always there for me. He's fast; not the fastest guy, but he runs really good routes which gives him the separation. He's got really good hands. I trust him in a one-on-one matchup with pretty much anyone in the country."

Spruce also returned punts during his career and once scooped up an onsides kickoff and took it to the end zone for a touchdown. While he never enjoyed a winning season at CU, Spruce left as the school's most prolific receiver—and perhaps its most reliable.

"That's why you play football, to be the best," he said. "Setting those records, it's something I'm always going to remember."

66 Steve Jones

Had it not been for the remarkable Hale Irwin, Steve Jones would be the most famous golfer to come out of CU. Frankly, had it not been for a collection of unfortunate injuries, Jones might have challenged Irwin's success on the links.

A native of New Mexico, Jones grew up in Yuma, Colorado, played at CU from 1977 to 1981, and had a remarkable career with the Buffs. He's the only player in program history with four top-10 finishes in the conference championships and the only one to lead the team in stroke average four consecutive years. He was also All-Big Eight four times and a second-team All-American as a senior.

Jones turned pro in 1981 and won eight events on the PGA Tour, with 44 top-10 finishes. Since 2011, Jones has played on the Champions Tour, with two top-10 and 14 top-25 finishes to his credit through 2018.

The greatest moment of his career came on Father's Day in 1996, June 16. At Oakland Hills Country Club in Bloomfield Hills, Michigan, Jones rolled a two-foot putt into the cup for a par on the 18th green to defeat Davis Love III and Tom Lehman for the United States Open championship.

"It was amazing," said Jones, who joined Irwin as the only Buffs to win the U.S. Open. "I thanked God right away after I won and raised my arms with my ball in one hand my putter in one hand. I have a picture, looking up to the heavens and, 'Thank you, Lord.' Probably my favorite memory. I can still see and feel the solid tee shot I hit on 18. I hit the driver really well all week and wasn't hooking the ball. I was just hitting a little draw. I just took it over the right bunker and hit a little draw into the fairway. I can still feel how solid that Covert driver, how solid I hit it."

While the 1996 U.S. Open was a moment he will never forget, his career was beset with injuries. His rookie year in 1981 was cut short with a broken thumb. He also spent three-and-a-half years recovering from a 1991 motorcycle accident; suffered another injury in 2003; another one in 2007 that cost him almost four years of his career; and an elbow injury in December of 2015 that wiped out another two years.

"A third of my career I've been injured and it seems like another third of it I've been coming back from an injury," he said. "I just haven't had a lot of good years. I think I've had maybe nine or 10 years is all in my career that were healthy years, where it felt like I could do something."

Despite his injuries, Jones' good years were memorable. He's been inducted into the CU Athletics Hall of Fame, the Colorado Sports Hall of Fame and the Colorado Golf Hall of Fame. And, he won a U.S. Open and was still playing professionally at the age of 60 in 2019.

"I truly believe it's a gift from God that enables you to do certain things that your dreams come true," he said. "It's been great. It's been a great game."

Aside from Irwin and Jones, CU's golf history has included Dale Douglass, who won three PGA Tour events and 11 times on the Champions Tour; 1953 NCAA champion Merle Backlund; and a dozen inductees to the Colorado Golf Hall of Fame.

CU's also had remarkable stability with coaching. Les Fowler coached the Buffs for 29 years from 1948 to 1976 and was succeeded by Mark Simpson, who coached for 29 years until 2005, when he lost a year-long battle with cancer. Since 2006, Roy Edwards has led the program.

In women's golf, Anne Kelly was in her 22nd season as head coach in 2019, and the program has featured several stellar players, including Emily Talley and Esther Lee.

67 Bill Mallory

Between Bill McCartney, Eddie Crowder, Dal Ward, and Fred Folsom, CU has had several football coaches who left a long-lasting impression on the program. Bill Mallory generally isn't mentioned among the CU legends, but his five-year tenure may be the most underrated in CU annals.

Mallory was hired in January of 1974 after leading Miami of Ohio to an 11–0 record in 1973. Mallory replaced Crowder, who retired from coaching but remained the Buffs' athletic director.

Most remembered for becoming the all-time wins leader at Indiana, where he coached from 1984 to 1996, Mallory enjoyed a successful run in Boulder, too. From 1974 to '78, he posted a record of 35–21–1 at CU, led them to a share of the Big Eight Conference title in 1976 and took them to a pair of bowl games.

Mallory led CU to a 9–3 record in 1975, a year that included a crushing loss at No. 1 Oklahoma. The No. 19 Buffs scored in the closing moments to pull within 21–20 and Mallory elected to kick the extra point for the tie. Tom Mackenzie's kick hooked left, however. In 1976, the Buffs beat Oklahoma in Boulder en route to a share of the Big Eight title. Mallory produced winning records in 1977 and 1978, as well, but the Buffs went 1–5 in their last

Tragedy in 1974

During the first few days of Bill Mallory's inaugural fall camp with the Buffaloes, tragedy struck. On August 23, sophomore quarterback Polie Poitier, a 19-year-old from Coral Gables, Florida, collapsed during a training run. The Buffs were in shorts and T-shirts and going though an 880-yard run on the track when Poitier suddenly slowed down, then stopped and knelt down. After being treated for several hours, Poitier seemed to be recovering. Early in the evening, however, he went into cardiac arrest. The next morning, on August 24, he died. It was determined he died of cardio-pulmonary arrest, but doctors believed the sickle cell trait (SCT) played a role. Poitier, a star quarterback in high school, played for CU's freshman team in 1973. He went through that season and spring practices in 1974 without incident and he passed a physical before the workout in August. The Poitier family was unaware he carried SCT, which is most common in black people. Poitier's was the first SCT-related death to be documented by the NCAA and it heightened the awareness of SCT in the sporting community. That fall, many teams around the country began to test athletes for SCT.

six games of 1978. Shortly after the season ended, Crowder fired Mallory because he wasn't seeing the type of progress he wanted in the program.

"I'm sorry to see it end this way," Mallory said. "I want to make it clear that I was released. I didn't resign. There was no way I was going to quit."

Mallory passed away May 25, 2018. Several of his former CU players attended a memorial the next month and remembered him as a tough, but highly respected coach.

"The Mallory men that were here needed to do that because he had a tremendous impact and influence on shaping our lives and shaping us as men," said Brian Cabral, who played linebacker at CU from 1975 to '77 and later spent more than 20 years as an assistant coach with the Buffs. "He shaped my life from what I accomplished playing, but also as a coach. He was a tough dude, but you knew he cared because all he cared about was your best, getting the best out of you and he knew what that was. He demanded only the best and nothing less."

After going 5–6 in 1974, Mallory had a winning record in each of his final four seasons with the Buffs. After he was fired, CU had six consecutive losing seasons.

"It was just such a great honor to play for him," said Tom Tesone, a CU safety from 1973 to '77. "He toughened us all up. We were all kind of soft in that Boulder era back in the '70s. He taught us a lot how to be men and how to work hard. I came back from three knee injuries and learned how to fight through all of that."

68 Pearl Street Mall

For decades, Boulder has been highly attractive for outdoor enthusiasts, runners, bikers and, of course, fans of the Colorado Buffaloes. No visit to Boulder would be complete without a stroll through the Pearl Street Mall—a four-block pedestrian mall in the heart of Boulder. The Mall is filled with shops, dining options and exceptional people watching.

In June of 1976, Pearl Street was closed to vehicle traffic between 11th and 15th streets, with the Mall opening in August of 1977. Since then, it has drawn thousands of patrons on a daily basis. The Mall features shops for everything from jewelry to outdoor gear; dozens of restaurants, bakeries, and ice cream shops; and four local breweries. There are also built-in play areas for the kids, street vendors, and entertaining street performers.

"Pearl Street represents what Boulder is all about," said Marcus Washington, who played football at CU from 1995 to '98. "If you want to know what Boulder is all about, if you want to know what the people are like, if you want to know what the atmosphere is like, Pearl Street is the place to go. Pearl Street is the center of Boulder. It's eclectic. It's what Boulder embodies as a whole because the people are so vast and so different and the shops are nice. When I was in school, I'd walk around down there and, more than anything, it's great people watching."

Pearl Street is also the place to be the night before a CU football home game. For more than a decade, the Pearl Street Stampede has kicked off home football weekends. Typically beginning around 7 p.m., the Stampede includes the CU Golden Buffalo Marching Band, with players and coaches also on hand for festivities.

In addition to Pearl Street, several restaurants are popular destinations in Boulder. Among the favorites:

Foolish Craig's Café: About a block east of the Mall, this is a good spot for breakfast, lunch and dinner, and it's a great place to get crepes.

The Mediterranean: Known as "The Med" and located near the Mall, there is a wide variety of options, from Italian, Spanish, French, and even Greek foods.

Pasta Jay's: Located on Pearl Street, a block west of the Mall, this is a favorite for those who love old style Italian cuisine.

The Sink: Located on The Hill in Boulder, The Sink has been serving Boulder residents since 1923. It's known for its burgers and pizza. U.S. President Barack Obama made a surprise visit here in 2012 and ordered a pizza.

69 Women's Lacrosse

U.S. President Richard Nixon signed Title IX as a federal civil rights law in 1972. In part, it required equal educational and athletic opportunities for men and women. Since its implementation in 1975, higher education institutions have had to make sure they are in compliance with Title IX and that led to an important addition to the CU athletic department in 2012.

CU had an imbalance of participation numbers and money being spent on men's sports compared to women's so, in February of 2012, athletic director Mike Bohn announced the addition of women's lacrosse. The sport was rapidly growing at lower levels around the country and especially in Colorado, and adding it as the

10th women's sport at CU made it a natural fit. It was the first time in 16 years that CU had added a sport.

Given two years to get the program running, 27-year-old Ann Elliott was hired as head coach. Elliott had won three national championships as a player at Northwestern and then three more as an assistant with the Wildcats. CU's fledgling program took flight in 2014 and instantly became a winner. The Buffs won their inaugural game, 12–4 against Stetson University, and finished 11–8 that season.

The Pac-12 conference didn't sponsor the sport at the time, so the Buffs joined the Mountain Pacific Sports Federation (MPSF) and reached the conference semifinals in each of the first three years. In her fourth season, 2017, Elliott guided the Buffs to the NCAA Tournament for the first time.

The 2018 season was a breakthrough campaign. For the first time, the Pac-12 formed its own women's lacrosse conference. CU won the regular season title, qualified for the NCAA Tournament again and advanced to the second round.

During CU's first six seasons, the program had six All-Americans and several All-Conference players. Elliott was named the regional coach of the year and conference coach of the year twice. As the Buffaloes concluded their sixth season in 2019, it was clear that CU had succeeded not only in becoming Title IX compliant, but in building a winning program that stood up against some of the nation's best teams.

"Since I started building this program, the goal has been to get better every year and every season," Elliott said. "I think we have done that."

70 Daniel Graham

During the summer of 1997, a 6-foot-3 true freshman tight end showed up to an offseason workout with the Colorado football team. As a graduate of Denver's Thomas Jefferson High School, making the trek to Boulder was easy for Daniel Graham, and it gave him an opportunity to get a jump-start on his college career. Although it was just a 7-on–7 passing practice with no pads and helmets, Graham made his veteran future teammates take notice.

"He ran a pass route against one of our linebackers and beat him soundly and caught the pass," said Marcus Washington, who was a junior starting cornerback that year. "I'm standing on the sideline going, 'Wow, okay.' Then, it was my turn in the rotation to cover him. The kid comes off the line faster than I thought a tight end could come off the line of scrimmage, does a double move and runs a post route by me and catches a touchdown pass. I knew right then this kid was going to be good. He hadn't even officially started school yet."

Yeah, Graham was pretty good. In fact, he's arguably the best tight end in CU history, or at least the most decorated. After red-shirting in 1997, Graham caught 106 passes for 1,543 yards and 11 touchdowns from 1998 to 2001. As a senior in 2001, Graham was the sixth unanimous All-American in CU history and he won the John Mackey Award, presented to the nation's top tight end.

"I knew he was going to be good, but I didn't imagine he was going to be that good," Washington said.

The son of seven-year NFL veteran Tom Graham, who played linebacker for the Denver Broncos, San Diego Chargers, and Buffalo Bills, Graham began to make a name for himself at Thomas Jefferson High. He was an All-State performer, playing linebacker

Tight Ends in the Draft

Daniel Graham is one of several CU tight ends to be selected in the NFL Draft over the years:

1962—Jerry Hillebrand, New York Giants, 1st round
1967—Sam Harris, New Orleans Saints, 8th round
1974—J.V. Cain, St. Louis Cardinals, 1st round
1977—Don Hasselbeck, New England Patriots, 2nd round
1981—Bob Niziolek, Detroit Lions, 8th round
1984—Dave Hestera, Kansas City Chiefs, 9th round
1987—Jon Embree, Los Angeles Rams, 6th round
1995—Christian Fauria, Seattle Seahawks, 2nd round
2002—Daniel Graham, New England Patriots, 1st round
2006—Joe Klopfenstein, St. Louis Rams, 2nd round
2006—Quinn Sypniewski, Baltimore Ravens, 5th round
2013—Nick Kasa, Oakland Raiders, 6th round

and tight end for the Spartans. Several schools, including Arizona State and Southern California, wanted Graham, but he was set on becoming a Buffalo. His attraction to CU began during his sophomore year of high school, when he came to Boulder for a debate conference with his school.

"I skipped out on that and I walked into the stadium right when Rashaan Salaam rushes for 2,000 yards," Graham said. "I just remember what an atmosphere Folsom Field was and to see that. I had the 2,000 sign hanging up in my room. That was my earliest memory of Folsom Field."

The opportunity to play at CU was one he didn't want to pass up.

"It's just a great atmosphere and the best mascot in college football," he said. "There's nowhere else where you can play a game and see the foothills right behind you. It's just an exciting time playing there."

Graham proved to be an all-around tight end with the Buffaloes, excelling as a blocker and as a receiver. Through 2018,

Graham's 51 catches in 2001 were still tied for the most in a single season by a CU tight end. He shares the mark with Jon Embree, who was Graham's position coach at CU.

"He was a quiet leader who did his job and just brought his hard hat and came to work every day," Washington said. "From the time he came to CU, he embodied professionalism, because he just did his job."

Graham was selected by the New England Patriots in the first round (21st overall) of the 2002 NFL Draft. He played 11 seasons in the NFL, including five with the Patriots and four with the Broncos. He also played with the Tennessee Titans and the New Orleans Saints, wrapping up his career in 2012 after compiling 224 catches for 2,490 yard and 25 touchdowns. A two-time Super Bowl champion with the Patriots, Graham returned to CU after his playing career and completed his degree. In 2018, he was inducted into the CU Athletics Hall of Fame.

"It means so much," he said of the Hall of Fame honor. "When I enrolled here, I never really imagined this would happen. I guess I did something special here when I was here to get this honor, and I'm appreciative of it."

71 Walton Breaks the Barrier

When Claude Walton came to the University of Colorado in 1933, he didn't have any grand ideas of becoming a pioneer or a Buffaloes' legend.

"I was just trying to go to school," he said in 2008.

That, in itself, was a challenge during a time when the world was going through the Great Depression and racial segregation was a way of life in the United States. Nevertheless, Walton became one of the first black students in CU history, while breaking barriers in athletics. A graduate of Denver West High School, Walton, who died in 2014 at the age of 100, became the first black student-athlete in CU history to earn a varsity letter and became the first CU athlete—regardless of race—to earn All-American honors in any sport.

An exceptional discus thrower for the track and field team, Walton lettered four times, was a two-time Rocky Mountain Athletic Conference champion and earned All-American honors as a senior in 1936. Walton might have competed in the 1936 Berlin Olympics had it not been for an injury. During a pick-up softball game, he sprained an ankle and was unable to participate in an Olympic qualifying meet.

A music major who excelled at playing the piano, Walton worked as a hasher at a CU fraternity house to pay for his room and board. He made extra money by playing the piano in local bands and orchestras. As one of the few black students on campus at the time, he also dealt with discrimination, in Boulder and on the road. Walton once told ESPN about a track team road trip to the Kansas Relays. The CU track team gathered for breakfast at the hotel dining room. A hostess told Walton he would have to eat in the kitchen, however.

"That turned out to be the most embarrassing moment," he told ESPN. "Here I was a member of the team, and the team was in the dining room. So I'm good enough to be on the team, but I'm not good enough to have accommodations with the team? It was the one time I rebelled. I did not go out to the kitchen. It just so happened that there was a black fraternity (house)... and I went down and spent the night. The coach never knew what happened to me, and I never said anything about it."

Typically, Walton dealt with the discrimination by putting his head down and pouring his energy into school, work, and athletics.

"We were products of accepted segregation, but it was acceptance with dignity," he said. "It was the fact that we acted like human beings and showed we weren't barbarians. It was because of that those who came after us had an easier time."

During his senior year, Walton received a job offer with the Chicago Parks Department (CPD). Despite being a few credits short of his degree, he accepted the offer because jobs were so hard to come by during the Depression. He spent the next 45 years working for the CPD. In 2008, Walton received an honorary degree and was inducted into the CU Athletic Hall of Fame.

"I've always had a good relationship with the school, and it's nice to be recognized," Walton said. "But all this attention that has been made about me being the first, I never thought about that then."

He will, however, forever be remembered as a pioneer and one of the greatest athletes to compete for the Buffaloes.

72 Frosty Cox

For 15 minutes, the start of the men's basketball game on March 6, 1950, was delayed as the crowd at CU Fieldhouse honored Forrest "Frosty" Cox. In the final home game of the season and of Cox's tenure as head coach, the Buffaloes wanted to send him off in style. During the celebration, "he received, among other things, a shotgun and honorary membership in the Colorado band," according to the game recap printed in *The Daily Oklahoman*. No word on what those other things might have been, but they were well-deserved gifts for the longest-tenured and most successful coach in CU basketball history at that time.

From 1935 to 1950, Cox coached the Buffs for 13 seasons, still the second-longest tenure in the program. CU did not field a team from 1942 to '44 because of World War II, but Cox coached before and after the war, compiling a record of 147–89. His .623 winning percentage is the best in CU history, and only three coaches have won more total games. Cox led the Buffs to four conference championships, the National Invitation Tournament (NIT) twice and to the NCAA Tournament three times. His 1941–42 team made the program's first appearance in the Final Four.

"He was a no-nonsense type of person," his son, Forrest Jr., told CUBuffs.com upon his father's induction to the CU Athletics Hall of Fame in 2014. "He was dedicated to perfection and discipline…. On the court, he was pretty intense."

Cox, who was born in Newton, Kansas, won several state titles as a high school player. He then was a two-sport star at the University of Kansas, earning All-Conference honors in football and All-American honors in basketball, playing for legendary coach "Phog" Allen. Upon graduation, Cox was hired by Allen as an assistant coach and he held that job for five years before coming to CU at the age of 28.

CU hired Cox, in part, because he agreed to be an assistant coach for the football team. He filled that role for seven seasons, 1935–41, under three different head coaches. Basketball was Cox's true passion, however, and he took CU to new heights. In addition to leading them to national tournaments, Cox coached four All-Americans at CU: Robert Doll, Jack Harvey, Leason McCloud, and Jim Wilcoxon.

Cox also coached Russell "Sox" Walseth in the 1940s and later hired him as freshman coach. Walseth would later become the program's all-time leader in wins (261) and seasons coached (20).

During World War II, Cox served with the Army's special service forces. At the end of the war, he coached in basketball clinics in Europe for three months before returning to CU.

At just 42 years old, Cox retired from CU and started a ranching business in Kansas. His love for basketball, however, pulled him back into coaching. In 1955, he took the head coaching job at the University of Montana, going 80–85 before he was fired after the 1962 season. Just a couple months later, he died suddenly from a heart attack, at just 54 years old.

Although a tough coach, Cox often got the best out of his teams. According to CUBuffs.com, Walseth once said of Cox, "He was tough-nosed… but he was a good guy."

73 In the Trenches

In front of every good running back is a talented offensive line and CU has been fortunate with the amount of exceptional linemen to come through Boulder. It's probably no coincidence that CU's glory days on the football field coincided with arguably the best line the program has ever seen. It was a group led by Joe Garten and Jay Leeuwenburg.

In 1990, Garten became the first CU offensive lineman to earn unanimous All-American honors. A year later, Leeuwenburg became the second.

Garten, a 6-foot-3, 280-pound guard from Placentia, California, was a two-time first-team All-American, in 1989 and 1990, and was runner-up for the Outland Trophy—presented to the country's best offensive lineman—in his senior year. Leeuwenburg, from Kirkwood, Missouri, was a 6-foot-3, 265-pound center who earned All-American honorable mention in 1990 and was one of six finalists for the Outland Trophy in 1991.

Garten and Leeuwenburg were the anchors of the offensive line during CU's remarkable run in 1989–90, when it went 22–2–1 and won a national title. Three different players—Eric Bieniemy, J.J. Flannigan and Darian Hagan—rushed for over 1,000 yards behind them.

Four of the five starting offensive linemen in 1990 were drafted by the NFL, including Garten (sixth round in 1991 by Green Bay) and Leeuwenburg (ninth round in 1992 by Kansas City). Tackles Mark Vander Poel (fourth round in 1991 by Indianapolis) and Ariel Solomon (10th round in 1991 by Pittsburgh) were also drafted.

CU's history of great linemen goes back decades and includes legends such as Mike Montler, Joe Romig, and John Wooten in the 1950s and 60s; and Mark Koncar, Matt Miller, Don Popplewell, Leon White, and the Brock brothers in the 1970s.

Some of the recent great linemen:

David Bakhtiari: Second-team All-Pac-12 twice, he was a fourth-round pick of the Green Bay Packers in 2013. Named second-team All-Pro in 2016 and 2017 and first-team All-Pro in 2018.

Brad Bedell: Second-team All-American in 1999, he was a sixth-round pick of the Cleveland Browns in 2000.

Tony Berti: Third-team All-American in 1994, he was a sixth-round pick of the San Diego Chargers in 1995.

Andre Gurode: First-team All-American in 2001, he was drafted by the Dallas Cowboys in the second round. Named to the Pro Bowl five times in his 12-year career.

Heath Irwin: A first-team All-American in 1995, he was a fourth-round pick by the New England Patriots.

Ryan Miller: Third-team All-American in 2011, he was a fifth-round pick by the Browns.

Chris Naeole: Consensus All-American in 1996, he was the highest drafted lineman ever from CU, going 10th overall to the New Orleans Saints. Started 150 of his 154 NFL games.

Nate Solder: Consensus All-American in 2010, he was selected 17th overall by the Patriots and won two Super Bowls.

Bryan Stoltenberg: Consensus All-American in 1995, he was a sixth-round choice of the Chargers.

74 Cliff Branch

At his own 32-yard line, Cliff Branch fielded an Ohio State punt, avoided a tackler, made a move to his right, and raced down the sidelines for a 68-yard touchdown that gave Colorado a 13–0 lead in what eventually became a 20–14 upset of the sixth-ranked Buckeyes.

"We worked for two weeks on making it difficult for him and we made just one mistake today and it cost us," Ohio State coach Woody Hayes said.

Branch played just two seasons at Colorado, but he was the type of player that could change a game in an instant. His 97-yard kickoff return for a touchdown helped the Buffs upset Penn State in 1970, and his punt return touchdowns against LSU and Ohio State in 1971 were pivotal in those upset wins.

"He made some of the most exciting runs I've ever seen," longtime CU administrator Fred Casotti wrote in 1972. "Literally, breathtaking. I've never seen a player who could bring the entire Colorado cheering section to its feet by just fielding a punt."

A Houston native, Branch attended Wharton County Junior College in Texas before his dynamic two seasons with the Buffs, from 1970 to '71. CU ran the run-oriented triple option offense, which makes it tough for a receiver to pile up statistics, but Branch caught 36 passes for 665 yards and three touchdowns, while rushing for 354 yards and five touchdowns. His 18.5-yards per catch average is among the best in CU history.

As a returner, he was the first Division I player in the country with eight career touchdowns (six on punts, two on kickoffs). Everyone else with eight return touchdowns played at least three seasons.

Branch holds CU records for career punt return average (16.7), career punt return touchdowns (six) and single-season punt return touchdowns (four). No other player in CU history has had more than three career return touchdowns.

Branch was arguably the fastest player ever at CU, not only in football, but on the track. Branch set several school records in track, including running the 100-meters in 10.0 seconds in the preliminaries of the 1972 NCAA championships. Newspaper accounts at the time wrote about Branch tying the world record in the 60-yard dash (5.9 seconds) and clocking a record-setting time of 9.2 seconds in the 100-yard sprint. He was also part of a 4x400 relay team that still holds the CU record. At the 1971 United States Track and Field Federation championships, he tied meet records in the 100-yard sprint (9.2) and 220-yard sprint (20.2).

Branch's true passion, however, was football.

"Playing on a team is more gratifying than an individual sport because it's about a group of guys trying to achieve the same goal," he said years later. "You have to be unselfish."

In the spring of 1972, Branch was selected in the fourth-round of the NFL Draft by the Oakland Raiders. He spent his entire 14-year career, from 1972 to 1985, with the Raiders, catching 501 passes for 8,685 yards and 67 touchdowns. A four-time Pro Bowler, he helped the Raiders win the Super Bowl three times.

Branch is considered one of the best players to be excluded from the Pro Football Hall of Fame, but in 2018 he was inducted into the California Sports Hall of Fame. In 2010, he was inducted into the CU Athletics Hall of Fame.

"It's a very special honor to be recognized by your alma mater," he said at the time. "I feel truly blessed. I'm a Buff all the way."

75 Boyd Dowler

As a youth, Boyd Dowler knew the expectations for him in athletics were high. His father, Walter, was a star football player at the University of Wyoming from 1931 to '33 and later became a longtime high school coach. Walter coached football, basketball, and track and is one of the few coaches in Wyoming history to lead two different high schools to football championships.

"I was really raised to be a good player," Dowler said during a 2016 interview with the National Football Foundation. "He was a little disappointed for a while because it took a long time to happen."

It may have taken a while, but when it happened, Dowler became a legendary football player, not only at CU but in the NFL. Playing at CU from 1956 to '58, Dowler started as a single-wing quarterback—throwing, blocking, running, and catching—while also handling punting duties and playing defense.

"(Walter) instilled in me a passion for competition and basically what I developed into was a pretty good player and I could do a lot of things," Dowler said.

A three-year starter at quarterback, Dowler threw for 727 yards and six touchdowns, ran for three touchdowns and caught 41 passes for 628 yards and six touchdowns in his career. He still ranks among the best in CU history for career punting average (43.61 yards) and interceptions on defense (10). As a senior in 1958, he was first-team All-Big Seven and received UPI All-American honorable mention.

"Boyd was a very talented athlete," Green Bay Packers legend Jerry Kramer said of his former teammate in 2017. "He led Colorado in passing, running, receiving, and punting. But when you think about that, how the hell could you lead the team in both passing and receiving? You can't throw to yourself!"

Certainly, Dowler didn't throw to himself, but he was an expert in running coach Dal Ward's single-wing. In that offense, the quarterback is typically more of a blocker than a thrower and he was almost as likely to run a route than drop back to throw. At 6-foot-5, 220 pounds, Dowler was a mountain of a man and perfect for the offense.

A third-round selection of the Green Bay Packers in 1959, Dowler focused on being a receiver and became an immediate star, earning NFL rookie of the year honors.

"Boyd was a mature kid," Kramer said. "He understood the game and what we were doing and he was just a bit ahead of most rookies. I think his father coaching him played a part in that. I think Boyd's confidence was one of the big reasons why he was accepted so quickly and completely."

Dowler played 12 years in the NFL, the first 11 with the Packers. He caught 474 passes for 7,270 yards and 40 touchdowns and helped the Packers win five NFL championships and victories in Super Bowls I and II. Dowler was a two-time Pro Bowler, was selected to the NFL's All-Decade team for the 1960s, and is a member of the Packers Hall of Fame.

Early in his NFL career, he also served in the Army reserves and he was called to active duty during the 1961 season. "I played in games on weekends, either on a weekend pass or leave," he said. "I never missed a play. Two terms on active duty with the Army and I never missed a game. That was kind of unusual. I was a private with the Red Arrow 32nd Division from Wisconsin, attached to an artillery unit out of Milwaukee."

After retirement, Dowler worked as an assistant coach in the NFL for 15 years before going into scouting.

"It's fortunate that I got to do something I love for a lifetime," he said when inducted to the CU Athletics Hall of Fame in 2012. "I got great friends and family and I've got football to thank for all of that. I've got real fond memories. And it all started at CU."

76 Women's Basketball Stars

Ceal Barry was eight years into her successful tenure as the Colorado women's basketball coach when a 5-foot-6 point guard from Kennedy High School in Cedar Rapids, Iowa, chose to play for the Buffaloes.

"When Shelley Sheetz made a commitment to come to Colorado, I think we elevated," Barry said. "We went from Big Eight and regional [success] to national. She was our first and only All-American. She gave us the opportunity to recruit better players."

A high school All-American who was recruited by nearly 70 colleges around the country, Sheetz played at CU from 1991 to '95 and put together the most decorated career of anyone in the program. In 1995, Sheetz became the first and only player in CU history to earn first-team All-American honors from the Associated Press. She was the Big Eight Conference player of the year that season and a finalist for the Naismith Award. She was also first-team All-Big Eight three times and second team as a freshman;

MVP of the 1995 Big Eight tournament; and the Big Eight new-comer of the year in 1992.

"She hit big shots for us and she understood the game," Barry said. "She also was very respectful of the seniors when she was a freshman and sophomore. She respected the leadership and she bought into the culture. She loved the culture that we had."

Statistically, Sheetz is still among CU's all-time leaders in points (1,775), assists (514), steals (287), made 3-pointers (252), starts (127) and minutes played (4,236). She started each of her 127 career games.

Sheetz's greatest impact, however, was in elevating the winning culture at CU. During her time with the Buffs, they went 106–21, won three Big Eight regular season titles and two conference tournaments. They also went to the NCAA Elite Eight twice and the Sweet 16 three times.

"Shelley wanted to win more than any player that I've ever coached," Barry said. "She aspired to win. Winning mattered to Shelley Sheetz and she would do whatever it took."

CU has had dozens of exceptional players throughout its history in women's basketball, but the ultra-competitive Sheetz, who later played professionally before embarking on a long career in coaching, is arguably at the top of the list.

Other top players in CU women's basketball history:

Sandy Bean (1978–82): One of the program's first stars, she earned all-region honors twice and was one of only three players to rank top 20 in scoring and top 10 in rebounds and assists in school history.

Tera Bjorklund (2000–04): Ranks fourth in scoring (1,858 points) and her final two years were sensational. She was first-team All-Big 12 twice and a finalist for the Wade Trophy, presented to the nation's top player, as a senior.

Isabelle Fijalkowski (1994–95): The 6'5" center from France played just one season at CU, but was remarkable. She earned AP

All-American honorable mention, first-team All-Big Eight and NCAA West Regional MVP honors.

Crystal Ford (1985–89): A three-time All-Big Eight performer, she's top 20 in CU history in points and rebounds. In 1989, she was Big Eight tournament MVP.

Chucky Jeffery (2009–13): Dynamic point guard ranks sixth in CU history in points and fifth in assists and rebounds—the only player to rank top six in all three. She's also third in steals and earned first-team All-Pac-12 honors twice.

Jamillah Lang (1990–94): Named co-Big Eight player of the year in 1994, she earned All-Conference honors twice and All-Big Eight tournament honors three times, including tournament MVP in 1992.

Kennedy Leonard (2015–19): Closed her career as the program's all-time leader in assists, while ranking top 10 in scoring and steals. Earned first-team All-Pac-12 honors twice.

Amy Mathern (1989–93): Tough player from nearby Lyons wasn't asked to be a scorer, but started nearly every game and ranks top 15 in history in steals and assists.

Jackie McFarland (2004–08): Athletic forward is third in CU history in points and rebounds and second with 46 double-doubles. Earned All-Big 12 honors three times, twice on the first team.

Mandy Nightingale (1998–02): Exceptional point guard who ranks fourth in CU history in assists and top 15 in scoring. She earned All-Big 12 honors twice.

Erin Scholz (1993–97): One of the best all-around frontcourt players CU has had, she leads all "bigs" in assists (11th overall), while ranking second in rebounds and eighth in scoring. Earned All-Conference honors four times and was All-American honorable mention as a senior. Was also Big Eight tournament MVP as a junior.

Brittany Spears (2007–11): CU's all-time leading scorer (2,185 points), she's also fourth in rebounds (997) and earned All-Big 12 honors four times. Scored in double figures in more games (111) than anyone in CU history.

Tracy Tripp (1985–89): One of only six players to rank top 15 in scoring and top 10 in assists, she's also among the leaders in steals, starts and minutes played. Earned All-Conference honors twice.

Bridget Turner (1985–89): She and Jeffery are the only players to rank top 10 in points, rebounds and assists. She held the assist record until Leonard broke it in 2019. She was All-Big Eight four times and the Big Eight player of the year in 1989. She later became one of the first women to play for the Harlem Globetrotters.

Lisa Van Goor (1980–85): In the conversation with Sheetz for the best player in program history, she's second to Spears in points (2,067), but first in scoring average (18.0), rebounds (1,127), blocks (281) and double-doubles (59). She was All-Conference three times and a two-time finalist for the Wade Trophy.

77 Hike the Flatirons

On a crisp, 40-degree day in December of 2018, CU athletics personnel picked up newly hired head football coach Mel Tucker from the airport and knew just where to take him for his introductory interview. Despite the chill in the air, CU filmed the segment with Tucker at Chautauqua Park, with the Flatiron mountains in the background.

"The Flatirons, to me, are the most iconic natural structure that has relevance to a university," said Curtis Snyder, who grew up in Boulder and works in the CU sports information department. "The Flatirons are Boulder."

The Flatirons are flat rock formations that are located on the east side of Green Mountain. Rising above the background of Folsom Field, the Flatirons provide breathtaking views and pictures of Boulder and the CU campus, but they are also a destination for many outdoor enthusiasts. There is a long history of rock climbing at the Flatirons, with three main areas that are visited each year. The first and third Flatirons are the most popular for climbing, but each of the areas offer something different. Exploring the Flatirons could be a full day of adventure.

"I think it's a must for visitors," Snyder said. "As a high school kid growing up in this city, we did that on the weekends."

In addition to the Flatirons, Boulder offers many options for those looking to enjoy the outdoors, including:

Boulder Creek: Flowing out of Boulder Canyon and into the heart of the city, Boulder Creek is a popular destination for residents and visitors. Walkers, joggers and bikers frequent the path that runs for miles along the creek. People also enjoy fishing, tubing, and swimming in the creek.

Boulder Falls: One of the more well-known destinations along Boulder Canyon, the Falls are located about halfway between Boulder and Nederland. It is a short, 100-yard hike, leading to a picturesque, 70-foot waterfall.

Chautauqua Park: Located at the base of the foothills and only about a mile and a half from downtown Boulder, Chautauqua has a family-friendly park, perfect for picnics and other activities. Nearby is the trailhead, frequented by hikers, bikers and rock climbers.

Flagstaff Mountain: About 20 minutes from the heart of Boulder is Flagstaff Mountain, which offers a variety of hiking trails, from easy to moderate. The top of the mountain is a popular location for stargazing.

Walker Ranch Loop Trail: A moderate mountain hike just a short, 25-minute drive from downtown Boulder, Walker Ranch is filled with spectacular views along its 7.9-mile loop. Near the trail-head, there are picnic areas.

78 The Hawk Era

Following the tumultuous end to the Gary Barnett era at CU, the Buffaloes felt they had hit a home run when luring Dan Hawkins to Boulder in December of 2005. CU was reeling as a program, but Hawkins was coming off a five-year run at Boise State in which he went 53–11 and won four Western Athletic Conference titles. In a previous stint, he had won three conference titles in five years at NAIA school Willamette University. Hawkins was tabbed as the man to get the Buffs back on track.

"There have been some scars, but we'll get over that," he said during his introductory press conference. "So let's throw a little 'Hawk Love' out there and let's get going."

CU was overflowing with optimism as the Hawkins era was set to begin in 2006—and then reality set in. In Hawkins' debut, the Buffs hosted Division I-AA Montana State, and walked off the field with a 19–10 loss. CU lost its first six games that year and finished 2–10. Hawk Love quickly faded. Although he did lead the Buffs to a bowl appearance in 2007, he had a five-year record of 19–39.

Hawkins' tenure featured some spectacular wins, including upsetting No. 3 Oklahoma (2007), No. 21 West Virginia (2008), and No. 17 Kansas (2009) and a dramatic 29–27 win against Georgia on ESPN in 2010. His tenure also featured monumental losses and unfulfilled promises. He declared the Buffs would win 10 games in 2009, and then went 3–9 and was nearly fired. CU brought him back for 2010, but many people saw the end as being near.

After the win against Georgia, the Buffs were 3–1, but then lost their next four. Next up was a trip to Kansas, which had lost 11 conference games in a row. CU led 45–17 in the fourth quarter before an epic meltdown. Kansas scored 35 consecutive points to hand the Buffs a 52–45 loss. The next day, athletic director Mike Bohn pulled the plug and fired Hawkins with three games left in the season.

"Really, ending the negativity was what it was all about," Bohn said. "The divisiveness and the disenfranchisement of our fan base… we just felt it was time to end that."

Head coach Dan Hawkins holds up the Centennial Cup after winning the 2007 Rocky Mountain Showdown against Colorado State. (Getty Images / Doug Pensinger)

Cody Hawkins

For much of Dan Hawkins' time at CU, his starting quarterback was his son, Cody. The 5-foot-11, 190-pounder was probably better suited for playing in a smaller conference and was nearly headed to Boise State before his father got the job at CU. With the Buffs, his limitations as a player were evident at times and fans often felt that Dan favored his son. Cody started every game in 2007 (leading them to a bowl game), but then shared the job with Tyler Hansen from 2008–10. Although not an overwhelming fan favorite—in part because of his father—Cody handled a tough situation with maturity and class and was actually a talented quarterback who gave everything he had to help the Buffs win. He left CU as the program's all-time leader in passing yards (7,409) and touchdown passes (60).

Hawk Love had fully dried up at that point and few fans were sad to see him go. Hawkins had cleaned up the program off the field, but the losses piled up and he upset some of the alumni, who felt he didn't respect all of the program's traditions. Ultimately, Hawkins' tenure will be remembered for the epic losses, the failure to turn the program around and one unforgettable press conference tirade.

Speaking to local reporters before spring practices in 2007, Hawkins talked about an anonymous letter from the parent of a player who complained about the lack of time off before summer conditioning. He then calmly said, "Here's my point …"

Hawkins then raised his voice and yelled, "It's Division I football! It's the Big 12! It ain't intramurals! You've got two weeks after finals, you've got a week at July Fourth and you get a week before camp starts. That's a month! That's probably more vacation than you guys (in the media) get! And, we're a little bummed out that we don't get three weeks?!"

Hawkins then lowered his voice and finished the rant with, "Go play intramurals, brother. Go play intramurals."

79 Rae Carruth

Wearing a white T-shirt, leather jacket, and skull cap, Rae Carruth walked out of Sampson Correctional Institution in North Carolina and into the passenger seat of a Chevy Tahoe. For the first time in 19 years, the former CU receiver was a free man.

Once possessing star potential, Carruth's story took a turn that shocked many people. Carruth, who grew up in Sacramento, California, came to CU in the fall of 1992 and immediately wowed his teammates with talent and blazing speed.

"He kicked my ass every time I lined up in front of him," said Marcus Washington, a cornerback who went on to play in the NFL after his CU career.

During his four years with the Buffs, Carruth caught 135 passes for 2,540 yards and 20 touchdowns—numbers that still rank among the best in CU history. He earned All-Conference honors twice and All-American honors as a senior. He was twice voted as the team's offensive MVP.

"Being a teammate of Rae Carruth and watching him on the field was almost like being a fan in the stands, waiting for them to throw him the football, because you knew it was either going to be a touchdown or a big play," Washington said. "The guy was dynamic."

The guy was also a great teammate, with a sense of humor.

"Truth be told, as a teammate, Rae actually was very caring," Washington said. "If you needed a ride home from practice, if you had a question about something, he'd help. Even going up against him, he would beat me several times on plays and then on our way back to the huddle, he would give me advice. As a teammate, he was cool as hell. He was somebody, personally, I looked up to."

Carruth was selected in the first round (27th overall) of the 1997 NFL Draft by the Carolina Panthers and wound up playing 22 games, with 62 catches for 804 yards and four touchdowns. His football career came to a sudden end, however. On November 16, 1999, Carruth's girlfriend, Cherica Adams, who was eight months pregnant, was shot several times while in her car near Carruth's home in Charlotte. Adams' baby boy was delivered through emergency C-section and survived, but Adams died on December 14.

Carruth was later captured in the trunk of a car at a motel in Tennessee. While acquitted of first-degree murder, he was convicted in 2001 of conspiracy to commit murder after he hired Van Brett Watkins and Michael Kennedy to kill Adams. Watkins confessed to being the gunman and was sentenced to a minimum of 40 years in prison. Kennedy was the driver of the car from which Watkins shot and was released from prison in 2011.

"I was floored at hearing about the arrest and the whole situation," Washington said. "I was surprised. It was completely out of the character of the person that I knew as a teammate. Completely in shock."

Most of Carruth's CU teammates and coaches were shocked, but Carruth would wind up spending nearly 19 years in prison before his release on October 22, 2018. The baby, Chancellor Lee Adams, was born with cerebral palsy and raised by his grandmother, Saundra Adams. Although Carruth has never admitted to the crime, he wrote a letter to Saundra Adams in February of 2018 and in that letter said, "I want to sincerely apologize to you for the senseless act that led to the death of your daughter Cherica and the permanent mental and physical difficulties that Chancellor has to suffer through.... Having had time to look back and ponder on how the events of that night unfolded, I want you to know that I take full responsibility for everything. I could have done a better job of keeping Cherica and Chancellor out of harms way. And it's something that will definitely weight on me for the rest of my life."

80 Cross Country & Track Olympians

At the 2016 Summer Olympics in Rio de Janeiro, Brazil, two former Buffaloes claimed bronze medals in their events. Jenny (Barringer) Simpson won bronze in the 1,500 meters, while her training partner, Emma Coburn, took home the bronze in the 3,000-meter steeplechase. They were the first American women to medal in those events.

The success of Barringer and Coburn continued a long tradition of Olympic performances by former CU athletes. From 1948 to 2016, CU's track/cross country programs produced 22 Olympians. Unless noted, all competed for the United States.

Men

David Bolen (1948 Olympics): In London, he was fourth in the 400 meters.

Art Burns (1984): He threw the discus at the games in Los Angeles.

Alan Culpepper (2000 and 2004): In Sydney, Australia, he ran the 10,000 meters, and in Athens, Greece, in 2000 he was 12th in the marathon.

Jeremy Dodson (2016): Representing Samoa, he competed in the 200 meters in Rio de Janeiro.

Adam Goucher (2000): Competing in Sydney, he reached the finals in the 5,000 meters, placing 13th.

Bill Jankunis (1976): He competed in the high jump in Montreal.

Billy Nelson (2008): In Beijing, China, he finished 29th in the 3,000-meter steeplechase

Dathan Ritzenhein (2004, 2008, and 2012): After competing in the 10,000 meters in Athens, he was ninth in the marathon in Beijing in 2008 and 13th in the 10,000 meters at London in 2012.

Bill Toomey (1968): In Mexico City, he won gold in the pentathlon, the only gold ever won by a former Buff.

Jorge Torres (2008): Running in the 10,000 meters in Beijing, he placed 25th overall.

Ted Woods (1960): He was on the 1,600-meter relay team in Rome.

Women

Jenny (Barringer) Simpson (2008, 2012 and 2016): She was ninth in the 3,000-meter steeplechase in Beijing, reached the semifinals in the 1,500 meters in London and then won bronze in the 1,500 in Rio de Janeiro. She set an American record in the 1,500 in 2016.

Emma Coburn (2012 and 2016): She was ninth in the 3,000-meter steeplechase in London before winning bronze in the event in Rio de Janeiro. Her bronze medal race set an American record—which she broke a year later.

Hannah Cooper (2000): She competed for Liberia in the 100-meter hurdles in Sydney.

Shayne (Willie) Culpepper (2000 and 2004): She ran in the 1,500 meters in Sydney and then in the 5,000 meters in Athens.

Mary (Decker) Slaney (1984, 1988, and 1996): Competed in the 3,000 meters in Los Angeles and was one of the leaders 1,700 meters into the race until she fell after making contact with Zola Budd. She didn't finish the race.

Jane Wardwell Frederick (1972 and 1976): In Munich, Germany, in 1972, she was 21st in the pentathlon. Four years later, in Montreal, she was seventh.

Kara (Grgas-Wheeler) Goucher (2008 and 2012): The only Buff to compete in two events in the same Olympiad, she was ninth in the 5,000 meters and 10th in the 10,000 meters in Beijing. She was 11th in the marathon in London in 2012.

Shalaya Kipp (2012): Competing in the 3,000-meter steeplechase in London, she reached the semifinals.

Karol (Damon) Rovelto (2000): In Sydney, she competed in the high jump.

Yvonne Kanazawa Scott (1996 and 2000): She competed for Japan in the 100-meter hurdles in both Atlanta and Sydney, Australia.

Annette Tannander (1976 and 1984): Competing for Sweden, she was seventh in the high jump in Montreal in 1976 and 14th in the heptathlon in Los Angeles.

81 Big 8 Champs... and A Scandal

When CU joined the Big 7 Conference in 1948, it knew the step up in competition was significant, but the Buffaloes likely didn't figure the journey to the top would take so long. Dal Ward led the Buffs through their first 11 seasons in the Big 7, from 1948 to 1958, and enjoyed some success, but only four winning seasons in conference play. The CU Board of Regents wanted someone to take CU to the next level and Ward was fired.

Enter Sonny Grandelius, a 29-year-old Michigan State assistant who signed a four-year, $14,000 per year contract with the Buffs.

"I'm no genius and there'll be no miracles," he said when hired. "It's going to take a lot of hard work to build a winner."

Short on experience in 1960, the Buffs went 5–5, with a 3–3 record in the Big 7. In 1959, Oklahoma State began playing in the conference, now known as the Big 8. CU lost three of its last four, but finished 6–4 and posted a 5–2 record in conference play. Going into 1961, the Buffs had confidence with All-Conference quarterback Gale Weidner and end Jerry Hillebrand, All-American lineman/linebacker Joe Romig, and other veterans.

"We truly expect to have a better football team than in our previous two years at Colorado," Grandelius said. "But we feel that's all relative because everybody else in the conference will be that much better, too. We'll have the biggest team I think they've ever had at Colorado and a more balanced attack. You can see I'm fairly optimistic."

The optimism was warranted, as the Buffs opened with a 24–0 rout of Oklahoma State and a 20–19 win against Kansas. A 21–12 loss to Utah in a non-conference game was the only blemish on the regular season. Victories against Nebraska and Oklahoma highlighted a 9–1 regular season that included a 7–0 mark in Big 8 play. The Buffs won their first conference title since joining a "major" conference. It was CU's only outright conference title from 1945 to 1988 The seeds for that season were planted when CU fired Ward, who was popular among the players.

"I think what happened was, in the middle of the Dal Ward firing when we were sophomores, everyone was pretty upset," punter Charlie McBride told the *Boulder Daily Camera* when the group celebrated the 50th anniversary of that season. "There was a lot of talk about, 'Let's go transfer,' as there usually is during a coaching change…. Going through that episode made us closer. A lot of the guys who played the most for Sonny were recruited by Dal. We just had fun together and it was a great group."

The season didn't end like the Buffs wanted, though. Ranked No. 6 going into the Orange Bowl, CU was routed by No. 4 Louisiana State, 25–7, to finish 9–2 overall. The loss to LSU was the least of CU's worries, though.

Throughout the season, the NCAA had been investigating CU's program for rules violations. The CU regents didn't wait for the NCAA to finish its investigation, however. After conducting its own investigation, the regents voted 5–1 on March 17, 1962, to fire Grandelius for "numerous violations of Big Eight and NCAA rules and regulations." Grandelius was accused, among other things, of operating a recruiting "slush fund" to provide financial assistance to players and recruits.

CU hoped that proactively firing Grandelius would ease the NCAA punishment. The next month, the NCAA put CU on two-year probation, and the Buffs were not allowed to participate in bowl games or play on national TV for those two years.

William "Bud" Davis, a CU alumni secretary, was named head coach for 1962. His only coaching experience had come in the high school ranks, and most of his staff were high school coaches.

The scandal also depleted the roster for 1962, as nearly 20 players were ruled ineligible. CU went 2–8 in 1962, and then hired Eddie Crowder as head coach. The scandal lingered, though, as the Buffs went 2–8 in 1963 and 1964, as well, before discovering winning ways again in 1965.

82 Mark Haynes

Coming out of Harmon High School in Kansas City, Kansas, in 1976, Mark Haynes flashed the ability to be a standout running back at the college level, rushing for 1,380 yards and 19 touchdowns in his senior year. Haynes had other ideas, though.

"I felt my best position would be as a defensive back," Haynes said during his senior year at CU in 1979. "I had no aspirations to be a running back then, and I have none now."

Good thing for the Buffs. Haynes was more interested in delivering hits than absorbing them and he wound up as one of the best defensive backs to ever play at CU. Voted to CU's All-Century team in 1989, Haynes was a first-team Associated Press All-American in 1979 and he received honorable mention in 1978.

A four-year starter, Haynes played "Apache" back—a type of safety—under coach Bill Mallory during his first three seasons. He then switched to cornerback when Chuck Fairbanks was hired as head coach for the 1979 season. Regardless of where he played, Haynes shined. During his first three seasons at CU, the 5-foot-11, 185-pound Haynes was a big hitter, posting 82 tackles in 1977 and 89 more in 1979. As a senior, he was voted team MVP. The switch to cornerback in his senior year was a new experience, but the Buffs wanted to take advantage of his 4.4-second speed in the 40-yard dash.

"Chuck Fairbanks told me that if I did well with the switch to cornerback, I could have a chance to get drafted into the NFL," Haynes said.

In the 1980 draft, Haynes was the highest-selected defensive back in CU history, going No. 8 overall to the New York Giants.

Secondary Stars

For decades, CU has had several defensive backs earn All-American honors and several become high draft picks in the NFL. Since 1980, CU has had 30 defensive backs drafted, including three in the first round: Mark Haynes (1980), Deon Figures (1993) and Jimmy Smith (2011). The All-Americans:

First-team: Dick Anderson (1967); Cullen Bryant (1972); Deon Figures (1992); Mark Haynes (1979); Chris Hudson (1994); Ben Kelly (1999); Pat Murphy (1970)

Second-team: Mickey Pruitt (1987); Steve Rosga (1996); Damen Wheeler (1999)

Third-team: Chris Hudson (1993); Michael Lewis (2001)

Honorable mention: Mark Haynes (1978); Tim James (1990); Odis McKinney (1977); Mickey Pruitt (1986); Victor Scott (1983); Mike Spivey (1976); Damen Wheeler (1998)

He wound up playing six seasons with the Giants and four with the Denver Broncos. He was a three-time Pro Bowler and two-time All-Pro with the Giants. From 1986 to '89, he helped the Broncos get to the Super Bowl three times in four seasons.

Haynes was inducted into the CU Athletics Hall of Fame in 2017.

"I think it's a great honor," he said of going to the Hall of Fame. "We've had some great football players back here and to be recognized as one of the guys that's having an opportunity to go in is just a tremendous honor. I always wanted to play college football and this was great [at Colorado]."

83 Zimmer and KOA

Most CU football games since the 1940s—and every game since 1985—has been broadcast on the airwaves of KOA Radio, at 850 AM. With the exception of the 1982–84 seasons, when CU went with a different station on an experimental basis, KOA has been synonymous with the Buffaloes.

"KOA has been with us for all but three years since 1940," CU sports information director David Plati said, adding that getting back on KOA in 1985 was a big deal for the school. "It was the most respected AM radio station in the region and still is. It was important to get back on KOA. We were tired of jumping around on the AM dial."

There's been no jumping around the dial since 1985, and for many years, it's been easy to find the Buffs simply by the recognizable voices of Larry Zimmer and Mark Johnson.

From 1971 to 2015, Zimmer was a part of CU broadcasts for 42 of 45 years (all but the 82–84 seasons). For 26 years, he broadcast CU and Denver Broncos games in the same seasons. He often dealt with some interesting travel arrangements to get from a CU game on Saturday to a Broncos game on Sunday.

"Half his battle would be, 'How am I going to get from Stillwater to Seattle?'" Plati joked.

It was a labor of love for Zimmer, though, because Zimmer loved college football and despite growing up in Louisiana, he grew to love the Buffaloes. In all, Zimmer was on the air for 486 CU football games and 525 men's basketball games. He was a part of 22 CU bowl games and watched each of the first five Ralphies run. Zimmer was presented with the prestigious Chris Schenkel Award, given to a broadcaster who has worked in college football at the same school for number of years.

"That was a big deal to him and a really big deal to the school," Plati said. "They haven't handed out many of those. There were so many different people during the years doing our games and Larry became the constant."

On November 28, 2015, Zimmer called his final game, one day after his 80th birthday.

"The fact that I can look back on a half century of doing college football is very, very special to me," Zimmer said. "I've had a lot of great experiences in my career."

Johnson hasn't been in the booth nearly as long, but the "voice of the Buffs" has become iconic in his own right. Johnson became the Buffs' play-by-play man for football and basketball in 2004, teaming with Zimmer on football broadcasts for 12 years. Following Zimmer's retirement, former CU head coach Gary Barnett took over as color commentator in 2016, working alongside Johnson.

84 Linebacker U

As a two-time All-American and winner of the Butkus Award, Alfred Williams is arguably the greatest linebacker to ever play for the Colorado Buffaloes. Throughout CU history, however, there has been a long list of exceptional linebackers.

Two CU linebackers have won the Butkus Award, five have been first-team All-Americans, 14 have earned some sort of All-American honor and, from 1963 to 2018, there were 26 CU linebackers taken in the NFL Draft.

Here's a look at some of the best linebackers to ever play for the Buffs:

Greg Biekert (1989–92): Finished his career second in CU history in tackles and was just the second player to lead the team three times. He was semifinalist for the Butkus Award—given to the nation's top linebacker—in 1992, when he was also All-Big Eight and honorable mention All-American. Biekert, who grew up in nearby Longmont, had an 11-year NFL career.

Chad Brown (1989–92): Playing with Biekert, Brown was a star at both inside and outside linebacker. He finished his career fourth in CU history in tackles and racked up 30 tackles for loss and 14 sacks in his last two seasons. He was a second-team All-American in 1992 and All-Big Eight as a junior and senior. A second-round pick of the Pittsburgh Steelers, he played 15 years in the NFL.

Jordon Dizon (2004–07): As a senior in 2007, he was a consensus All-American and runner-up for the Butkus Award. He was also voted the Big 12 defensive player of the year. Just the fifth player in CU history with 400 career tackles (he had 440), his 160 in 2007 were the most by any CU player from 1997 to 2018. He was taken in the second round of the NFL Draft by the Detroit Lions, but a knee injury cut his career short.

Ted Johnson (1991–94): At the time of his graduation, he was third in CU history in tackles (409), and was the runner-up for the Butkus Award in 1994. He was also first-team All-Big Eight and third-team All-American. Taken in the second round of the draft by the New England Patriots, he played all 10 of his NFL seasons with them, winning three Super Bowls.

Bud Magrum (1971–72): Maybe a stretch to put him on this list, since he played primarily at defensive tackle. But in 1972, he played the first several games at linebacker before moving back to the line, and he became a first-team All-American that season. Before coming to CU, he was a Marine Corps veteran who won

Brian Cabral

As a player, Brian Cabral was a standout linebacker for the Buffaloes. His greatest impact, however, came in how many young men he mentored at CU. For 24 seasons, from 1989 to 2012, Cabral was an assistant coach for the Buffs—making him the longest-tenured assistant coach in school history, regardless of sport.

Working for five different head coaches, Cabral coached the Buffs' linebackers. Among the linebackers he mentored at CU: Greg Biekert, Chad Brown, Jordon Dizon, Ted Johnson, and Matt Russell. In all, 10 linebackers he coached at CU played in the NFL.

Cabral also coached the Buffs' punt return unit from 1999 to 2005, working with All-American Roman Hollowell. After Dan Hawkins was fired with three games to play in the 2010 season, Cabral took over as interim head coach, sparking the Buffs to a 2–1 record down the stretch.

A 1978 CU graduate, Cabral lettered three times. He was a captain as a senior and played for the 1976 Big Eight championship team. A fourth-round pick of the Atlanta Falcons in 1978, he played nine seasons in the NFL. He was the Chicago Bears' special teams captain 1985, when they won Super Bowl XX.

two purple hearts in Vietnam, honored for his bravery under fire as a demolitions expert.

Kanavis McGhee (1987–90): He teamed with Alfred Williams to form the best outside linebacker duo in CU history. He and Williams were both first-team All-Americans in 1989. He was also second-team All-American in 1988. McGhee earned All-Big Eight honors three times and was named to the Big Eight All-Decade team for the 1980s. A second-round pick of the New York Giants, he played 50 games in the NFL.

Barry Remington (1982–86): A Boulder native and graduate of Fairview High School, he was still, through 2018, the all-time leading tackler in CU history, with 493. He earned All-American honorable mention as a senior. He was the first player in CU history to record three consecutive 100-tackle seasons.

Joe Romig (1959–61): One of the toughest men to ever player for CU, he was two-way star, at guard and linebacker. He was the first two-time, first-team All-American in CU history, and is one of just four players in school history to have his number retired. In 1984, he was enshrined in the College Football Hall of Fame.

Matt Russell (1993–96): As a senior in 1996, he was a consensus first-team All-American and joined Alfred Williams as the only Buffs to win the Butkus Award. He was also a third-team All-American as a junior and earned first-team All-Conference honors twice. In 1997, he was a fourth-round draft choice of the Detroit Lions. Knee injuries cut his career short. The 2018 season was his 10th working in the Denver Broncos' front office.

Alfred Williams (1987–90): Williams was the school's first Butkus Award winner and the only CU linebacker to earn first-team All-American honors twice. A feared pass rusher, he established CU career records for career sacks (35) and career tackles for loss (59)—records he still owned through 2018. Drafted in the first round of the 1991 NFL Draft, by the Cincinnati Bengals, he played nearly a decade in the NFL—also with the San Francisco 49ers and Denver Broncos. He helped the Broncos to back-to-back Super Bowl wins.

Ron Woolfork (1991–93): Taking over at outside linebacker after Williams graduated, Woolfork carved out a great career of his own. Although never an All-American, he was first-team All-Big Eight twice, in 1992 and 1993. Finished his career second in CU history in tackles for loss (53) and sacks (33), and was a fourth-round draft pick of the Miami Dolphins.

In recent years, CU hasn't had the dominant linebackers it had in the past, but players such as Rick Gamboa, Jimmie Gilbert, Addison Gillam, Nate Landman, Drew Lewis, Derek McCartney, and Kenneth Olugbode have been standouts and fan favorites.

85 Don Campbell

Compared to other battles during World War II, the Battle of Luzon was not among the biggest, but it was significant. Fought in the jungles of Luzon, the largest island in the Philippines, from January to August of 1945, it wound up being a strategic victory for the United States and Allied forces against the Empire of Japan. There were reportedly 230,000 casualties for Japan, while the U.S. had 10,380 killed and 36,550 wounded.

It was during that battle that young Don Campbell, a private in the Army, saw his running career nearly come to an end. A graduate of Sterling High School in northeast Colorado a year before, Campbell's leg and hip were wounded during the battle in May of 1945. He was later awarded a Purple Heart, but was told at the time that he wouldn't run again. For Campbell, nicknamed the "Sterling Flash" after winning several state titles in the sprints, this was devastating to hear, but he had a question for the doctor.

"Will it hurt me to try?" he asked. "He told me, 'No, it won't hurt to try.' So that was my goal, to run again."

Less than a year later, in April of 1946, Campbell was on the track in a CU uniform. During a meet at the University of Denver, he won the 100-yard dash and 220-yard run. The next month, in the first post-war Mountain States Conference championships, he clocked a lifetime-best 9.7 seconds in winning the 100-yard dash. He also won the 220 in 21.3 seconds, helped CU win the mile relay, and was a key to the Buffaloes' team championship.

Earning a new nickname, the "Colorado Comet," at CU, Campbell won seven conference titles during his time with the Buffaloes. He was also an All-American in 1948 and in 1949 earned the Russell Memorial Award as the region's top amateur athlete.

While Campbell was in high school, All-American hurdler Phil Cope inspired Campbell when he told him, "You may not be the world's best, but you can be among the world's best and you'll have an opportunity to run all around the world."

Motivated by that goal, Campbell represented the United States in the 1951 Pan American Games in Buenos Aires, Argentina, and in other competitions around the world, in places such as New Zealand, Norway, Finland, and South Africa.

"I loved to run fast," he said when inducted to the CU Athletic Hall of Fame in 2008. "My goal was to be able to run fast enough to travel the world, and by golly, I could."

86 Nate Solder

Going into his senior year at Buena Vista High School, located nearly three hours southwest from Boulder, Nate Solder knew he would be a college athlete. He just wasn't sure where he'd go, or which sport he'd wind up playing. Dartmouth College of the Ivy League wanted him for basketball. A few other schools wanted him for football. Then, CU called and offered him a football scholarship and his decision was made.

"If I hadn't gotten that offer from Colorado, I probably would have gone basketball," Solder told *The Denver Post* in 2010. "But that offer from CU, that was an offer from a big-time program. I wasn't getting offers like that for basketball."

It's safe to say that Solder made the right choice in picking CU, as he went on to become an All-American at tackle, a first-round NFL Draft choice and a two-time Super Bowl champion with the New England Patriots.

A stellar tight end at Buena Vista, Solder was a 6-foot-8, 245-pound senior who caught 31 passes and helped the Demons to the Class 2A state championship game. While his size suggested he might be better suited for offensive tackle, the Buffs signed him as a tight end. As a true freshman in 2006, Solder redshirted and excelled at tight end on the scout team. He earned a team award for his efforts on the scout special teams unit. In 2007, he remained a tight end, playing in all 13 games on special teams and offense.

"When Nate got here as a tight end, he got people's attention for the way he could hit, even being so tall and skinny," quarterback Cody Hawkins, who played five years at CU with Solder, told *The Post*. "He was a good tight end, but the coaches thought he would be a great left tackle."

Nate Solder high-fives fans after beating Colorado State 24–3 in 2010.
(AP Photo / Matt McClain)

All-State game in Pueblo. CU freshman team coach Dan Stavely was in attendance and was impressed by Brundige.

"He asked me if I had signed a letter of intent," said Brundige, who told Stavely he had not signed.

Just a few hours later, Stavely showed up to Brundige's motel room.

"He said they found a scholarship that they had overlooked," Brundige said. "So a week before school started, I got a scholarship."

After spending the 1966 season on the freshman team, he played varsity for the Buffs from 1967 to '69. At 6-foot-5, 235 pounds, he was an imposing figure, playing defensive tackle and end for the Buffs.

There was nothing spectacular about Brundige's first two seasons on varsity, however. In fact, before his senior season on the gridiron, his greatest athletic accomplishment may have come in track and field. In March of 1969, he had a shot put of 56 feet, 1.5 inches. It was the second-best mark in CU history at the time and, as of 2018, ranked eighth-best all-time.

In the fall of 1969, Brundige absolutely terrorized CU opponents on the football field. In helping the Buffs to a 7–3 record during the regular season, Brundige recorded 70 tackles, including 24 tackles for loss (for 123 yards) and 13 quarterback sacks. He actually had 18 sacks that season—including five in a Liberty Bowl win against Alabama—but bowl statistics did not count toward single-season and career records at CU. That season, Brundige earned first-team All-American honors and was named the Big Eight Conference defensive player of the year.

"Bill Brundige made more progress this season than any player we've ever had," head coach Eddie Crowder said in 1969. "He was amazing. He was responsible, in large part, for our defensive success."

Brundige's 13 sacks remained a CU single-season record until 1985, when Dan McMillen had 14. Through 2018, Brundige still held the school record for tackles for loss in single season. He was inducted into the CU Athletics Hall of Fame in 2016.

During the 1970 NFL Draft, Brundige was selected by the Washington Redskins in the second round (43rd overall). He spent his entire eight-year career with the Redskins, playing 107 games, with 75 starts. He started every game during his rookie season and then helped the Redskins reach Super Bowl VII in 1972. In 2002, the Redskins celebrated their 70th anniversary by honoring the 70 greatest in their history, and Brundige was on the list.

Through all his success at CU and in the NFL, Brundige never forgot where he grew up. It was on the Colorado plains, after all, that he developed his work ethic and toughness.

"The school system was phenomenal, and also working on the farm," he said years after his playing career. "Whenever I was out on the practice field in the hot sun I would remember walking up and down those rows of beets over at Brush and driving that tractor and breaking up hay bales. I didn't want to do any of it. Some of my pro football buddies would have a hard time being a farmer."

92 Frank Prentup

At Colorado, Frank Prentup is known for his association with the baseball program. The Leavenworth, Kansas, native was well-rounded in athletics, however, and he left a lasting impression on many.

For 24 seasons, from 1946 to 1969, Prentup was the head coach of the CU baseball team, compiling a record of 257–255–2. He led the Buffs to a tie for the Mountain States Conference title in 1946 and had 13 winning seasons. He also guided the Buffs through the

93 Women's Soccer

Seemingly from the moment she first touched a soccer ball as a youth in Mead, Colorado, Nikki Marshall had a knack for putting the ball in the net. A record-setting scorer at Skyline High School, where she notched 100 career goals, Marshall continued to shine when she played for CU, from 2006–09, becoming arguably the greatest player in the history of the program.

"Nikki is going to be one of those players that I will be telling stories about for a long time," former CU head coach Bill Hempen said prior to Marshall's senior year in 2009.

In her four seasons with the Buffs, Marshall set 20 school records and became CU's all-time leader in goals (42), points (93), and game-winning goals (18). Marshall scored a stunning 17 goals as a freshman in 2006, earning Big 12 Newcomer of the Year honors. She earned first-team All-Big 12 honors four times and helped the Buffs post a 47–29–12 record with three NCAA Tournament appearances during her career.

In addition to her stellar career with the Buffs, Marshall played on the international level. She was in the U.S. Women's national team program for several years and helped the U.S. Under–20 team to a silver medal in the 2007 Pan American Games and to the FIFA World Cup championship in 2008. Following her career at CU, Marshall was selected in the first round (seventh overall) of the 2010 Women's Professional Soccer (WPS) draft by the Washington Freedom. She played professionally until retiring after the 2014 season.

If Marshall isn't the best player in CU soccer history, that title would go to Fran Munnelly, a brilliant playmaker for the Buffs from 2002–05. The lone soccer player in the CU Athletics Hall of Fame, Munnelly was the only Buff to be named conference player of the year, honored by the Big 12 in 2003. That season, she guided the Buffs to their only conference title in soccer. Munnelly is the program's all-time leader in assists (24); earned third-team All-American honors from the United Soccer Coaches in 2004 and second-team in 2005; and was first-team All-Big 12 four times.

In addition to Marshall and Munnelly, the Buffs have relied on other stars, such as Katie Griffin, Laura Munnelly, Michelle Wenino, Jessica Keller, Amy Barczuk, and Taylor Kornieck to keep them competitive annually.

CU's inaugural season in women's soccer was in 1996, and the Buffs posted their first winning campaign in 1999. Led by Hempen and Fran Munnelly, the Buffs reached the NCAA Tournament for the first time in 2003. That was the start of a six-year run of NCAA Tournament appearances. Hempen had a 114–88–28 record in his 11 seasons coaching the program, from 2001–11.

After joining the ultra-competitive Pac-12 in 2011, the Buffs went through an adjustment period, but got back to their winning ways in 2013. Led by head coach Danny Sanchez, who was hired in 2012, the Buffs reached the NCAA Tournament four times in five seasons from 2013–17.

94 Bo Goes No. 2

Colorado has had dozens of All-Americans, a Heisman Trophy winner and numerous others who earned national or conference awards. Bo Matthews didn't earn any of those honors during his football career at CU, but he has the distinction of being the highest draft pick in school history. During the 1974 NFL Draft, the 230-pound fullback was selected with the second overall pick, by the San Diego Chargers.

By the 2010s, the fullback was a seldom-used position; some NFL teams haven't employed a fullback in recent years. In 1974, however, fullbacks were a key position—and Matthews was a player San Diego felt it could build around.

"Champions have the character," Chargers coach Tom Prothro said after drafting Matthews. "When the going gets tough the others fold. Bo Matthews and those like him will form the nucleus of this team."

Defensive end Ed "Too Tall" Jones, who played 15 years for the Dallas Cowboys, was the only player taken ahead of Matthews. Heisman Trophy-winning running back John Cappelletti, from Penn State, went nine picks later. (Also in 1974, CU tight end J.V. Cain went seventh overall, to the St. Louis Cardinals.)

"I didn't think I'd be the first back to go," Matthews said after signing his first contract. "There was [Woody] Green who you hear a lot about and Cappelletti—who knows Bo Matthews? I looked to go third or fourth down the line."

During his childhood, the NFL didn't appear to ever be an option. Growing up just outside of Huntsville, Alabama, Matthews was one of 14 children in his family and he worked hard on the farm. If he wasn't feeding cows and hogs, he was likely gathering crops of corn, cotton, and beans.

"The most disappointing part was when you would look over the fence into the next pasture and you would see kids playing football and baseball," Matthews said in 1974, just ahead of his rookie season with the Chargers. "You're in the next field, driving a tractor. That's pretty tough. You get up pretty early to do the chores and then you are in the fields till sundown."

With that, there wasn't any time for football.

Top Picks

Through 2019, CU had produced 24 first-round NFL draft picks. Here's a list of the top 12, in terms of their overall spot in the draft:

No. 2—Bo Matthews, FB, San Diego (1974)
No. 4—Byron White, HB, Pittsburgh (1938)
No. 4—Michael Westbrook, WR, Washington (1995)
No. 7—J.V. Cain, TE, St. Louis (1974)
No. 8—Mark Haynes, CB, N.Y. Giants (1980)
No. 10—Chris Naeole, OG, New Orleans (1997)
No. 11—Bobby Anderson, TB, Denver (1970)
No. 12—Pete Brock, OC, New England (1976)
No. 12—Stan Brock, OT, New Orleans (1980)
No. 13—Jerry Hillebrand, TE, N.Y. Giants (1962)
No. 13—Troy Archer, DT, N.Y. Giants (1976)
No. 13—Mike Pritchard, WR, Atlanta (1991)

"We all helped with the work," he said. "My father was a little old-fashioned. He didn't believe in sports. He always wanted me to go to college but not to play football."

It wasn't until his sophomore year of high school that he played football. After some problems within the family, he left his old high school and enrolled at Butler High School in Huntsville. He earned All-State, All-Conference and even high school All-American honors.

After high school, Matthews originally signed to play at Alabama, and was the first African American to ever sign with the Crimson Tide. He was unable to get into Alabama, though, and instead went to CU. During his career at CU, he lettered three times from 1971 to '73. While he was mostly a blocking back, he rushed for 1,339 yards and 11 touchdowns for the Buffs.

"Colorado was good to me," he said.

Matthews played eight years in the NFL, including his first six with the Chargers, helping them win a division title in 1979.

He also played for the New York Giants and Miami Dolphins. He totaled 1,566 yards and 11 touchdowns, while also catching 75 passes for 488 yards during his career.

95 Wrestling

Although CU has not sponsored a wrestling team since 1980, it is a sport that was contested for decades and produced some great Buffs.

Leading the list of great grapplers in CU history is Dean Lahr, who dominated competition in the 177-pound weight class from 1962 to '64. Posting a 58–4 career record, Lahr was the national runner up in 1962 and back-to-back national champions in 1963 and 1964. At the NCAA championship in 1964, Lahr built a comfortable lead against Bill Harlow of Oklahoma State and then wore him down for an 8–4 victory. Lahr was named the most outstanding wrestler at the meet.

A 1960 graduate of Denver North High School, where he was a football star and state wrestling champion, Lahr originally went to CU on a football scholarship. Following the 1961 season, however, he turned his focus to wrestling. Lahr credits much of his success in those years to Joe Klune, his coach at North, and Linn Long, who coached him at CU.

"When I was wrestling I was really fortunate as far as coach Long and coach Klune developing skills and that sort of thing," he said years later.

Lahr took that coaching and became a star in the sport. At the 1964 Olympic trials, he won at 171.5 pounds and was named most outstanding wrestler. He also represented the United States at the

World Freestyle Championships in 1963 (placing fourth) and 1966 (fifth). He also was a two-time AAU national champion.

In 2000, Lahr was inducted to the CU Athletics Hall of Fame. In 2014, he was inducted in the National Wrestling Hall of Fame.

"I always felt like sooner or later I might make it," he said. "I was very pleased to receive the honor."

Led by Lahr's championship and Jim Hanson's second-place medal at 130 pounds in 1964, the Buffs had their best team finish, placing fourth. That team was led by Long, the Buffs' head coach from 1961 to '68.

A Boulder native, Long wrestled for CU from 1952 to '55, placing third nationally at 130 pounds in his senior year. During his tenure as head coach, Long tutored the only two national champions in CU history: Lahr and Bob Justice, who won the 177-pound title in 1968. Over the years, CU won 18 medals at the national meet, nine of those with Long as coach. In addition to Lahr's three medals, Hanson won two. Long remained involved with wrestling for years after leaving CU and, in 2014, joined Lahr in the CU Athletics Hall of Fame.

"If it weren't for the University of Colorado my life wouldn't be what it is; it gave me a platform of education that gave me a terrific life," Long said.

Justice became the third wrestler in the CU Athletics Hall of Fame in 2016, providing yet another reminder of CU's great history in the sport. It's a history that included CU's first national qualifiers in 1949, when five grapplers went to the NCAA Tournament. From 1952 to 1980, the Buffs scored points at nationals in 27 of 29 years. In 1980, Derek Glenn placed third at 134 pounds, giving CU its final medal winner before shutting down the program.